CRIME & SECURITY
in Trinidad and Tobago

CRIME & SECURITY
in Trinidad and Tobago

Randy Seepersad
& Dianne Williams

IAN RANDLE PUBLISHERS
Kingston • Miami

First published in Jamaica, 2016 by
Ian Randle Publishers
16 Herb McKenley Drive,
Box 686
Kingston 6
www.ianrandlepublishers.com

© Randy Seepersad, Dianne Williams

ISBN: 978-976-637-910-0

National Library of Jamaica Cataloguing-in-Publication Data

Seepersad, Randy
    Crime and security in Trinidad and Tobago / Randy Seepersad and
Dianne Williams

    pages; cm
Bibliography : p . – Includes index
ISBN 978-976-637-910-0 (pbk)

1. Crime – Trinidad and Tobago   2. Criminology – Trinidad and Tobago
3. Crime analysis – Trinidad and Tobago
I. Williams, Dianne   II. Title

364.972983   dc 23

Cover and Book Design by Ian Randle Publishers
Printed and Bound in the United States of America

Table of Contents

List of Figures

List of Tables

Preface

This book offers an in-depth analysis of crime and security in Trinidad and Tobago, and has been specifically developed for students of criminology and criminal justice and related disciplines, and for practitioners and policymakers in the areas of crime control, prevention and security. The areas focused upon have been chosen such that they address how to understand and deal with crime in Trinidad and Tobago. These include a focus on the criminal justice system with particular attention to the nature of, and the problems in, the police service, courts and prisons service. It looks at the nature and extent of criminal victimization in Trinidad and Tobago, paying particular attention to data from 1990 to 2014, which examined vulnerable groups in Trinidad and Tobago, including women and juveniles, with a special emphasis on the juvenile justice system, criminal gangs and interventions for dealing with gang violence, risk factors which are relevant for understanding crime, the responses of the population to insecurity, and the policy environment in Trinidad and Tobago. In examining these areas, this book provides several policy recommendations for dealing with crime and insecurity.

Crime is one of the leading social problems facing Trinidad and Tobago and is one of the most important threats to citizen security. Concerns about crime and violence are expressed daily in the news media and rank high among citizens' concerns in public opinion polls. An increase in crime and violence, particularly after 2000, has intensified perceptions of insecurity among citizens. The result has been a decline in the public's trust in the capacity of government, and specifically law-enforcement agencies, to deal with this problem, intensifying their sense of insecurity and weakening the country's social fabric. For the period 2000–2010, the average annual murder rate in Trinidad and Tobago was 26 murders per 100,000 inhabitants, compared to an average of 22.1 for the Caribbean, as a whole, and 5.4 for the US. The only Caribbean countries with murder rates which exceeded Trinidad and Tobago's for this period were Jamaica, with an average rate of 51.7; Belize, with an average rate of 35.8; and St Kitts/Nevis with an average rate of 29.2. In the case of Belize and St Kitts/Nevis, the absolute number of murders was small compared to that of Trinidad and Tobago. Belize recorded an average of 86 murders per year for the period under consideration while St Kitts/Nevis recorded an average of 14. Trinidad and Tobago, in contrast, recorded an average of 328 murders per year while Jamaica recorded an average of 1,349. The only crimes which declined significantly in Trinidad and Tobago over the 20-year period ending in 2014 were burglary and breaking and entering. In contrast, murders, woundings and shootings, robberies and kidnapping exhibited some level of stability from 1990 to 2000, and thereafter began to increase. Within very recent times, however, there have been notable declines in murders, woundings and shootings, robberies and kidnappings (since 2005 in the case of kidnappings, and 2008–2009 in the case of murders, woundings and shootings, and robberies). The annual number of sexual offences increased from 1990 to 2006 and, with the exception of 2012, thereafter started to decline. Despite these recent declines, crime levels are still relatively high compared to the rest of the Caribbean, particularly so for violent crimes and, accordingly, public perception remains fixated on crime as the most pressing concern in Trinidad and Tobago.

No single empirically supported reason exists to account for the rapid growth and persistence of crime and violence that has been observed in Trinidad and Tobago within the last decade. Studies on crime and violence have, however, highlighted a range of factors which may be plausible explanations. Abusive family conditions that have transferred violent tendencies to new generations have been offered as one reason. The legacy of colonial domination and underdevelopment and their impact on governance post-independence have also been offered as causes for social apathy and resignation and consequent violence. So too have the structural adjustment prescriptions imposed by international financial institutions that severely undermined the ability of the state to offer social welfare, which generated significant cultural changes and lessened the influence of conventional institutions of socialization such as the family, the school, the workplace and community organizations in shaping the habits and behaviours of individuals; a high proportion of youths in the population, generally a group that has a higher than average propensity for aggression; social exclusion of specific groups; high levels of poverty and income inequality, and the proliferation of drugs and arms through organized crime. Other plausible predisposing factors include deteriorating living conditions, especially in urban areas, a culture that excuses and rationalizes familial relations based on dominance and violence against women and children, high rates of unemployment particularly among youths, lack of capacity in the institutions of the criminal justice system, the judiciary, the police and the penal system, and high levels of corruption among law enforcement officials. Many of these factors may be important in explaining crime in Trinidad and Tobago and are critically discussed in the various chapters.

This book utilizes primary as well as secondary data and a wide variety of previous research. The primary data utilized in this book were collected from a random sample of 1,595 adults in Trinidad and Tobago, from November 2009 to January 2010. The questionnaires which were administered to the sample of adults collected data on a number of areas, including demographics, satisfaction with living conditions and the level of development in the community and country as a whole, problems in Trinidad and Tobago, criminal victimization within the last year and within the last ten years, utilizing a 19-item measure: physical injury occurring as a result of criminal victimization, reporting behaviour of respondents, police action, satisfaction with police action, victimization of family members, domestic violence, crimes in the community, responses to crime in the community and country, gang violence, fear of crime, fear related behaviour, the policy orientation of the population, performance of the police, confidence in the police and in the courts/justice system, community cohesion, societal cohesion, informal social control and self-reported criminal behaviour. This primary data offered a range of rich and detailed information relevant to many of the substantive topics treated in this book. The important role of the United Nations Development Programme (UNDP) in collecting this data must be acknowledged.

Technical consultations with experts in various governmental and non-governmental organizations were also carried out to aid in the development of this book. These experts included the acting Commissioner of Police, the Commissioner of Prisons, and representatives of the Ministry of National Security, the Ministry of Trade and Industry, the Judiciary, CARICOM IMPACS, the Trinidad and Tobago Police Service, the Institute for Criminology and Public Safety, and the University of Trinidad and Tobago. Key informants were selected based on their expertise and experience in various topic areas relevant to this study. The authors express their deep gratitude to the technical committee members who gave willingly of their time and expertise and whose input contributed substantially to the content and quality of this book. In addition to key informant interviews, secondary sources of data were consulted; these include, but are not limited to previous studies done in Trinidad and Tobago, pre-existing data, documents and policy papers. The range of data sources as well as technical consultations allowed for a comprehensive and in-depth examination of each topic and assisted with triangulation of the findings and conclusions.

Chapter 1 critically examines the three arms of the criminal justice system in Trinidad and Tobago. The reader is provided with information on the structure and organization of the Police Service, the judicial system and the Prison Service in Trinidad and Tobago as a background to examining substantive issues within each of these systems. The high crime rate, coupled with very low detection rates, as well as allegations of corruption, have led to low levels of public confidence in the Trinidad and Tobago Police Service. Other problems discussed include a lack of accountability, difficulties with external and internal control, the excessive use of force, low levels of legitimacy, less than adequate training, failure to successfully implement a community policing approach and the less than optimum use of applicable technologies. Two primary issues facing the Judiciary include the excessive time required for trials to be completed and the very low conviction rates. Recent reforms are examined and recommendations offered to improve the efficiency of the judicial system. In chapter 1, the prison system is described as a tense environment which is the result of fragmentation, useless coercion, and obsolete and outdated policies. One of the most troubling manifestations of this is the high recidivism rate, which stood at 49 per cent in 2013. This chapter examines the utility of alternate approaches, including the use of selective incapacitation and a restorative justice approach, as possible solutions to the problems which affect the Prison Service.

Chapter 2 provides detailed statistics on crime and examines official crime data for Trinidad and Tobago for the period 1990–2014. Among other things, data are provided on murders, woundings and shootings, kidnappings, rapes and sexual offences, robberies and burglaries. This chapter also examines victimization survey data and estimates the extent to which official crime data underestimate the true extent of criminal offending. A comparison of official crime data with victimization survey data indicates, among other things, that the number of robberies occurring in Trinidad and Tobago is 4.6 times higher than indicated in official crime data; the number of sexual offences is 6.6 times higher; the number of burglaries and break-ins is 4.1 times higher; the number of motor vehicle thefts is 2.4 times higher, and the number of financial crimes is 7.2 times higher. Domestic violence, as a special case of victimization of a vulnerable group, is also discussed in chapter 2. Official crime data as well as data from other research are examined. Utilizing data on relative occupational earnings and gender disparities in labour force participation, the argument is made that societal and economic inequalities are important factors linked to domestic violence, especially where women are victims. Inadequacies in domestic violence laws are examined in detail, and several suggestions for reducing the incidence of this crime and for dealing with it when it occurs are discussed. The importance of this area of study is underscored by the fact that 8.4 per cent of all murders for the period 1995–2013 were the result of domestic violence.

Chapter 3 focuses on juvenile justice in Trinidad and Tobago. This chapter draws upon available empirical evidence to assess the nature and extent of youth crime and violence in Trinidad and Tobago, and among other things, demonstrates that the public's perception that youth crime is out of control is misguided and has been exaggerated and misinformed by media reporting. Official data examined in this chapter indicate, for example, that for the period 2007–2010, youths committed only 1.5 per cent of all murders, 1.2 per cent of all woundings and shootings, 2.8 per cent of all sexual offences, 2.2 per cent of all kidnappings and 1.1 per cent of all robberies. It is also shown in chapter 3 that a large proportion of the youths who are institutionalized in Trinidad and Tobago have not committed illegal acts, but instead have committed status offences or are in need of protection. This chapter hopes to transform the narratives about youth violence and provides a platform upon which reasonable interventions may be developed and utilized. It is argued, consistent with the empirical data presented, that a preventative as opposed to a suppressive approach to reducing youth violence may be the most cost-effective and appropriate approach for Trinidad and Tobago. It is further argued that, even where preventative approaches fail, policymakers must use incapacitation strategies only in the most extreme of cases and only as a last resort where youths are concerned.

Chapter 4 examines the troubling issue of criminal gangs in Trinidad and Tobago. This chapter examines the nature and extent of the gang problem in Trinidad and Tobago and assesses the impact of criminal gangs on violent crime. Among other things, it is shown using official crime data, that the spatial distribution of gangs is very closely related to the spatial distribution of several violent crimes. This chapter also examines the consequences of the presence of gangs and its impact on economic productivity, foreign investment, social exclusion and other such factors. Recommendations for dealing with the gang problem in Trinidad and Tobago are also developed. Recommendations focus on suppressive as well as preventative approaches, and also examine weaknesses in the criminal justice system, which diminish the state's capacity to deal with violent gangs. Recommendations which are developed are based on empirical evidence that is provided and critically examined. The discussion draws from a range of data sources, including official crime and gang data from the Trinidad and Tobago Police Service, data from the Besson Street Gang Intelligence Criminal History Project, and primary data gathered for this book.

Chapter 5 examines risk factors and determinants of crime and sets this discussion within the context of criminological theories, which may be applicable to the Caribbean region generally, and to Trinidad and Tobago specifically. The chapter critically examines some of the main risk factors which have been identified by past criminological research and theorizing, and assesses research in Trinidad and Tobago which has focused on risk factors. Coverage includes economic deprivation, social disorganization, strain theory, routine activities theory and subcultural theories. It is a fundamental assumption of this chapter that crime policy must be data driven and must be informed by a systematic understanding of the root causes of crime. Failure to do so will result in the continued implementation of policies which may be popular, but which may meet with little success since they lack connectedness to the main causal factors which are linked to crime. In examining risk factors which encourage crime and violence, chapter 5 offers an empirical basis upon which to design intervention strategies that are likely to yield successful results. Previous research and primary data are analysed to determine which risk factors are important for intervention purposes.

Chapter 6 focuses on the responses of the population to insecurity. This chapter argues that policy is influenced by the responses of the population to crime. These responses may set the agenda for action and demand greater responsiveness by state agencies and the political administration. They may, however, also lead to negative outcomes. The responses of the public are not always well-informed, and even when informed, are not always governed by reason. Violent crimes tend to evoke strong emotions. Reactions may be conditioned by the prejudices and biases of the population. These emotions, biases and prejudices may fuel inappropriate responses and even undemocratic ones. Indeed, misconceptions about the nature and extent of crime and about the solutions may encourage policies that support increasingly punitive responses to criminal activity without addressing the root causes of crime. Such policies may be entirely misplaced, and may do more harm than good. If policy is to be influenced in socially constructive and value-appropriate ways, then the responses and policy orientation of the population must be better understood. In an attempt to come to terms with the impact of the population on crime and security initiatives, this chapter evaluates the opinions of the Trinidad and Tobago population on crime, violence and insecurity. It also examines other aspects of citizens' subjective responses to insecurity, including levels of confidence in state institutions that are integral to the provision of citizen security. This chapter concludes by arguing that success in the fight against crime must not rely only on the functioning of the criminal justice system, but must employ preventative approaches that go beyond the remit of law enforcement agencies.

Chapter 7 focuses on the future of crime and security in Trinidad and Tobago. This chapter assesses the nature and extent of the problem, draws on linkages to human development, and offers recommendations for dealing with crime and insecurity in Trinidad and Tobago. This chapter argues primarily that proactive (preventative) as well as reactive (after the crime has occurred) measures are required if the nation is to be successful in its fight against crime. The chapter argues that a progressive criminal justice system is one which extends its focus to include preventative measures. Preventative approaches, for the most part, are lacking in Trinidad and Tobago, and are not given emphasis because their effects are usually in the medium to long term. Yet, reactive approaches deal only with the symptoms of the problem, and leave the underlying causes untouched. This chapter argues that several other institutions, such as schools, the family, and community organizations, are positioned such that their effective reach is wider than that of the criminal justice system, and many of these other institutions serve crime-reduction functions, but only incidentally or as a by-product of their functioning. Such institutions do not have purposive strategies which aim to reduce or control crime. Chapter 7 argues that the criminal justice system could be positioned so that it interfaces with other institutions and assists with the development of such strategies which could be implemented within such institutions. This chapter also focuses on a range of additional issues, including youth crime and violence, gangs, the justice system, and other areas of concern. Several suggestions are offered for future development in these areas.

The research conducted in this book adds to the body of knowledge on the causes of crime, responses to crime and the institutional arrangements in place to control crime, reduce fear and improve security. Several strategies and solutions as well as proposals to reduce violence and insecurity are offered, and these apply within the range of substantive areas treated in the book. These recommendations are based on a careful examination of best practices and relevant empirical data, including the primary data utilized in the development of this book. The material presented is relevant to a wide audience, which goes beyond students of criminology and policymakers/practitioners in national security and related fields.

The Criminal Justice System in Trinidad and Tobago

Introduction

This chapter focuses on the criminal justice system in Trinidad and Tobago and looks specifically at the Trinidad and Tobago Police Service (TTPS), Trinidad and Tobago Prison Service (TTPrS) and the Trinidad and Tobago Judiciary.

Trinidad and Tobago Police Service

The first police force in Trinidad and Tobago was established by Spanish settlers in the then capital of St Joseph. At that time, the Office of the Cabildo or Town Council controlled the police force, which, between 1592 and 1792, never numbered more than six. In this early period, police officers operated only within the main city itself. After slavery was abolished in 1838 and over 22,000 men and women were given their full civil rights, the responsibility of the police increased and a 'rural system of police' had to be established. By the end of 1842, there were 12 police stations and approximately 100 officers comprising inspectors, sergeants and constables.

In the mid-19th century, members of the Metropolitan Police were brought to Trinidad on secondment. During this period, the Police Headquarters was housed at the corner of Abercromby and Hart streets in the present capital city, Port of Spain. The general procedure in the case of an arrest in the 1840s was that once arrested, the accused was taken to the station or, if he was recalcitrant, held while the sergeant was called. All police stations were courthouses as magistrates travelled from one police station to another; this was the case until 1844 when trial by jury began. In 1851, the police were appointed the country's first postmen and mail carriers, and the police stations were transformed into post offices; the Mounted Branch was established for this purpose. In 1860, the police force was relieved of some of these extra duties. By 1869, an ordinance was initiated for better organization and discipline of the police force.

With a more organized police force, greater police surveillance of residents was provided. The police headquarters at the corner of St Vincent and Sackville streets, Port of Spain, was completed in 1876 housing approximately 452 men. Over the years, the number increased and other units were established, such as the Traffic Branch and Special Branch. By 1955, the need for policewomen to deal with juveniles and female offenders had arisen. Under Ordinance No. 6 of 1955, 12 females were drafted into the force. In 1966, the name was changed from police force to police service. The focus shifted from being a militaristic force to a service-oriented organization. By the 1970s, the police service had grown in strength to 3,399 members and was placed under the portfolio of the Ministry of National Security. Currently, there are 77 police stations located within nine police divisions in Trinidad and Tobago. These are staffed by approximately 6,500 police officers.

Over the last decade, crime statistics in Trinidad and Tobago suggest that the police service is struggling to execute its function as an agent of crime control. Nathan Pino (2009), in examining police statistics on the number of offences reported to the police during the period 1962–2007, argues that since independence in 1962 there has been a general increase in murders. From 1962 to 1980, there were approximately 50–60 murders per year. During the 1980s, the number gradually went up and remained at an average of 100 per year until 2000. As the data in table 1.1 indicate, within the last ten years, the majority of serious crimes in Trinidad and Tobago have increased, though there have been very recent declines in a number of offences. Despite the recent declines, however, crime rates remain relatively high compared to other Caribbean countries.

This rising crime rate has, on several occasions, been identified as a source of major concern for the citizens of Trinidad and Tobago. The United Nations Development Programme (UNDP) (2012) in the administration of a victimization survey in Trinidad and Tobago in January/February 2010 found that 63 per cent of respondents indicated that delinquency and crime were the issues of highest concern affecting the country. Stephen Mastrofski and Cynthia Lum (2008) also noted that public opinion surveys conducted in Trinidad and Tobago identified crime as the country's biggest problem and showed that confidence in the police was low. The less than favourable view of the Trinidad and Tobago police service is not confined to the adult population. Devon Johnson et al. (2008) in their analysis of *Youth Perceptions of the Police in Trinidad and Tobago* administered a questionnaire to 2,376 secondary schools students ranging in age from 13 to 18 years old. Respondents had a relatively negative view of the police, regardless of whether they were asked about service quality, fairness of treatment or police misconduct. It was discovered that 36.8 per cent of respondents agreed that they were satisfied with the services provided by the police while a somewhat larger proportion (41.5 per cent) expressed dissatisfaction with the police service.

The increasing crime rate brought into focus the need for an effective and efficient response from the Trinidad and Tobago police service. William Wells, Charles Katz and Jeorglim Kim (2008) noted that while homicides were on the increase, the Trinidad and Tobago detection rates were far from ideal, suggesting that the police service was struggling to manage the crime situation in the country. Stephen Mastrofski, Roger Parks and Craig Uchida (2008) argue that this low detection rate negatively impacts citizens' level of confidence in the ability of the police to ensure their safety. They further noted that a substantial portion of the public believed that many police officers are corrupt or use excessive force. Pino (2009) further argues that while citizens are fearful of crime, they are at the same time afraid to go to the police due to lack of trust and fear of retaliation by criminals. The Bureau of Democracy, Human Rights and Labour (2004) indicated that the US State Department expressed concerns about police killings during apprehension, death of persons in police custody and police abuse of prisoners.

Detection rates based on TTPS arrest data reveal strengths and weaknesses (see table 1.1). While the average detection rate for sexual offences is relatively high (61 per cent for the period 2000–2014), detection rates for murder (24 per cent), woundings and shootings (33.7 per cent), kidnapping (46.2 per cent), burglaries and break-ins (13.3 per cent), and robberies (14.9 per cent), leave much to be desired. Even more troubling is the fact that for almost all crimes reviewed, detection rates have been decreasing over time (see figure 1.1). For example, while the average detection rate for murder for the period 2000–2003 was 45.2 per cent, this decreased to 17.9 per cent for the period 2010–14. Similarly, for woundings and shootings, while the detection rate for the period 2000–2003 was 45.9 per cent, this declined to 22 per cent for the period 2010–14. Available data indicate that the only crimes with temporary improvements in detection rates are kidnapping and sexual offences. Detection rates for kidnapping peaked in 2005 and 2006 (58 per cent and 57 per cent respectively), but then declined until 2010. Detection rates for kidnapping exhibited a fluctuating pattern after 2010. Detection rates for sexual offences declined from 2000 to 2011, but have exhibited an increase from 2011 to 2014. The detection rates discussed here are based on arrest data. The number of persons convicted is far fewer than the number of persons arrested. Very low conviction rates reduce confidence in the criminal justice system and indicate that there may be challenges not only within the police service but in other institutions such as the courts.

Table 1.1:   Detection Rates in Trinidad and Tobago, 2000–2014[1]

	Murder		Woundings and shootings		Sexual offences		Kidnapping		Burglaries and break-ins		Robberies	
	Rep.	Det.	Rep.	Det.	Rep.	Det.	Rep.	Det.	Rep.	Det.	Rep.	Det.
2000	120	68	387	217	545	409	156	61	5623	867	4094	767
2001	151	69	499	223	545	383	135	69	5016	807	4269	689
2002	171	74	655	296	641	451	235	110	4930	740	4675	704
2003	229	92	784	333	643	468	235	96	4863	710	4590	758
2004	261	69	643	265	581	414	177	83	5214	894	3885	751
2005	386	94	795	282	738	546	280	163	4548	659	4883	911
2006	371	100	657	243	903	646	214	121	4973	719	5633	921
2007	391	74	680	286	825	550	178	92	4958	676	4965	849
2008	547	99	771	205	724	405	155	67	4855	464	5043	567
2009	506	137	689	196	760	393	155	55	5744	560	6040	743
2010	473	104	623	140	696	346	119	41	5207	521	5075	515
2011	352	77	535	128	650	257	122	57	4220	533	3718	435
2012	379	61	579	116	933	456	185	82	4321	431	4436	528
2013	407	53	542	131	550	223	116	39	2967	349	2958	420
2014	403	65	558	109	829	494	97	45	2592	382	2672	436
Average	343	82	626	211	704	429	171	79	4669	621	4462	666
% detected	24.0		33.7		61.0		46.2		13.3		14.9	

Source: Crime and Problem Analysis Branch of the Trinidad and Tobago Police Service

One of the earlier attempts at police reform in Trinidad and Tobago was the introduction of community-oriented policing, commonly referred to as community policing. According to Ramesh Deosaran (2002), the Association of Caribbean Commissioners of Police decided to implement community-oriented policing, in the region, in 1993. Roy Mitchell, a crime consultant to the Trinidad and Tobago Police Service from 1996 to 1998 and the architect of the *Implementation Proposal for the Community Policing Plan*, in an article in the *Newsday* newspaper of January 27, 2008, noted that the Plan was introduced in 1996. He defined community policing as 'a consultative process', which required a rethinking of the old top-down approach to police-citizen relations. He argued that policing under this concept allowed citizens to articulate their problems. He noted that under traditional policing 'strategies to deal with crime are being handed down and the people are not being allowed to come up with strategies'.[2]

Figure 1.1:   Trends in Detection Rates, 2000–2014

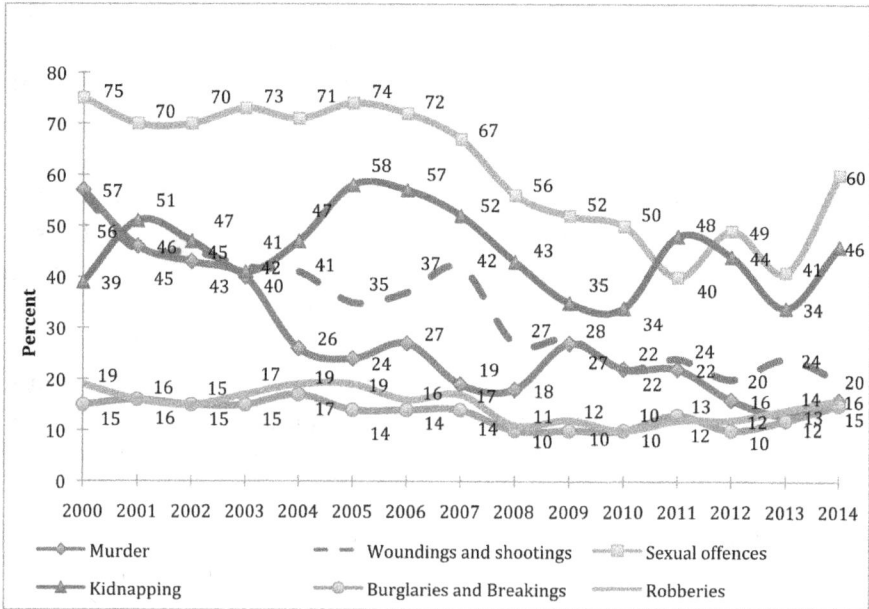

Source: *Crime and Problem Analysis Branch of the Trinidad and Tobago Police Service*

Notwithstanding its good intentions, community policing as the vehicle of change in the Trinidad and Tobago police service, began to 'fizzle out' in 2002. When asked why this occurred, Mitchell indicated that he was unable to answer that question. The answer to this question could, perhaps, be found in a review of the recommendations advanced by Deosaran (2002) for the successful implementation of community-oriented policing. He argued that before the implementation of community policing could be executed, it was necessary to ensure the development of the human resource within the Service and the democratization of the command structure away from the old colonial and paramilitary style. He also argued that to improve community policing it would be necessary to institute oversight and evaluation, build awareness and train all officers in the concepts of community policing. These recommendations were never implemented and community-oriented policing was implemented under the old colonial structure. This greatly reduced the potential of the community-oriented policing approach to be a successful long-term initiative. French criminologist, Marie-Emmanuelle Pomme-rolle, in responding to the *Newsday* newspaper query as to why community policing failed, used the example of a Kenyan experiment. In critiquing the effectiveness of the new community policing plan in Kenya, she adamantly stated that the scheme had failed. Similar to the Trinidad and Tobago experience, she indicated that the Kenyan police force remain the inheritors of colonial authoritarian forces and have not changed since the experiment of community policing began. She argued that, first and foremost, the overall police system has to be democratized in order to facilitate the introduction of community policing.

In 2007, Stephen Mastrofski and Cynthia Lum were contracted as consultants by the Trinidad and Tobago government to assist in devising and implementing policy to reform the Trinidad and Tobago police service and improve their standard of performance. Mastrofski and Lum (2008), in their analysis of the original administrative structures in the Trinidad and Tobago police service, argued that the distribution of governing authority was dysfunctional. They noted that the Ministry of National Security had the responsibility for general policy oversight and budgetary authority over the TTPS. The Police Service Commission (an independent five-member board) made key personnel decisions such as hiring, promotion, discipline and dismissal. This meant that although the Commissioner of Police was considered the head of the organization, his office had little authority to exercise internal control that would ensure the execution of his operational decisions. They also argued that there was no independent authority to monitor the performance of the service. This function was carried out by the Ministry of National Security and the police service, the very entities held accountable for its success. Mastrofski and Lum also noted that the staff of the Police Complaints Authority, which was charged with receiving complaints from the public and monitoring the investigation of the complaints, lacked the professional and technical competence to effectively carry out their assigned functions. The Commissioner's lack of internal control, coupled with the lack of a proper monitoring and evaluation system for the TTPS, resulted in less than adequate performance.

The analysis of Mastrofski and Lum (2008) substantiated previous findings on the Trinidad and Tobago police service. The Committee on the Restructuring of the Police Service (1984) reported that leadership was seen as extremely weak due to managerial inefficiencies, a lack of communication among senior officers, ineffective disciplinary procedures, high turnover among supervisors, uneven and unclear workload among officers and a lack of respect for senior officers among junior officers. Graham Seaby (1993) conducted a thorough investigation into accusations of police corruption and found that corruption was endemic and existed at all ranks. He reported the same issues of inadequate leadership, management, discipline and accountability that previous reports on the TTPS had identified.

In 2007, in response to the crisis of an increasing crime rate and lowered public confidence in the Trinidad and Tobago police service, the government embarked on a package of reforms intended to transform the governance and ultimately the performance of the police service through the provisions of new legislation aimed at addressing the inconsistencies and imbalances in the system (Mastrofski and Lum 2008). In discussing the model adopted by Trinidad and Tobago, Mastrofski and Lum (2008) explained that the reforms consolidated more administrative authority in the office of the Commissioner of Police. The Commissioner was given authority over personnel matters such as hiring, promoting, transfers and the dispensation of discipline. This provided the opportunity for the Commissioner to exert more influence over the conduct of his subordinates. The Ministry of National Security was given the responsibility to guide the policy direction of the police service and monitor its performance. Under the new reforms, provisions were made for external and independent oversight of the Trinidad and Tobago police service by the Police Service Commission and the Police Complaints Authority. The Police Service Commission was assigned the role of 'watchdog' over the TTPS and that of an independent check on the Ministry of National Security. The Commission was now expected to evaluate the performance of the TTPS according to the expectations established by the Ministry of National Security. The power to hire, discipline and review the performance of the Commissioner of Police and deputy commissioners were also vested in the Commission. The Police Complaints Authority was given the responsibility to investigate reports of serious police misconduct and corruption. They were also given a range of investigative powers aimed at providing this independent entity with the authority to investigate and report on the matters reported by members of the public. This reform was geared towards offering an element of transparency and legitimacy in the process.

Mastrofski and Lum (2008) argue that these reforms strengthen the legitimacy of all governing entities, and provide greater internal and external control, transparency and effective technical management. They advised that the success of the reforms was hinged on the ability of the government and its agencies to improve governance through committed leadership, which is reflected in selecting the right calibre of individuals for employment in the service, developing effective managers and ensuring accountability to the citizenry.

Despite the implementation of the reforms, Trinidad and Tobago continues to experience a high crime rate and there has been limited improvement in the relationship between the police and the citizenry. Pino (2009), in critically analysing the attempt at police reform in Trinidad and Tobago, argues that the model adopted was flawed in its application. He postulates that, while Mastrofski and Lum (2008) noted the problems of capacity, corruption and the like, hindering the prospect for successful reform, it appears that the foreign trainers and advisors, Mastrofski included, did not or could not create a reform programme that took into account the complex political, social and economic difficulties unique to the Trinidad and Tobago experience.

The Judicial System in Trinidad and Tobago

The judiciary of the Republic of Trinidad and Tobago comprises the Supreme Court of Judicature and the magistracy. The Supreme Court of Judicature is made up of the Court of Appeal and the High Court. The court system includes one appeal court, three supreme courts, one family court and magistrates' courts located within 13 districts. The Judicial Committee of the Privy Council in the United Kingdom continues to function as the highest court in Trinidad and Tobago. The judiciary is guided by the vision that 'The Judiciary of Trinidad and Tobago provides an accountable court system in which timeliness and efficiency are the hallmarks, while still protecting integrity, fairness, equality and accessibility and attracting public trust and confidence'. However, in December 2010, then President of the Law Association of Trinidad and Tobago, Martin Daly, admitted that the Trinidad and Tobago judicial system was confronted by challenges in relation to preliminary enquiries and the backlog of cases. This situation negatively impacted the ability of the judiciary to operate in an efficient and timely manner. He further noted that these challenges were not unique to Trinidad and Tobago but common to other jurisdictions in the Caribbean.

The Honourable Chief Justice of Trinidad and Tobago, Ivor Archie, in delivering the feature address at the ceremonial opening of the 2010–11 law term, admitted that the judiciary was confronted by challenges in the execution of its functions. In analysing the performance of the Criminal High Court, he noted that the findings were not very encouraging. There was a 14 per cent increase in indictments filed compared to the same period in 2008–2009. The number of capital matters in the High Court declined even as the numbers in the magistrates' courts for preliminary enquiries continued to increase. The number of matters disposed of fell by 30 per cent. Clearance ratios also declined in the past year from 0.87 to 0.53 and acquittals accounted for the largest share of dispositions at 40 per cent. This was followed by discontinued matters or dropped charges. In the magistrates' courts, new filings remained high, dropping marginally from 90,437 matters in 2008–2009 to 89,416 in 2009–2010 and disposition rates improved from 79,226 in 2008–2009 to 88,907 in 2009–2010.

Archie (2010) pointed out that, although the judiciary was seen as central, it was not the only institution involved in the administration of justice. The core process of the judiciary is case management but, in order to facilitate the speedy and efficient execution of this process, the necessary information and resources must be in place at the appropriate time for the judicial officer to dispense with the matter before him or her. The necessary information and resources are, in many instances, outside the direct control of the judiciary or may reside with other stakeholders or agencies whose priorities may be different from that of the judiciary. Archie (2010) noted that this was further compounded by the external challenges posed by overburdened police, prison and social services and environmental challenges such as new technologies, increased filing, reduced national income, customer expectations and most importantly, threats to the security of court officers, jurors and witnesses.

Despite these challenges, Archie (2010) argued that there had been some improvements in the system that led to an improvement in the delivery of service. He noted that the judiciary had restructured the internal management structure along three distinct lines. These included the setting of performance standards that would inform management decisions, the reengineering of the organizational culture into one of professionalism and one which was performance driven, and articulating a clear understanding of the core processes that are being managed and the things that impact their efficient execution. He further pointed out that the judiciary had focused on the nurturing of strategic partnerships that resulted in the successful introduction of the new 'remand via videoconferencing' pilot project. This project involves the cooperation of the prison and police services, the Bar, the ministries of the Attorney General and Public Administration and the judicial technology service provider. It was suggested that the technology be expanded to include bail applications. These advances in the delivery of service should improve the efficiency of the judiciary. Another noted improvement was the increase in the physical space allotted to the judiciary. The Industrial Court building in San Fernando was handed over for use by the Supreme Court with the promise of more accommodation. The increase in physical space enhances the ability of the judiciary to conduct the business of the court.

In December 2010, interviews were conducted with magistrates to identify and explore improvements required to facilitate greater efficiency and effectiveness in the administration of justice in Trinidad and Tobago. Magistrates offered the following recommendations:

- Improvements are needed in the legal aid system. There is need to increase the remuneration package for legal aid cases in order to attract more attorneys into the system. This will reduce the three-to-four-month delay currently experienced in appointing legal aid counsel.

- An increase in the number of scientific officers, particularly firearms and narcotics analysts at the Forensic Science Centre, is required. This will facilitate the timely analysis of court exhibits thereby ensuring that the prosecution is prepared to proceed with cases.

- The replacement of police prosecutors with qualified state attorneys or alternatively the use of police officers who are qualified attorneys to prosecute cases in the magistrates' courts is an absolute necessity. This will improve efficiency in the system in that fewer cases will be referred to the Director of Public Prosecution for the assignment of a prosecuting attorney and it will allow for a higher standard of prosecution.

- The implementation of the video link remand system between the courts and the prison facilities. This will remove the need to transport remanded prisoners to and from the courts. This recommendation is currently being piloted.

- The provision of additional physical space to accommodate the increased workload of the judiciary.

- The replacement of the preliminary enquiry at the magistrates' courts with paper committals. Through the submission of reports and statements instead of the physical appearance of witnesses, the magistrate will make the decision of whether the accused should be committed to stand trial at the next sitting of the High Court. This will facilitate the timely administration of justice.

- The introduction and implementation of plea bargaining legislation to facilitate the speedier disposition of cases. The prosecution will be authorised to offer the defendant the opportunity to plead guilty to the original or lesser charges with the recommendation of a reduced sentence. This will assist in reducing the current backlog of cases in the judicial system.

- The implementation of a victim compensation programme which addresses victims' emotional, physical, psychological and financial needs.

- The provision of competitive remuneration packages for all judicial officers. This will motivate existing officers and encourage applications from competent qualified individuals.

- The review of the sentencing legislation that will provide the judiciary with a wider range of options such as mediation, community service, drug rehabilitation and counselling.

The Trinidad and Tobago Prison Service

The TTPrS is an enforcement arm of the criminal justice system in Trinidad and Tobago. It is a division of the Ministry of Justice, though prior to 2010 it came under the purview of the Ministry of National Security. The TTPrS is headed by the Commissioner of Prisons, who has delegated powers under the Constitution of the Republic of Trinidad and Tobago, and who is ultimately responsible to the Ministry of Justice. There are seven prisons and institutions under the authority of the TTPrS. These include: the Carrera Convict Prison, the Maximum Security Prison, the Women's Prison, the Tobago Convicts' Depot, the Port of Spain Prison, the Golden Grove Prison, the Remand Centre, the Eastern Correctional and Rehabilitation Centre and the Youth Training Centre. The total number of inmates for the period 1992–2001 is shown in table 1.2, while the number of inmates in each of the country's prisons as of July 2013 is shown in table 1.3.

The TTPrS was initially established in the then capital of Trinidad and Tobago, St Joseph, in 1592. It was later relocated to the new capital, Port of Spain, in 1757 at the corner of George and Kings Streets, now Independence Square, but was destroyed by fire in 1808. In 1812, the prison now known as the Port of Spain Prison was completed at its present location at 103a Frederick Street, Port of Spain. In time, the TTPrS expanded to include several district prisons throughout the country. The Carrera Convict Island Prison was established in 1877 off the coast of Chaguaramas. The Young Offenders' Institute was established, in 1926, in St James. By 1949, it was relocated to a 17-acre site on the western side of the Golden Grove Road, opposite to the present site of the Golden Grove Prison, declared an industrial institution and renamed the Youth Training Centre (Youth Training Centre, Quarterly Report January–March 2010).

Table 1.2:   Daily Average Prison Population, 1992–2001

Prisons	1992	1993	1994	1995	1996	1997	1998	1999	2000	2001
Carrera Convict Prison	483	493	529	567	575	570	583	561	501	524
Golden Grove Prison	1097	1053	1023	1073	1284	1407	1443	1456	1341	1189
Maximum Security Prison	0	0	0	0	0	0	116	413	772	815
Port of Spain Prison	916	978	1100	1052	1076	1236	1327	1114	873	884
Remand Centre	437	405	676	922	944	908	837	814	863	795
Tobago Convict Depot	42	49	49	48	50	59	46	59	70	56
Women's Prison	115	114	126	123	128	148	162	155	154	142
Total	3090	3092	3503	3785	4057	4328	4514	4572	4574	4405

Source: The Trinidad and Tobago Prison Service, Administrative Report 2001

Table 1.3:   Total Number of Inmates as of July 2013

Prison	Total No. of Inmates	Total Convicted	Total Remand
Carrera Convict Prison	291	291	0
Eastern Correction & Rehabilitation Centre	105	105	0
Golden Grove Prison	461	461	0
Maximum Security Prison	1089	701	388
Port of Spain Prison	490	95	395
Remand Centre	1051	0	1051
Tobago Convict Depot	47	23	24
Women's Prison	115	47	68
Total	3649	1723	1926

Source: The Trinidad and Tobago Prison Service

During colonial times, Her Majesty's Royal Navy occupied the compound upon which the Golden Grove Prison is presently situated. In 1947, the site was formally converted to a penal institution for men and occupancy thereof officially commenced. The Golden Grove Prison is the only medium security prison in Trinidad and Tobago. It is located on approximately

146 hectares of land, in the ward of Tacarigua, county of St George. The Golden Grove Prison is situated approximately 4.4 kilometres from the Piarco International Airport and 20.9 kilometres from Port of Spain. At the commissioning of the Golden Grove Prison in 1947, the initial facilities comfortably accommodated 300 inmates. The Remand Centre, Golden Grove, was subsequently opened at the Golden Grove Prison Complex in 1974, while the Maximum Security Prison was built and finally occupied in 1998 (The Golden Grove Prison Annual Administrative Report 2002).

Earliest records show that the Women's Prison was first housed at the St James Police barracks in the late 1960s–1970s. It was moved to the Port of Spain Prison in the 1970s and later relocated to the compound of the Golden Grove Prison Complex on the Golden Grove Estate, where it remains to date. Initially, the Women's Prison occupied a very modest building catering to a mere fraction of the inmate population. To meet growing demands, a new building was commissioned in August 1989 by the then prime minister, the Honourable A.N.R. Robinson. This building eventually made way for the new Women's Prison Complex, which was partially opened in the year 2000 (Administrative Report, Women's Prison 2006). Other offices include the Prison Administration Building, Philip Street, Port of Spain, Prison Training College, Tumpuna Road, Arima and the Prison Sports Club, Maximum Security Prisons Grounds, Arouca. The administrative structure of the TTPrS as of 2013 is shown in figure 1.2.

According to the Prison Service mission statement:

> The Trinidad and Tobago Prison Service, as an arm of the criminal justice system, is committed to the protection of society and crime prevention by facilitating the opportunities for habilitation/rehabilitation of offenders while maintaining control under safe, secure and humane conditions.[3]

Cipriani Baptiste et al. (2002) note that the mission statement advocates that the best way to protect society is to ensure the successful reintegration of prisoners such that they become law-abiding citizens. He further notes that the rehabilitative efforts of the TTPrS are founded on a model that incorporates correctional education, cognitive development and spiritual restoration.

Figure 1.2:   Organizational Structure of the Trinidad and Tobago Prisons Service, 2013

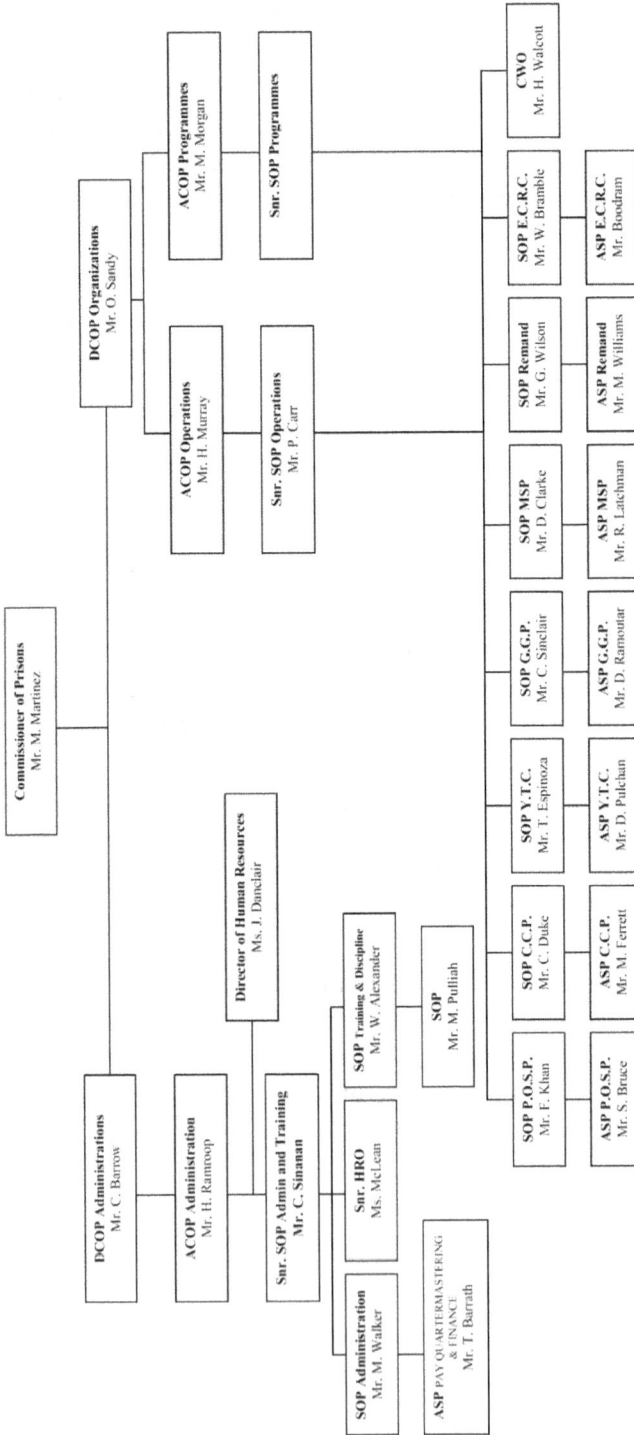

Commissioner of Prisons — Mr. M. Martinez

DCOP Organizations — Mr. O. Sandy
- ACOP Programmes — Mr. M. Morgan
  - Snr. SOP Programmes
    - CWO — Mr. H. Walcott
    - SOP E.C.R.C. — Mr. W. Bramble
      - ASP E.C.R.C. — Mr. Boodram
- ACOP Operations — Mr. H. Murray
  - Snr. SOP Operations — Mr. P. Carr
    - SOP Remand — Mr. G. Wilson
      - ASP Remand — Mr. M. Williams
    - SOP MSP — Mr. D. Clarke
      - ASP MSP — Mr. R. Latchman
    - SOP G.G.P. — Mr. C. Sinclair
      - ASP G.G.P. — Mr. D. Ramoutar
    - SOP Y.T.C. — Mr. T. Espinoza
      - ASP Y.T.C. — Mr. D. Pulchan
    - SOP C.C.P. — Mr. C. Duke
      - ASP C.C.P. — Mr. M. Ferrett
    - SOP P.O.S.P. — Mr. F. Khan
      - ASP P.O.S.P. — Mr. S. Bruce

DCOP Administrations — Mr. C. Barrow
- ACOP Administration — Mr. H. Ramroop
  - Director of Human Resources — Ms. J. Danclair
  - Snr. SOP Admin and Training — Mr. C. Sinanan
    - SOP Training & Discipline — Mr. W. Alexander
      - SOP — Mr. M. Pulliah
    - Snr. HRO — Ms. McLean
      - SOP Administration — Mr. M. Walker
      - ASP PAY QUARTERMASTERING & FINANCE — Mr. T. Barrath

Source: The Trinidad and Tobago Prison Service

Keron King and Terrence Bartholomew (2007) argue that despite the claims of a rehabilitative approach, the present penal system operates primarily according to a retributive model. According to the *Final Report of the Cabinet Appointed Task Force on Prison Reform and Transformation*, the current prison system is characterized by a 'tense setting...which is the result of fragmentation, useless coercion, and obsolete and outdated policies' (Baptiste et al. 2002, 416). To date, the philosophical conceptualization of the prison as a rehabilitative instrument has not fully materialized. This argument is supported by the finding that Trinidad and Tobago has a recidivism rate of 49 per cent (Seepersad 2013).

According to the World Prison Brief (2010) compiled by the International Centre for Prison Studies, King's College, London, Trinidad and Tobago had a prison population of 3,591 as of January 2010, with a prison population rate of 276 per 100,000 inhabitants. A comparison of world prison population rates indicated that Trinidad and Tobago ranked 38 out of a total of 216 nations. Presently, Trinidad and Tobago has a prison population rate of 275 per 100,000 inhabitants. These statistics suggest that there is a need to devise mechanisms to address the level of incarceration and recidivism within our society. This change would be in keeping with a less punitive and more restorative approach.

José Cid (2009) examined the effects of custodial versus non-custodial sentences on recidivism. His findings revealed that prison sanctions do not reduce recidivism more effectively than suspended sentences; however, the risk of recidivism increases when the offender is imprisoned. He argued that the results of his research were compatible with labelling theory, which proposes that prison is likely to lead to higher rates of recidivism compared to a suspended sentence. In order to reduce recidivism it seems reasonable to replace prison with non-custodial sentences. This he postulated is especially important when the offender has no previous conviction or no previous imprisonment. With high-risk offenders, on the other hand, the risk of recidivism is high regardless of whether the penalty is imprisonment or a suspended sentence. Cid (2009) differentiated between the high-risk offender who has a higher risk of reoffending whether incarcerated or not, and those with no exposure to imprisonment. He essentially advocated discretionary sentencing or alternative sanctions for first-time offenders to reduce the possibility of recidivism among this category of persons.

Imprisonment of offenders who are unlikely to reoffend increases the likelihood that they will reoffend for a number of reasons. Once imprisoned, such persons are exposed, on a continual basis, to values and attitudes which support illegal behaviour. They become enmeshed in pro-criminal social networks and may be referred to criminal contacts outside of prison. Further, such offenders may develop new 'skills' which facilitate reoffending and may develop a hatred for conventional society and justifications for committing illegal acts against society. In addition, the loss of employment, disruption of social networks, and labelling and stigmatization by the wider society limits the possibility of successful reintegration into and acceptance by conventional society upon release. Such persons may have no option but to resort to criminality once released.

In 2002, the government of Trinidad and Tobago appointed a task force to review the penal system in Trinidad and Tobago. Their report was seen as a framework of reference for modernizing the penal system in Trinidad and Tobago. One of the key recommendations advanced by the task force was the implementation of a restorative justice philosophy throughout the criminal justice system in Trinidad and Tobago. The task force defined restorative justice as a vision, a public policy, and a criminal justice model that link social justice and criminal justice. They argued that the ultimate restorative justice goal is to keep people out of prison by dealing with them in the community without compromising public safety. The ultimate purpose of restorative justice measures is to heal torn relationships and to restore justice. This means promoting responsibility, safety and peace, so that offenders become stakeholders in society.

Despite these and a series of other recommendations, the prison service, through its website, admits that it is an ongoing challenge to move its operations, objectives, policies, rules and culture from retributive to restorative justice. They are nevertheless committed to ensuring its complete implementation. Evidence of the present government's attempts to expand the restorative approach can be discerned in the previous Minister of Justice, Herbert Volney's views on the penal system. In a *Trinidad Guardian* article dated January 6, 2011, he indicated that prisoner management, which hinges on the notion of reformation and restoration, was one of his main priorities. Minister Volney further noted that:

> The policy of the government is to move the approach of prisoner management from the retributive to the restorative in that not only is punishment a primary facet of incarceration but reforming prisoners for their return to society as better persons. (*Trinidad Guardian* 2011, A8)

Peter Greenwood and Allan Abrahamse (1982) alluded to the concept of discretionary sentencing in their analysis of selective incapacitation.

Incapacitation refers to the use of various punishment restraints to debilitate or remove criminals from society, and thus prevents the crimes that they would have committed, were they still free (Wright 1994). Greenwood and Abrahamse (1982) developed a dangerousness assessment instrument which enables criminal justice practitioners to determine which offenders should receive lengthier prison sentences and which offenders can be sentenced to alternative programmes or safely released into the community. Risk assessment instruments such as this rely on either clinical or actuarial procedures to estimate the risk of reoffending. People with a high risk of reoffending should be incapacitated while those with a low risk of reoffending should be subject to alternative, usually non-custodial dispositions.

Selective incapacitation may represent a framework from which the TTPrS can benefit. The newly appointed prisons inspector, Daniel Khan, in a *Guardian* article dated January 22, 2011, articulated his concerns with the Trinidad and Tobago prisons. He asserted that sub-par conditions such as overcrowding, unsanitary cells, denial of airing time, limited prison visits and numerous concerns relating to food were some of the complaints received from prisoners. He further noted that there have been several local judgments discussing whether these conditions are unconstitutional. The courts have used adjectives such as *distressing, appalling* and *sub-human* and the Court of Appeal emphasized that such conditions were *completely unacceptable in a civilized society*. These conditions pose a major challenge to the rehabilitative process and create an environment where prisoners are not segregated according to their level of dangerousness or the seriousness of offences committed. This situation creates opportunities for seasoned criminals to interact with and influence first-time offenders contributing to a high rate of recidivism.

Conclusion

The criminal justice system in Trinidad and Tobago is currently confronted with the challenge of dealing with very high crime rates. The demand for action and the failure of the criminal justice system to effectively respond has ushered in an era of ongoing reform within each of the arms of the system.

The TTPS, through the implementation of legislative changes, has sought to positively impact the overall performance of the Service. It has been argued that even with the new reforms the Service has not been able to effectively arrest the crime situation. It was argued that the minimal success was due to the failure of the drafters of the plan to consider and incorporate the cultural, social, and economic context of Trinidad and Tobago. It was also noted that the failure to recognize the citizenry as a valid contributing stakeholder both to the restructuring process and the drafting of a 'citizen security' crime plan undermines the success and ultimate purpose of the reform efforts.

The Trinidad and Tobago judiciary is also confronted with the challenge to respond to the changing needs of the society. The demand for timely justice is negatively impacted by the inability of the judiciary to effectively manage backlogged caseloads. This has resulted in the judiciary being described as time-consuming and non-responsive to the needs of citizens. To address the inefficiencies in the system a number of recommendations were advanced.

Over the last decade, the TTPrS has been engaged in the process of reforming its culture, goals and methodology from a retributive to a restorative orientation. The challenges in its implementation are made evident by the high recidivism rate within the system. With the recent change in government and their stated support for the restorative approach it is hoped that the prison service will achieve its goals of reforming its organization and contributing to the rehabilitation of individuals in the system.

Notes
1. Detection rates are based on arrest data.
2. Retrieved from: http://www.newsday.co.tt/crime_and_court/0,72228.html
3. http://ttprisons.com/

Criminal Victimization

The overall level of criminal victimization in Trinidad and Tobago sets the context for an examination of citizen security. Victimization, however, may be assessed in different ways, and contrasting measures may offer very different indications of the extent of victimization. Generally, it has been found that official crime statistics underestimate the level of victimization when compared to self-reported victimization data gathered through victimization surveys. A large proportion of crimes is never reported to the police and thus is not included in official statistics. The 2013 Jamaica National Crime Victimization Survey, for example, found that less than 15 per cent of all incidents of violent criminal victimization were reported to the police. Non-reporting of victimization may occur for a number of reasons. For example, people may think that the police will not be able to solve the crime or that the crime is not a serious one, people lack confidence in the criminal justice system, and victims are afraid of retaliation by perpetrators, etc. It is nevertheless the case that official crime data are important in estimating the level of victimization since the most serious crimes tend to be captured in such data. It is widely accepted, for example, that murder statistics tend to be fairly accurate because of the seriousness of the crime. As the seriousness of the crime decreases, or if there is only a minor loss sustained by the victim, then such crimes may not be reported and official crime statistics become less reliable as a measure of victimization. This chapter will examine official crime data in Trinidad and Tobago for the period 1990–2014,[1] and will compare these data to the findings of self-reported victimization. Self-reported victimization data derive from the United Nations Development Programme's 2012 Human Development Report on crime and insecurity in the Caribbean. The examination of general crime trends will be followed by an in-depth examination of domestic violence, which represents an area which has been under researched in Trinidad and Tobago.

Official crime data for Trinidad and Tobago for the period 1990–2014 are shown in table 2.1 and graphically represented in figures 2.1 and 2.2. These data indicate that there are long-term increases over time for all crimes considered except burglary. Within the last five to six years, however, there have been observed decreases in a number of crimes. For the period 1990–2014, there has been an average of 248 murders per year, with that average increasing to 403 per year within the last five years. On average for the last 24 years, the number of murders has increased by 13.3 per year. This represents an average annual increase of 8.2 per cent.[2] In the case of murders, the rates were relatively stable from 1990 to 1999, but thereafter increased steadily to 2008. Murders thereafter began to decline until 2011, after which there was a gradual increase until 2014.

Demographic data for murder victims are available for the period 2001–13.[3] The data indicate that males very consistently outnumber females as murder victims. When all murders for this period are considered, 89.9 per cent of the victims were male, while 10.1 per cent were female. Almost three-quarters (73.7 per cent) of all murder victims for the period were of African descent. People of East Indian descent made up the next largest group of victims (17.7 per cent) followed by people of mixed descent (6.6 per cent) and 'other' ethnicities (two per cent). Persons of Caucasian (n = 19 or 0.4 per cent), Chinese (n = 15 or 0.3 per cent), and 'Spanish' descent (n = 11 or 0.2 per cent) were numerically the largest groups in the 'other' category. With respect to age, 1.7 per cent of murder victims were aged 14 or younger, 28.8 per cent were 15–24, 17.1 per cent were 35–44, 15.8 per cent were 45–64, and 3.2 per cent were 64 or older.

From 2001 to 2013, during which time 4,624 murders occurred, data on the ages of the perpetrators were available for 24.1 per cent of all murders, while data on the sex of the perpetrators were available for 17.5 per cent, and data on the ethnicity of the perpetrators were available for 21.8 per cent.[4] During this period, 94.9 per cent of perpetrators were male while 5.1 per cent were female. This gender disparity holds for each year of the period under consideration, with some years having no female perpetrators. For the same period, 66.9 per cent of perpetrators were of African descent, 26.1 per cent were of East Indian descent, 6.3 per cent of mixed decent, and 0.7 per cent of other ethnicities. A similar distribution holds for each year of the period under consideration. With respect to age, the majority of perpetrators were between 15 and 24 years of age (34.5 per cent) and 25 and 34 years of age (33.8 per cent). The data also indicate that 0.6 per cent of perpetrators were 14 or younger, 16.6 per cent were between the ages of 35 and 44, 12.3 per cent were between 45 and 64, and 2.2 per cent were 65 and older.

Table 2.1: Crime in Trinidad and Tobago, 1990–2014

	Murder	Wounding/ Shooting	Sexual Offences	Kidnapping	Burglaries and Break-ins	Robbery
1990	84	391	221	13	7,546	3,115
1991	97	453	228	16	7,313	3,099
1992	109	420	274	16	7,938	3,786
1993	111	608	284	41	8,419	4,722
1994	140	533	254	46	7,635	4,490
1995	122	501	309	56	6,542	3,858
1996	107	505	295	81	6,835	4,075
1997	101	370	514	80	6,682	3,393
1998	97	319	572	100	6,112	2,780
1999	93	340	476	136	5,475	3,629
2000	120	387	545	156	5,623	4,094
2001	151	499	545	135	5,016	4,269
2002	171	655	641	235	4,930	4,675
2003	229	784	643	235	4,863	4,590
2004	261	643	581	177	5,214	3,885
2005	386	801	738	280	4,548	4,883
2006	371	657	903	214	4,973	5,633
2007	391	680	825	178	4,958	4,965
2008	547	771	724	155	4,855	5,043
2009	506	689	760	155	5,744	6,040
2010	473	623	696	119	5,207	5,075
2011	352	535	650	122	4,220	3,718
2012	379	579	933	185	4,321	4,436
2013	407	542	550	116	2,967	2,958
2014	403	558	829	97	2,592	2,672
Avg. all years	248.3	553.7	559.6	125.8	5,621.1	4,155.3
Avg. last 5 years	402.8	567.4	731.6	127.8	3,861.4	3,771.8
Avg. increase	13.3	6.9	25.3	3.5	-206.4	-18.5

Source: Crime and Problem Analysis Branch of the Trinidad and Tobago Police Service

Figure 2.1:   Murders, Woundings and Shootings, Sexual Offences and
              Kidnapping, 1990–2014

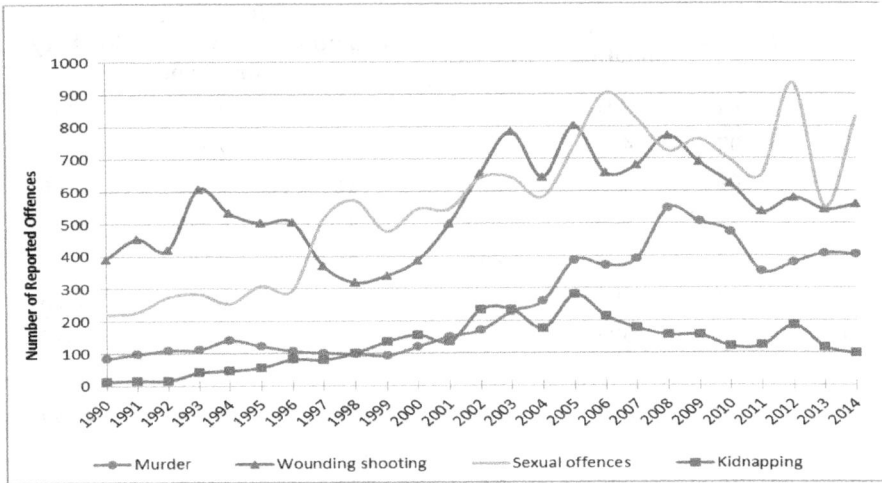

Source: Crime and Problem Analysis Branch of the Trinidad and Tobago Police Service

Figure 2.2: Robberies and Burglaries and Break-ins, 1990–2014

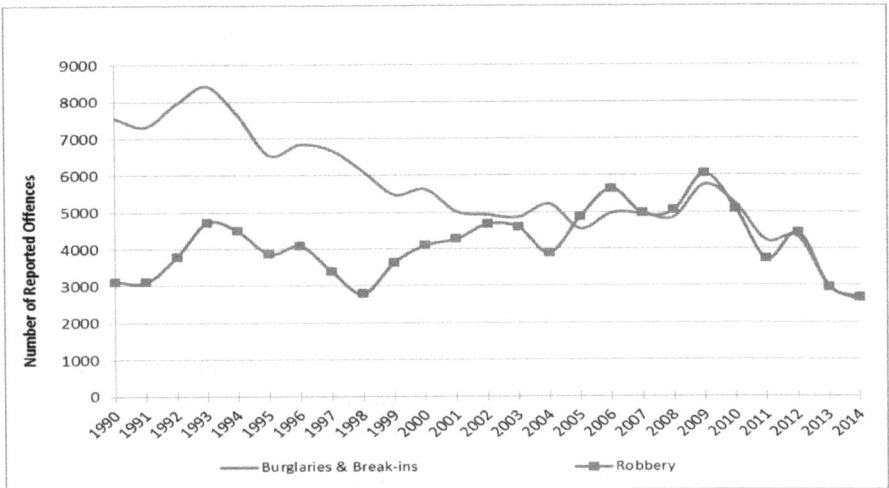

Source: Crime and Problem Analysis Branch of the Trinidad and Tobago Police Service

From 1990 to 2014, an average of 554 woundings and shootings occurred per year, with this increasing to an average of 567 in the last five years; the number of woundings and shootings increased by an average of 6.9 per year (an average increase of three per cent per annum) over the last 24 years. While there is an overall increase in the number of woundings and shootings during this time period, long-term trends indicate that there were two clearly discernible periods in which there was a rise then a fall in the number of incidents. The first period was from 1990 to 1998, while the second period was from 1999 to 2014. With respect to the first period, the number of woundings and shootings increased over the period 1990–93, and then declined up to 1998. In the second period, there was an increase from 1999 to 2003, with some fluctuation between 2003 and 2008, and then a decline to 2014.

Data on kidnappings indicate that an average of 126 kidnappings occurred per year in Trinidad and Tobago for the period 1990–2014, with an average of 128 per year in the last five years. On average, there was an increase in the number of kidnappings by 3.5 per year for the period 1990 to 2014. This represents a 14.6 per cent increase per year over the last 24 years. The total number of kidnappings increased steadily from 1990 to 2005 and only began to decline after 2005. From 2005 to 2014, Trinidad and Tobago has seen a steady decline in the total number of kidnappings. From 1997 to 2013, there were 2,778 kidnappings, of which 257 or 9.3 per cent were for ransom. During the last five years of this period, there were 697 kidnappings, of which 25 or 3.6 per cent were for ransom.

Figure 2.3: Kidnappings, 1997–2013

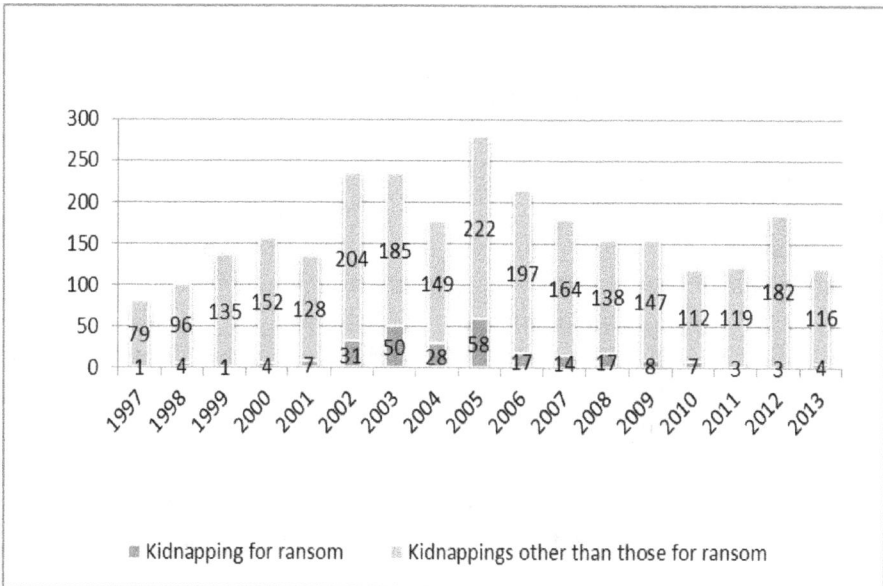

Source: Crime and Problem Analysis Branch of the Trinidad and Tobago Police Service

Time trends for kidnapping for ransom indicate that the number of such kidnappings was stable from 1997 to 2001, but increased dramatically from 2001 to 2005. In the latter year, 58 kidnappings for ransom were recorded, the highest number on record for the period for which data are available. Subsequent to 2005, there was a consistent decline in the number of kidnappings for ransom, with the number being less than ten per year after 2008 (figure 2.3).

An average of 560 major sexual offences[5] occurred annually during the period 1990 to 2014, with the average increasing to 732 per year in the last five years; the number of sexual offences increased by an average of 25.3 per year during the last 24 years. This represents an average annual increase of 10.7 per cent. The number of sexual offences increased steadily from 1990 to 2006 and then declined from 2006 to 2011, increased sharply in 2012 only to decline again in 2013, but thereafter increase in 2014. When rape alone is considered, data for the period 1993–2013 indicate that there was an average of 247 rapes per year in Trinidad and Tobago. For this period, rapes represented 41.8 per cent of all sexual offences. These data indicate that there was a gradual increase in the number of rapes from 1993 to 2005, with a gradual decrease from 2005 to 2013, with the only exception to this trend occurring in 2012.

For the period 1990 to 2014, there was an average of 4,155 robberies per year, with this decreasing to an average of 3,772 per year in the last five years. On average, the number of robberies has decreased by 18.5 per year. This represents an average annual decline of 0.93 per cent. While the number of robberies has fluctuated from year to year, there is a clearly discernible upward trend in the number of robberies from 1990 to 2009, and thereafter a decline until 2014. On average over the last 24 years, there were 5,621 burglaries and break-ins per year, with this average decreasing to 3,861 per year in the last five years. Overall, the number of burglaries and break-ins has decreased by 206 per year from 1990 to 2014. This represents an average annual decline of 3.8 per cent.

The decrease in the number of burglaries and break-ins may not necessarily indicate that something is being done correctly to address this specific crime. By definition, burglaries and break-ins are non-violent crimes which take place in the absence of the victim. The simultaneous increase in robberies from 1990 to 2008 suggests that the decrease in the number of burglaries and break-ins may indicate that people who were once content to take property via non-violent means, are now becoming more violent. Robbery incorporates a property crime with an element of actual or threatened violence. These data may indicate that people who were once engaged in burglaries and break-ins are 'graduating' to the more violent crime of robbery. Despite this possibility, however, there could be other factors, such as increased usage of burglar proofing and private security devices and personnel, or even a decrease in the reporting of burglaries and break-ins, which may account for the decrease that were noted. The sharp decline in robberies after 2009 is also noteworthy and may be due to changes in policing and other law enforcement tactics.

Table 2.2 shows the annual average number of crimes and the percentage of crimes that occurred in each police division for the period 2000 to 2014. The Port of Spain division accounted for the largest proportion of murders (26 per cent) during this time period with an average of 89.3 murders occurring annually in this division. This was followed by the Northern division (19.5 per cent), North Eastern division (13.4 per cent) and Western division (12.3 per cent). The divisions with the lowest proportion of murders were Tobago (1.8 per cent) and the South Western division (4.4 per cent). The Port of Spain and Northern divisions also stand out as the two with the highest proportion of woundings and shootings (24.4 and 17 per cent respectively). In these divisions there were, respectively, an average of 153 and 107 woundings and shootings annually. Tobago and the Eastern division had the lowest proportion of woundings and shootings for the period under consideration. The Northern (18.4 per cent), Southern (16.2 per cent) and Eastern (13.3 per cent) divisions had the highest proportions of sexual offences. The Northern (23.8 per cent), Port of Spain (18.9 per cent) and Southern (15.9 per cent) divisions had the highest proportions of robberies while these same divisions had the highest proportions of burglaries and break-ins. When the data are examined for the period 2000–2014, there is considerable stability in the spatial concentration of each of the crimes under consideration.

In assessing official crime data it must be borne in mind that a far larger proportion of all crimes occur in Trinidad than in Tobago (table 2.3). For the period 2000–2014, 98.2 per cent of all murders, 97.2 per cent of woundings and shootings, 94.6 per cent of sexual offences, 97.7 per cent of robberies and 91 per cent of burglaries occurred in Trinidad. While a larger proportion of crimes occur in Trinidad, the relative population sizes of both islands must be taken into account to ascertain the risk of victimization in each island. Table 2.3 also shows the average annual crime rates for various crimes for the period 2000–2014.[6] While the rates for murder, woundings and shootings and robberies are higher in Trinidad than in Tobago, the rates for sexual offences and burglaries and break-ins are higher in Tobago than in Trinidad.

Table 2.2:   Crimes Occurring by Police Division, 2000–2014

Police Division	Murder		Woundings/ Shootings		Sexual Offences		Robberies		Burglaries/ Break-ins	
	Avg.	%	Avg.	%	Avg.	%	Avg.	%	Avg.	%
Port of Spain	89.3	26.0	152.9	24.4	53.8	7.6	843.5	18.9	610.3	13.1
Southern	28.9	8.4	74.3	11.8	113.9	16.2	707.2	15.9	705.7	15.1
Western	42.1	12.3	67.6	10.8	54.7	7.8	387.2	8.7	447.9	9.6
Northern	66.9	19.5	106.7	17.0	129.5	18.4	1060.9	23.8	875.3	18.7
Central	30.7	9.0	71.7	11.4	89.1	12.6	586.7	13.1	585.0	12.5
South Western	15.0	4.4	33.0	5.3	68.8	9.8	202.6	4.5	356.9	7.6
Eastern	17.9	5.2	32.6	5.2	93.5	13.3	155.5	3.5	268.4	5.7
North Eastern	46.0	13.4	70.4	11.2	63.2	9.0	413.7	9.3	401.1	8.6
Tobago	6.2	1.8	17.6	2.8	38.3	5.4	104.2	2.3	420.5	9.0

Source: Crime and Problem Analysis Branch of the Trinidad and Tobago Police Service

Table 2.3:   Comparison of Crime Rates for Trinidad and Tobago, 2000–2014

	Per cent Tobago	Average annual number of offences		Rate	
		Trinidad	Tobago	Trinidad	Tobago
Murder	1.8	336.9	6.2	26.6	10.2
Woundings and shootings	2.8	609.3	17.6	48.1	28.9
Sexual offences	5.4	666.4	38.3	52.6	62.9
Robberies	2.3	4357.3	104.2	343.9	171.2
Burglaries and break-ins	9.0	4250.5	420.5	335.4	690.7

Source: Crime and Problem Analysis Branch of the Trinidad and Tobago Police Service

Victimization survey data from a random sample of 1,595 adults in Trinidad and Tobago (UNDP 2012) were also available for use in estimating victimization rates. Respondents were asked to indicate the extent to which they had been victimized within the previous ten years. It was discovered that, in this period, 23.9 per cent of the sample (n = 381 respondents) indicated that they had been victims of a crime. Of these, 48.5 per cent had been victimized once, 27.3 per cent had been victimized twice, and 24.2 per cent had been victimized three or more times. Of those who had been victimized, 27.6 per cent were between the ages of 18 and 30, 33.6 per cent were between the ages of 31 and 45, 30.2 per cent were between the ages of 46 and 65, while 8.6 per cent were over 65 years of age. A larger proportion of males had been victims of crime within the previous ten years (57 per cent) than females (43 per cent). With respect to ethnicity, the majority of victims were of African descent (40.7 per cent), while 25.5 per cent were of Indian descent, 28.1 per cent were mixed, and 5.7 per cent were of other ethnicities. The most frequently occurring crime was robbery at gunpoint (5.6 per cent of the sample), followed by robbery with other types of weapons (3.8 per cent), break-ins in homes during the day (3.4 per cent), break-ins at night (2.5 per cent), assault with a weapon (2.3 per cent), theft from a motor vehicle (1.9 per cent), and motor vehicle theft (1.1 per cent). For 11 other crimes on which respondents reported, prevalence rates of victimization were less than one per cent (table 2.4).

Table 2.4:   Self-reported Victimization in Trinidad and Tobago

	Percentage Victimized within the Previous Ten years	Percentage Victimized within the Previous Year
Attempted murder	0.8	0.3
Assault with a weapon	2.3	1.1
Robbery at gunpoint	5.6	1.0
Robbery with other types of weapons	3.8	1.1
Sexual assault and or rape	0.4	0.4
Extortion/protection	0.3	0.2
Domestic violence involving a partner	0.9	0.6
Family violence	0.8	0.4
Break-in at your house in the day	3.4	1.8
A break-in at your house at night	2.5	0.2
Motor vehicle theft	1.1	0.3
Theft from motor vehicle	1.9	0.8
Kidnapping (for ransom)	0.1	0.0
Abduction	0.1	0.1
Financial crime/scam	0.6	0.3
Praedial larceny	0.9	0.9
A threat on your life by someone with a weapon	0.9	0.4
A threat on your life by someone without a weapon	0.5	0.2
Overall victimization level	23.9	10.2

Source: Victimization Survey of 1,595 Adults in Trinidad and Tobago

Respondents in the victimization survey were also asked to indicate whether or not they had been victimized within the previous year (this refers to crimes committed in 2009), and if they had been victims of a crime, to indicate which crimes (table 2.4). It was discovered that 10.2 per cent of the sample had been victims of a crime in the previous year. Of those who had been victimized in the previous year, 23.9 per cent were between the ages of 18 and 30, 37.4 per cent were between the ages of 31 and 45, 31.3 per cent were between the ages of 46 and 65, while 7.4 per cent were over 65 years of age. A larger proportion of males had been victims of crime in the previous year (60.7 per cent) than females (39.3 per cent). With respect to ethnicity, 43.6 per cent of the persons victimized within the last year were of African descent, while 26.4 per cent were of Indian descent, 25.8 per cent of mixed descent, and 4.2 per cent of other ethnicities. The most prevalent offences within the previous year were break-ins during the day (1.8 per cent of the sample), robbery with other types of weapons (1.1 per cent), assault with a weapon (1.1 per cent), robbery at gunpoint (1.0 per cent), praedial larceny (0.9 per cent), and theft from a motor vehicle (0.8 per cent).

Overall, within the previous year, 1.4 per cent of the sample had been victims of violent crimes, while five per cent had been victims of property crimes, and 0.5 per cent victims of financial crimes. Data collected indicate that younger people were more likely to become victims of violent crime than older people (figure 2.4). Of those who had been victims of violent crimes, 34.7 per cent were between the ages of 18 and 30, 30.4 per cent were between the ages of 31 and 45, 17.4 per cent were between the ages of 46 and 65, and 17.5 per cent were over 65 years of age. In contrast, older people were more likely to be victims of property crime than younger people. Of those who had been victims of property crime, 16.5 per cent were between the ages of 18 and 30, 40.5 per cent were between the ages of 31 and 45, 34.2 per cent were between the ages of 46 and 65, while 8.8 per cent were over 65 years of age. Interestingly, males and females were equally likely to be victims of violent crimes (52.2 per cent vs. 47.8 per cent, respectively), while males were more likely to be victims of property crimes than females (59.5 per cent vs. 40.5 per cent, respectively). Slightly more than half (52.2 per cent) of all victims of violent crimes within the previous year were of Indian descent, while 17.4 per cent were of African descent, 26.1 per cent were mixed, and 4.3 per cent were of other ethnicities (figure 2.5). In contrast, persons of African descent were more likely than any other group to be victims of property crimes. Fully 45.6 per cent of all people who had been victims of property crimes within the last year were of African descent, while 20.3 per cent were of Indian descent, 29.1 per cent were mixed, and five per cent were of other ethnicities.

Figure 2.4: Violent and Property Crime Victimization as a Function of Age

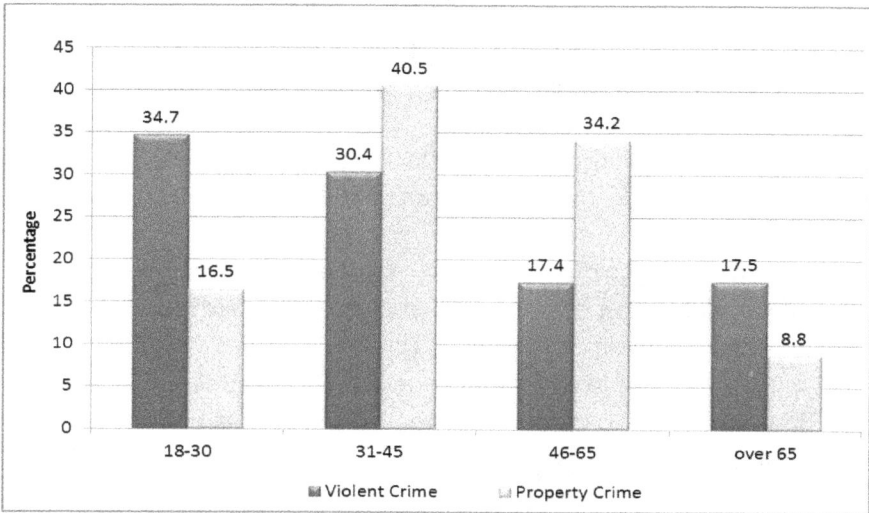

Source: Victimization Survey of 1,595 Adults in Trinidad and Tobago

Figure 2.5: Violent and Property Crime Victimization as a Function of Ethnicity

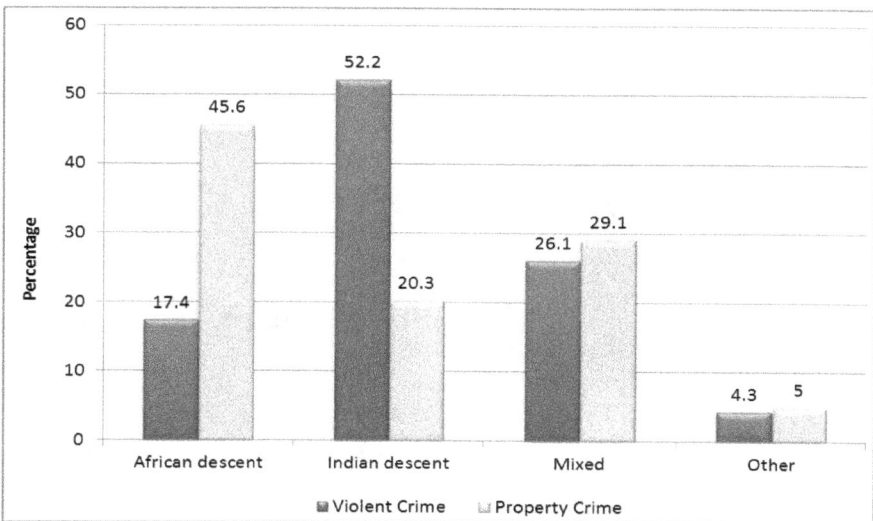

Source: Victimization Survey of 1,595 Adults in Trinidad and Tobago

Within the previous year, 2.6 per cent of the sample had been physically harmed when they were victimized and, for 1.9 per cent of the sample, the harm sustained was serious enough to seek medical attention. For those who had been physically harmed, 50 per cent had been harmed by a stranger, 10.8 per cent by an acquaintance, 15.2 per cent by a friend, and 24 per cent by other people. Data collected indicate that younger people, especially those in the 18–24 and 25–30 age groups, were more likely than older persons to sustain physical injury when they were victimized (figure 2.6). On average, as people became older, the chance of being physically harmed during the victimization incident decreased.[7] Males were more likely to be physically harmed during an incident of criminal victimization than females (59.5 per cent vs. 40.5 per cent). With respect to ethnicity, of those physically harmed, 38.1 per cent were of African descent, 40.5 per cent were of Indian descent, 19 per cent were mixed, and 2.4 per cent were of other ethnicities.

Respondents were asked to indicate whether or not other people in their households (i.e., not including themselves) had been victims of crime within the previous ten years and within the previous year (table 2.5).

Figure 2.6: Sustaining Physical Injury as a Function of Age

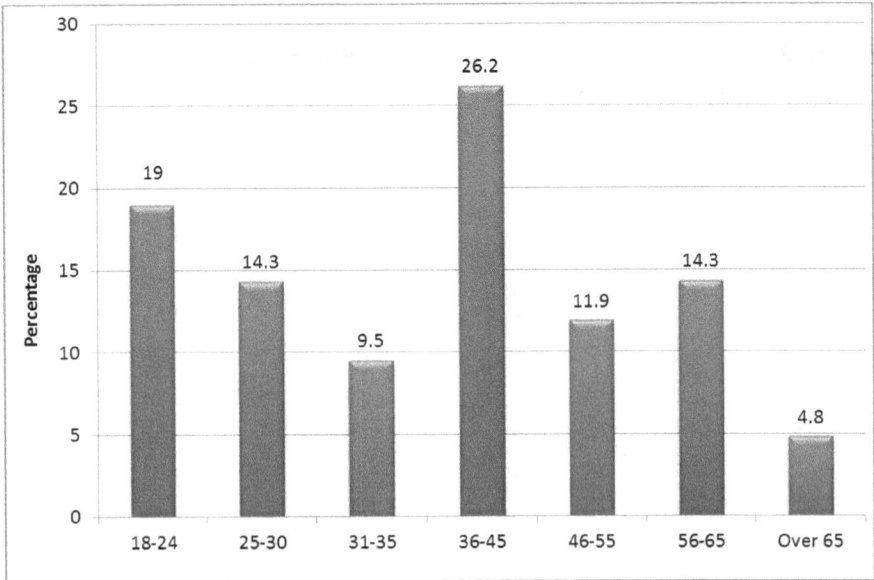

Source: Victimization Survey of 1,595 Adults in Trinidad and Tobago

Within the previous ten years, 16.5 per cent of the sample indicated that one other person in the household had been a victim of crime, 4.8 per cent indicated that two people had been victims of crime, 1.5 per cent indicated that three people had been victims of crime, and 1.3 per cent indicated that more than three people in their households had been victims of crime. Overall, 24.1 per cent of households had been victims of crime within the previous ten years. Within the previous year, 11.5 per cent of households had one person other than the respondent who had been victimized, 3.4 per cent had two people who had been victimized, 0.9 per cent had three people who had been victimized, and 0.6 per cent had more than three people who had been victimized. Overall, 16.4 per cent of households had been victims of crime within the previous year. Within the last year, the most prevalent types of victimization at the household level were robbery (11.5 per cent of households), assault with a weapon (3.9 per cent), motor vehicle theft (2.7 per cent), a threat on life (2.6 per cent), theft from a motor vehicle (2.5 per cent), and domestic violence involving a partner (1.9 per cent).

Table 2.5:   Members of Respondents' Households Victimized in 2009

	Percentage Victimized within the Last Year
Robbery	11.5
Assault with a weapon	3.9
Motor vehicle theft	2.7
A threat on their life	2.6
Theft from motor vehicle (motor vehicle break-in)	2.5
Domestic violence involving a partner	1.9
Murder	1.4
Attempted murder	1.4
Other family violence (other than your partner)	1.3
Sexual assault and/or rape	1.1
Extortion and/or protection rackets	0.6
Kidnapping	0.6
Abduction	0.5

Source: Victimization Survey of 1,595 Adults in Trinidad and Tobago

Table 2.6:   Official and Self-reported Crime Rates per 100,000 Inhabitants for 2009[9]

	Victimization survey data	Official crime data (TTPS)	Ratio of victimization survey vs. official crime rates
Praedial larceny	900	13.5	66.7
Assault with a weapon/wounding and shooting, and malicious wounding	1,100	92.1	11.9
Financial crime or scam/fraud	300	41.4	7.2
Sexual assault and rape	400	60.8	6.6
Domestic violence involving a partner	600	95.0	6.3
Robbery	2,100	456.7	4.6
Break-in and burglary	1,800	434.3	4.1
Motor vehicle theft	300	124.2	2.4

Sources: Victimization Survey of 1,595 Adults in Trinidad and Tobago and TTPS

Victimization data can be used to compute victimization rates for the population. Such rates can be compared to the rates indicated in official crime data to assess the extent to which official crime data represent an accurate picture of the crime situation.[8] Invariably, self-report data indicate that victimization levels are substantially higher than indicated by official crime statistics (see table 2.6). The largest discrepancy occurs with praedial larceny which is 66.7 times higher than indicated in official crime data. This is followed by assault with a weapon. According to the data the actual rate of assault with a weapon is 11.9 times higher than indicated in official crime data. Financial crimes or fraud are 7.2 times more prevalent than indicated in official crime data while the rate of sexual assault is 6.6 times higher than that indicated in official crime statistics. This is followed by domestic violence which is 6.3 times higher than indicated in official crime data. The number of robberies is 4.6 times higher than that indicated in official statistics while the number of break-ins and burglaries is 4.1 times higher. The number of motor vehicle thefts is 2.4 times higher than that indicated in official crime data.

Domestic Violence: A Special Case of Victimization

In a general sense, there may be many vulnerable groups in any given society, and vulnerability may be based on a range of things, including but not limited to a lack of financial resources, cultural differences, the lack of numerical strength of certain groups, sexual orientation and gender roles, cultural stereotypes and a comparative lack of physical strength (for example, children compared to adults).[10] Vulnerable groups by definition are less well protected under certain circumstances and thus may be victimized to a greater extent than non-vulnerable groups. Unfortunately as well, vulnerability may not be addressed at all, or adequately, by the legislative framework available. Even where there are legislative provisions to reduce vulnerability, social and cultural factors may nevertheless encourage behaviour that helps to perpetuate the vulnerability of some groups. For example, in the United States (US), while equal opportunity legislation is intended to protect the rights and privileges of minorities, many researchers have found that prejudice and discrimination exist, both external to and within the criminal justice system. This puts vulnerable populations at a disadvantage in American society.

Where women are concerned, vulnerabilities exist both within the society and family. Despite increases in the education level of females relative to males in Trinidad and Tobago, available data indicate that, for comparable occupations, women earn an average of 65 cents on the dollar compared to men. Data from the Trinidad and Tobago Central Statistical Office show, for example, that in 2000, women who were legislators and senior office managers earned 52.8 per cent of what males in similar jobs earned. For other occupations, the earnings of women were similarly lower than that of men (57.7 per cent for service workers, including Defence Force and shop sales workers, and 55.2 per cent for craft and related workers). For other occupational categories, the disparities were smaller, but nevertheless still apparent. In the case of plant and machine operators and assemblers and elementary occupations, women earned almost 65 cents on the dollar compared to men. For professionals, the figures were higher (73.5 per cent), while the smallest gender disparities were for technicians and associate professionals (84.1 per cent) and clerks (87.8 per cent). Data for 1998 and 1999 indicate similar gender disparities, with slight improvements over the period 1998–2000. Table 2.7 summarizes the relevant data for the period 1998–2000.

An examination of the percentage of males and females in different occupations further reveals the problem of lower earnings. Even where the same occupations are concerned women are concentrated in lower paying jobs, compared to men. Central Statistical Office data for 2000 (table 2.8) indicate, for example, that while 22.4 per cent of the female workforce are clerks, only 4.2 per cent of males are employed in this occupation.

Table 2.7:   Women's Average Income as a Percentage of Men's,
              1998–2000

Occupational group	1998	1999	2000
Legislators, senior officers and managers	52.9	52.3	52.8
Professionals	75.6	80.6	73.5
Technicians and associate professionals	76.7	79.7	84.1
Clerks	86.6	85.9	87.8
Service workers and shop sales workers	50.2	53.5	57.7
Agricultural, forestry and fishery workers	52.9	67.3	68.7
Craft and related workers	50.0	47.3	55.2
Plant and machine operators and assemblers	54.9	64.8	64.9
Elementary occupations	61.9	64.1	64.4
Average percentage	62.4	66.1	67.7

Source: Central Statistical Office of Trinidad and Tobago 2000 Census

Table 2.8:   Percentage of Economically Active Men and Women (2000 Data)

Occupational group	Women	Men
Legislators, senior officers and managers	6.6	6.3
Professionals	3.1	2.4
Technicians and associate professionals	13.6	7.2
Clerks	22.4	4.2
Service workers and shop sales workers	22.9	10.8
Agricultural, forestry and fishery workers	1	4.1
Craft and related workers	5.5	24.9
Plant and machine operators and assemblers	2.8	13
Elementary occupations	21.9	27

Source: Central Statistical Office of Trinidad and Tobago 2000 Census

Table 2.9:   Women and Men's Participation in the Labour Force, 1996–2000

Indicator	1996	1997	1998	1999	2000
Number of women as a percentage of the labour force	38.6	37.9	38.3	38.2	38.4
Number of men as a percentage of the labour force	61.4	62.1	61.7	61.8	61.6
Female unemployment rate	21.0	19.4	18.8	16.8	15.2
Male unemployment rate	13.2	12.3	11.3	10.9	10.2

Source: Central Statistical Office of Trinidad and Tobago 2000 Census

Similarly, 22.9 per cent of employed females are either service workers or involved in shop sales, while only 10.8 per cent of males are in similar occupations. There are some exceptions to this, however. More males than females are involved in craft and related occupations and elementary occupations. With respect to some of the higher paying occupations, females are making some headway relative to males. Of those who are legislators and senior officers and managers, 6.6 per cent are women while 6.3 per cent are men. Similarly, 3.1 per cent of professionals are female while 2.4 per cent are male, and 13.6 per cent of those who are technicians and associate professionals are female, compared to 7.2 per cent male. While the number of females relative to males is increasing for some of the higher paying occupations, these occupations account for only a small proportion of all occupations, indicating that many females are still restricted to low-paying occupations. In addition, as table 2.7 indicates, where there are females in high paying jobs, they still only earn a fraction on the dollar compared to males. Table 2.9 further indicates that overall, there are fewer females than males in the labour force, and the unemployment rate for females is higher than that for males for the entire period for which data are available.

Economic vulnerability is a reflection of culture and a belief system that perpetuates and accepts inequality. This vulnerability is also reflective of a legislative system that has not adequately addressed the issue of gender equality. While economic vulnerabilities have far-reaching implications in and of themselves, the larger sociocultural framework, which perpetuates such inequality, can also be conducive to other forms of inequality that perpetuate the vulnerability of females relative to males. Such a cultural system implicitly undervalues females and offers less to females in the way of opportunities for improvement and equality of treatment when they require assistance.

Economic inequality disempowers women and leaves them dependent. Economic dependence is a factor which has been linked to domestic violence (Lyon 2002; Strube and Barbour 1983). In the case of the family unit, economic dependency refers to the degree to which one person relies on another for financial support and is used to describe situations in which one member of a dyad (here the male) has exclusive or predominant control over financial resources (Alvi and Selbee 1997). The economic dependency of one member of a cohabiting couple may lead the dependent person to tolerate mistreatment because of a lack of viable living alternatives (Dearwater, Cohen and Campbell 1998; Dutton 1995).

Gender-based economic inequality also impacts upon single-parent families, and is especially important in a Caribbean setting where female-headed households are common. On average, female-headed families will face comparatively greater levels of hardship compared to male-headed single-parent families. Such hardships impact upon the children and mother and can have a number of negative implications.

Domestic violence refers to physical, psychological or sexual violence which occurs in families. W. Penn Handwerker (1997, 30) clarifies that violence 'encompasses anything that an individual experiences as the illegitimate exercise of what may be variously described as coercion, force, control or exploitation.' This definition includes, but is not limited to, kicking, shoving, pushing, slapping, clubbing, stabbing, shooting as well as verbal and psychological terrorization of the individual concerned. As well as causing physical damage, domestic violence can lead to psychological distress and trauma, with effects possibly lasting a lifetime. In addition, females who have been sexually abused as young girls may be in an especially vulnerable state, even many years later, and may never be able to make a full recovery (Browne et al. 1998). Abused women are often debilitated by anxiety, may suffer post-traumatic stress disorder, exhibit increased consumption of alcohol, tobacco, and illegal drugs, experience depression, and attempt suicide (Andrews and Brown 1998; Koss 1990; Plichta 1992; Rawlins 2000). Other researchers have found that victims of domestic violence are more prone to health complications since they have lowered immunity brought about by the stress of experiencing domestic abuse (World Health Organization 1997). Domestic violence impacts negatively on the lives of everyone who experiences it, witnesses it, or becomes aware of it. It 'affects society negatively, causing fear among those close to it, and a sense of helplessness among those who are unsure as to what needs to be done to reduce its incidence' (Rawlins 2000, 168).

One of the most important factors which prevent abused women from seeking help is their disadvantaged economic position. In addition to this, Michael Strube and Linda Barbour (1983) found that abused women's economic dependency is associated with a decreased likelihood of terminating an abusive relationship. Richard Gelles (1976) and Elaine Hilberman and Kit Munson (1978) found that women who are more economically dependent on their partners may be more tolerant of abuse and therefore, less likely to leave abusive relationships. Many abused women lack the education and skills to obtain employment; this is exacerbated in Trinidad and Tobago where there is a lack of equality to job access and remuneration. The responsibility for child care likewise can preclude the acquisition of work outside the home (Strube and Barbour 1983).

More recent studies suggest that the combination of poverty and violence in the household creates particular difficulties for women's well-being and ability to achieve self-sufficiency (Lyon 2002). In essence, abused women may never be empowered unless they are allowed sufficient access to gain resources (Busch and Valentine 2000). If a woman is not financially secure or lacks the opportunity to become financially secure, she may be unable to leave an abusive relationship. The rhetoric and ideology of empowerment have been provided as a guiding principle for interventions, at least to support abused women who are economically dependent on their abusive partners. Unfortunately, these efforts have a limited impact on changing abused women's status in the family because attempts to operationalize the means by which abused women can become empowered are scarce (Peled et al. 2000).

While economic dependency and the related factors of patriarchal sociocultural values and beliefs are important factors which increase women's vulnerability, other Caribbean research has linked domestic violence to a number of additional risk factors, including alcoholism and drug abuse, and the breakdown of the family structure, which here include changes which lead to matrifocality in the case of families with people of African descent, and changes in the extended family system in the case of families with people of East Indian descent (Gopaul and Reddock 1994). Other research suggests that women who have been involved in situations involving domestic violence are more likely to perceive their existing situations as hopeless. They adapt instead of leaving or exploring meaningful alternatives. Despite the fact that a number of risk factors have been identified, many service providers who are developing programmes and innovations to help with the problem fail to address the perceived and real difficulties of changing the internal dynamics of the family, the availability of social support, the lack of necessary social and economic resource programmes for abused women and their children, and the lack of enforcement of existing laws (McDonald 1989).

A number of researchers have attempted to assess the prevalence of domestic violence in Trinidad and Tobago. Joan Rawlins (1998) estimates that one in four women in Trinidad and Tobago has experienced some form of domestic violence. In a later study, Rawlins (2000) sampled 200 women in two communities in Trinidad – Barataria and Chaguanas – and found that 27 per cent of the sample had lived in homes in which they witnessed domestic violence when they were children. As children, eight per cent of the sample reported having been a victim of abuse in the home. Respondents indicated that their fathers were most likely to be the perpetrators of acts of domestic violence (61 per cent), followed by other males in the family (32 per cent). Rawlins further found that 16 per cent experienced domestic violence in adulthood. In adulthood, the majority of victims (77 per cent) were women, with the main perpetrators being their husbands. The data further indicated that there were no ethnic differences in the experience of domestic violence in childhood or adulthood. Other research found that over one quarter of the men on death row in Trinidad and Tobago were charged with killing their wives, girlfriends, or common-law spouses (Women and Development Studies Group 1994). Domestic violence has also been linked to child abuse (Anaya 2004; Humphreys et al. 2001; Jouriles et al. 2008). As such, where women are abused, other family members may also be at risk. Indeed, a study conducted in Trinidad and Tobago by S. Patel et al. (1999) revealed that of 200 antenatal women who were interviewed, 9.2 per cent had experienced abuse during their most recent pregnancy.

One of the most recent studies to assess the prevalence of domestic violence in Trinidad and Tobago is by Eugene Anyanwu (2011). Importantly, this study attempted to determine whether or not economic dependence is related to the level of domestic violence, as well as the willingness of abused women to leave their abusive relationships. A sample of 176 women between the ages of 18 and 61 years were asked to indicate the extent to which they had been the victims of nine different abusive acts in their relationships with male partners. Responses ranged from never to frequently. Lifetime prevalence for being attacked with a weapon was 17.6 per cent, threatened with violence, 26.2 per cent, punched/shoved, 33 per cent, hit, 34.6 per cent, forced to have sex, 16.5 per cent, having their life threatened, 19.3 per cent, being dominated, 25 per cent, experiencing violence against their children, 8.5 per cent, and being stopped from pursuing their choices and interests, 18.8 per cent (table 2.10).

The responses for all items were summed to compute a scale which reflected the total lifetime prevalence of domestic violence. While a number of predictors were used in this study (including age, number of children in the family, income, and level of education) the only significant predictor of total domestic violence was the willingness to leave the abusive relationship. Consistent with the findings of Rawlins (2000), there were no ethnic differences in the level of domestic violence experienced by participants. Transforming the total domestic violence variable to compensate for positive skewness did not change the findings.

Table 2.10:   Women's (n=176) Lifetime Experience of Domestic Violence

Type of Violence	Never	Once	More than Once	No Response
			(*Percentages*)	
Attacked you with weapon	79.0	7.4	10.2	3.4
Threatened you with violence	69.9	9.7	16.5	3.9
Punched/shoved	63.6	16.5	16.5	3.4
Hit you	61.4	19.3	15.3	4.0
Forced sex	77.8	8.0	8.5	5.7
Threatened to kill you	76.7	7.4	11.9	4.0
Dominated you	69.9	11.4	13.6	5.1
Violence against your children	76.7	2.8	5.7	14.8
Stopped you from pursuing choice/ interest	73.9	5.7	13.1	7.3

Source: Anyanwu (2011)

Anyanwu (2011) also examined the factors which predicted the willingness of respondents to leave abusive relationships. Important predictors were subordination due to gender and economic inequality. It was found that women who felt that their partners' actions made them subordinate in the relationship were more willing to leave, while women who experienced higher levels of financial equality expressed greater willingness to leave abusive relationships. This latter finding may be explained by the fact that women who are economically independent may have the means to allow them to leave such relationships.

Interestingly, Anyanwu (2011) found that perceptions of the ability of the criminal justice system to assist in cases of domestic violence were not related to the willingness of women to leave abusive relationships. In Trinidad and Tobago, the family is seen as a private sphere, and even in cases of domestic violence, the society and women themselves prefer to resort to personal solutions to resolve family disputes, rather than seeking the intervention of the criminal justice system. This cultural preference extends to personnel in the criminal justice system who are unwilling to intervene when incidents of domestic violence occur. The findings of Anyanwu (2011) are consistent with data uncovered by Rawlins (2000) who found, in her sample of 200 women from Trinidad that, of those who experienced domestic violence, only 35 per cent reported the incidents to the police. Rawlins also discovered that the police did nothing in 64 per cent of cases, took a report in 18 per cent of cases, and arrested the perpetrator in 18 per cent of cases.

A consequence of failure to seek the intervention of the criminal justice system in cases of domestic violence is the perpetuation of such violence and, indeed, its escalation to the point where victims may be killed. Trinidad and Tobago data indicate that an alarming proportion of all murder cases are a result of domestic violence (figure 2.7). For the period 1995–2013, a total of 5,264 people were murdered in Trinidad and Tobago and, of these, 442 cases or 8.4 per cent of all murders were because of domestic violence. Time trends indicate that the proportion of murders due to domestic violence declined from 1995 to 2013. This decline was not because of a decline in the number of murders due to domestic violence, but because of an increase in the overall number of murders over time. Figure 2.7 also shows the rates of murders due to domestic violence per 100,000 inhabitants for 1995–2013. The rates indicate stability for the period under consideration. For the period 1995–2013 there were 1.4 murders due to domestic violence per 100,000 inhabitants in Trinidad and Tobago. From 2009 to 2013, the rate stood at 1.8.

For the period 2000–2013, a total of 19,078 incidents of domestic violence were reported to the police. Of these, the majority (50.1 per cent) were due to assault and beatings. This was followed by threats, which accounted for 28 per cent of all reported cases. Breach of protection orders accounted for 5.6 per cent of cases, while woundings accounted for 3.5 per cent. Figure 2.8 gives a graphical representation of the various reasons for reports of domestic violence, with the data sorted according to prevalence. The data represent the collated data for the period 2000–2013. Figure 2.9 gives a graphical representation of the prevalence of each type of domestic violence incident for each year for the period under consideration. Here again, the most frequently occurring types of incidents stand out.

Figure 2.10 offers a graphical representation of the number of males and females who were victims of domestic violence from 2007 to 2012. For this period, there were 10,141 reported cases of domestic violence. Of these, in 7,328 or 72.3 per cent of the cases, the victims were female, while in 2,813 or 27.7 per cent of the cases the victims were male. The data indicate that this gender disparity applies for each of the years for which data are available. The Women and Development Studies Group (1994, 90) reported that from 1990 to 1992, 1,436 people reported offences under the Domestic Violence Act. Of these, 2.6 per cent were males and 97.4 per cent were females. This implies that in more recent times a larger proportion of males are reporting incidents of domestic violence than in the past.

Figure 2.7:   Percentage of Murders due to Domestic Violence and Rate per 100,000 Inhabitants, 1995–2013

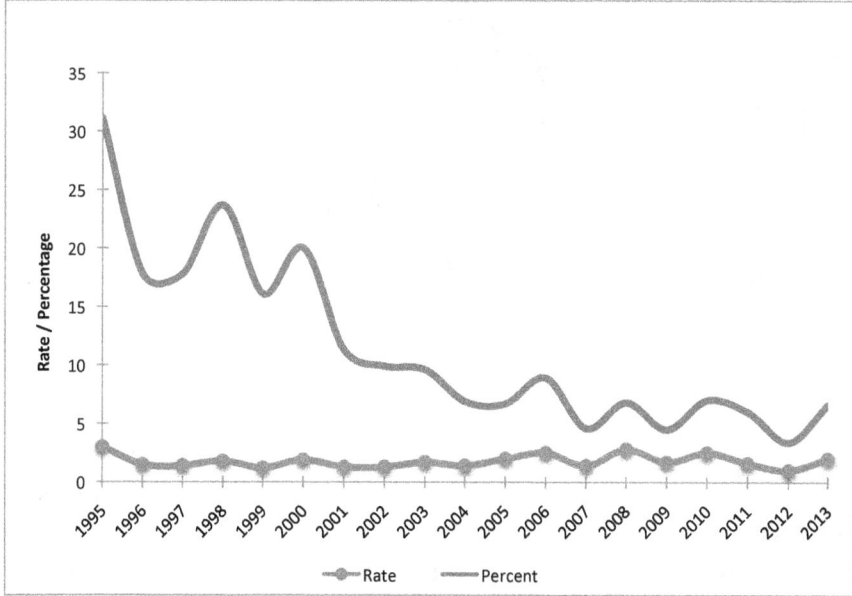

Source: Crime and Problem Analysis Branch of the Trinidad and Tobago Police Service

Figure 2.8:   Domestic Violence Incidents, 2000–2013

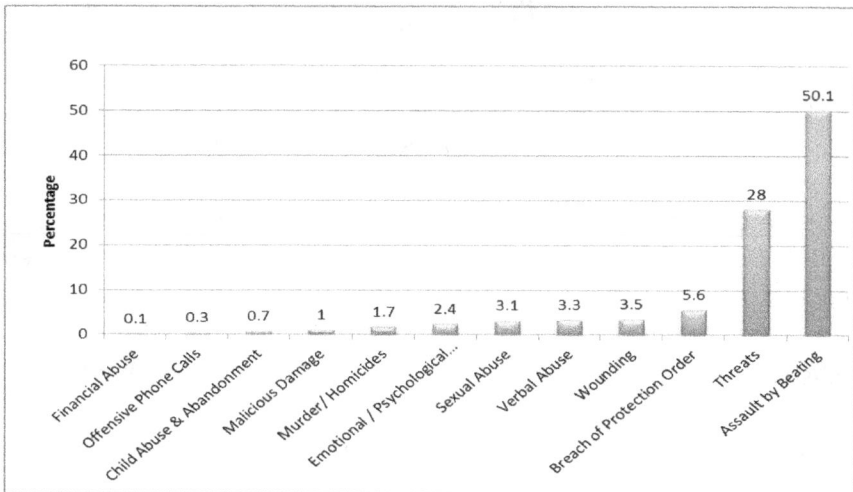

Source: Crime and Problem Analysis Branch of the Trinidad and Tobago Police Service

Figure 2.9:   Types of Domestic Violence, 2000–2013

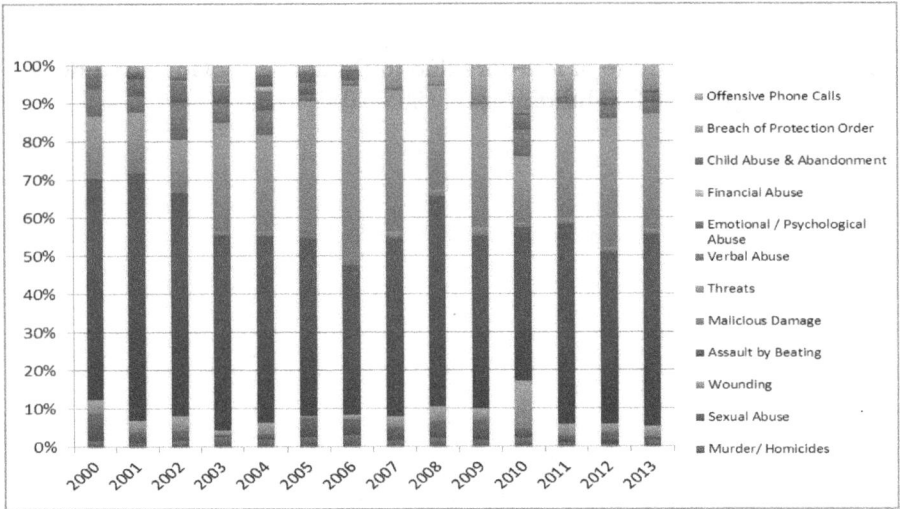

Source: Crime and Problem Analysis Branch of the Trinidad and Tobago Police Service

Figure 2.10 offers a graphical representation of the number of males and females who were victims of domestic violence from 2007 to 2012. For this period, there were 10,141 reported cases of domestic violence. Of these, in 7,328 or 72.3 per cent of the cases, the victims were female, while in 2,813 or 27.7 per cent of the cases the victims were male. The data indicate that this gender disparity applies for each of the years for which data are available. The Women and Development Studies Group (1994, 90) reported that from 1990 to 1992, 1,436 people reported offences under the Domestic Violence Act. Of these, 2.6 per cent were males and 97.4 per cent were females. This implies that in more recent times a larger proportion of males are reporting incidents of domestic violence than in the past.

Figure 2.11 shows the ages of victims of domestic violence from 2010 to 2012. During this period, there were 5,909 reported cases of domestic violence: 6.6 per cent of the victims were under 19 years of age, 29.2 per cent were between 20 and 29, 27 per cent were between 30 and 39, 17.2 per cent were between 40 and 49, 10.2 per cent were between 50 and 59, and 9.9 per cent were older than 59.

Figure 2.12 shows the ethnicity of victims of domestic violence for the period 2009–12. During this period, there were 7,415 reported cases of domestic violence. Of these, 3,058 of the victims or 41.2 per cent were of African descent, 2,987 or 40.3 per cent were of East Indian descent, and

987 or 13.3 per cent were mixed. Another three per cent of victims were of other ethnicities, while the ethnicities of 2.2 per cent of the victims were unknown.

Figure 2.10: Gender of Victims of Domestic Violence, 2007–12

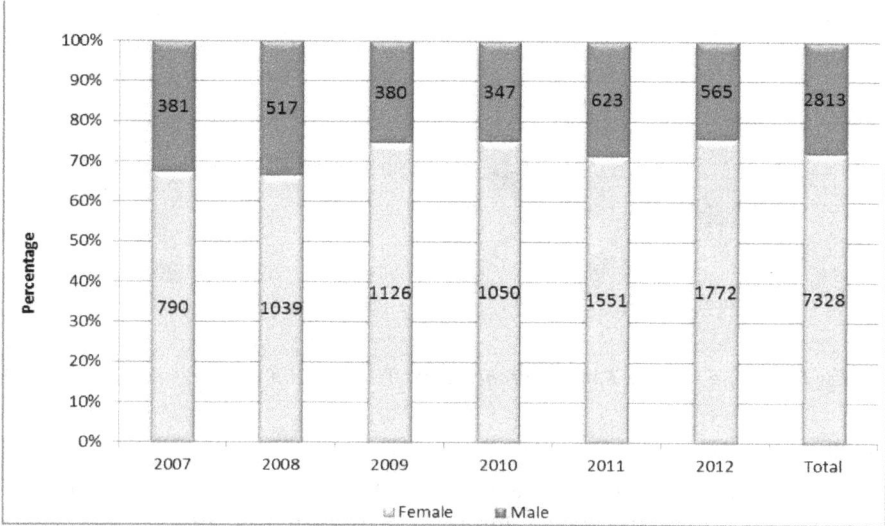

Source: Crime and Problem Analysis Branch of the Trinidad and Tobago Police Service

Figure 2.11: Ages of Victims of Domestic Violence, 2010–12

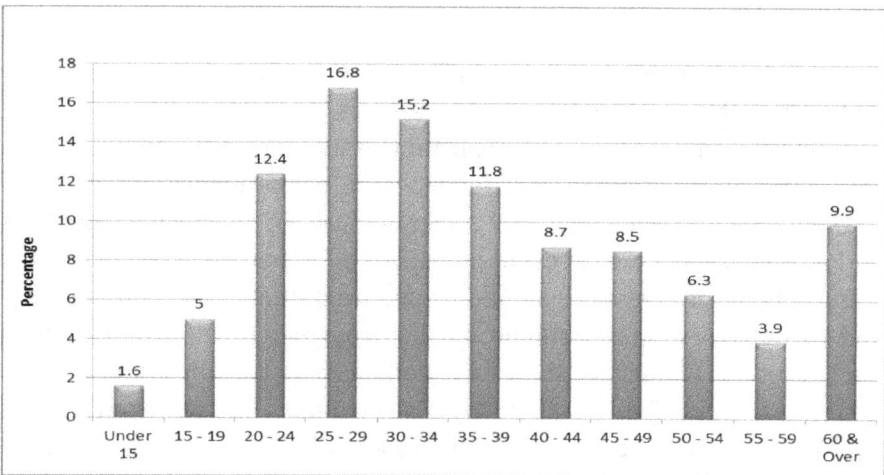

Source: Crime and Problem Analysis Branch of the Trinidad and Tobago Police Service

Figure 2.12:   Ethnicity of Victims of Domestic Violence, 2009-12

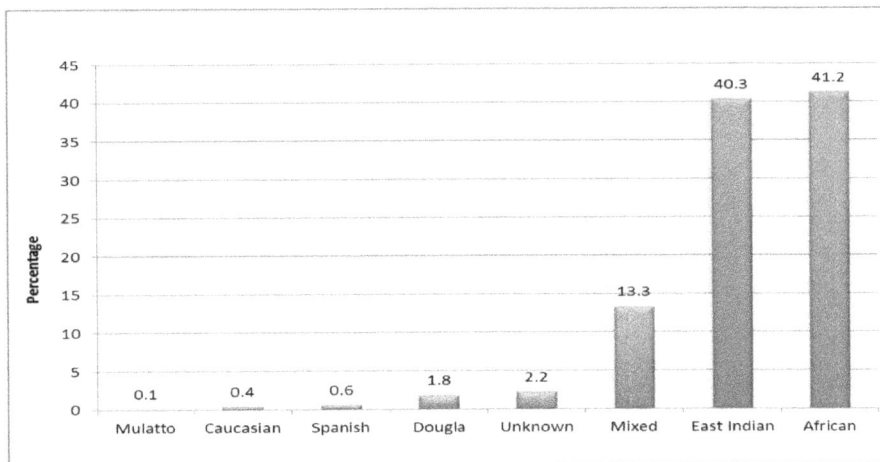

Source: Crime and Problem Analysis Branch of the Trinidad and Tobago Police Service

The incidence of domestic violence in Trinidad and Tobago is in all likelihood higher than is indicated in official statistics. Cultural norms which serve to justify male domination within the family, and which encourage the tolerance of domestic violence and decrease the willingness of victims to seek the intervention of the criminal justice system decrease the likelihood that abused women will report their abuse. Indeed, as self-report data previously cited from Anyanwu (2011), Rawlins (1998, 2000), and the Women and Development Studies Group (1994) indicate, the prevalence of domestic violence in Trinidad and Tobago is substantially higher than that indicated in official statistics.

Domestic violence is an important issue which requires careful consideration in Trinidad and Tobago. One of the biggest obstacles to dealing with this issue is lack of a criminal justice response to incidents of domestic violence. This could be explained in part by reference to the cultural belief that females should be subordinate to males in the family, and that family disputes should not be brought into the public sphere. These cultural beliefs are shared by women as well as men and, as such, even the victims of abuse – in many cases women – are not likely to seek the intervention of the criminal justice system. This results in the passivity of victims and limits the options which may be available to abused women. Domestic violence, however, intersects with the criminal justice system in the form of a number of criminal behaviours. The classification of a crime as domestic violence may result in a less serious charge for the abuser despite evidence that the injuries that abused people receive are at least as serious as injuries suffered in 90 per cent of violent felony crimes (Dutton 1986). Harm sustained as a result of domestic abuse include, but are not limited to, psychological and emotional abuse, assault and battery, harassment, breaking and entering, violation of an ex parte or protection order, malicious destruction of property, sexual assault, and stalking, as well as a number of other offences that may not be immediately recognizable as domestic in origin, such as arson, fraud, or embezzlement.

Legislation to deal with the issue of domestic violence was introduced in Trinidad and Tobago in 1991. The Domestic Violence Act of 1991 formally proclaimed that domestic violence was a crime and made provisions for the victim to get a protection order from any magistrate's court. According to this Act, anyone who contravened the legal order could be fined TT$5,000 or face a maximum sentence of six years in prison. In making these provisions, the aim of the Act was to stop threatened or actual abuse of victims. The explanatory note to the Bill, however, indicated that in Trinidad and Tobago there was the inclination to aim for a more conciliatory approach to dealing with domestic violence, rather than resort to criminal law. The explanatory note stated:

> The Bill is an attempt to provide legal protection for the victims of domestic violence. It does so in two ways. Firstly, by empowering the magistrate's court to grant protection orders irrespective of whether other relief is sought and secondly, it provides the police with powers to arrest and lay charges when there is a breach of the Court's Order or where a domestic violence offence is committed...The object of the Bill is to strike a right balance between the need to preserve an existing marital or other spousal or parental relationship on the one hand and the need to protect those persons from exposure to violence on the other. It seeks to achieve this objective by enacting provisions which can both punish and protect.

The Domestic Violence Act of 1991 did not appear to achieve its intended effect. While a large number of cases were brought before the courts, protection orders were not issued for the majority of such cases. Data from the Port of Spain Magistrate's Court for the period 1991–94 indicate, for example, that protection orders were granted in only 22.5 per cent of the cases. In addition, the number of crimes related to domestic violence continued to increase subsequent to the Act.

A number of problems reduced the effectiveness of the 1991 Act. With the introduction of the Act, there was a greater demand for legal assistance in obtaining protection orders. The state was severely constrained in its ability to provide such assistance. To compound the problem, the state's bureaucracy was incapable of dealing with the large influx of cases since additional personnel were not deployed to this sector. Another major problem with the 1991 Act was that protection orders were restricted mainly to the home, and did not apply to other settings such as the workplace or other locations. Even more importantly, the police service did not have the manpower to investigate every case of domestic violence, or many cases where people violated protection orders. Ann Marie Bissessar (2000) argues that, in many cases, police officers were reluctant to interfere in what was seen as essentially private family matters. Even in cases where applicants were able to get protection orders, there were no provisions made for families who may have lost their only source of financial support. State shelters for victims of domestic violence were not established and, where non-governmental facilities existed, they were small and funded by the private sector, and hence were incapable of dealing with the number of cases.

The Domestic Violence Act of 1999 was introduced in recognition of the many shortcomings of the 1991 Act. This new Act extended the range of protection afforded to include not only the home, but 'premises frequented by the applicant including any residence, property, business, school or place of employment'. The 1999 Act also made provisions to enable the spouse to 'make or continue to make payments in respect of rent or mortgage payments for premises occupied by the applicant.' It also ensured that 'reasonable care is provided in respect of a child or dependent person.' The courts also gained the power to award compensation not exceeding TT$15,000. In addition, it reduced the discretion of police officers and indicated that officers 'must arrest where they have reasonable grounds to suspect that a person has committed or intends committing an offence or breach of a protection order.' Importantly also, the new Act increased 'police powers of entry and arrest'. Part IV, 22 and 23 (1) and (2) allowed that:

> For the avoidance of doubt, a police officer may act in accordance with the provisions of the criminal law act where he has reasonable cause to believe that a person is engaging in or attempting to engage in conduct which amounts to physical violence and failure to act immediately may result in serious physical injury or death. Nothing in this section authorizes the entry onto the premises by a policeman, for the purpose of any search or the arrest of any person, otherwise than in connection with the conduct referred to in Subsection (1).

Despite the above, a number of problems remained. While one clause indicated that police officers could enter a building if they had reasonable cause, another indicated that they could only act in accordance with a warrant issued by a magistrate. Then senior superintendent of the police service pointed to the shortcoming by stating that 'By the time you go to a home and you know that, or you were told that an offence is taking place and you go to a magistrate to get a warrant, by the time you come back there you have four or five murders' (*Trinidad Guardian* August 9, 1999, 3). Another major shortcoming related to the length of time and complex nature of the procedures required to get a protection order. The Domestic Violence Act of 1999 outlined 13 steps which had to be followed in order to secure a protection order. A number of people had to be seen in completing these steps. These people included a justice of the peace, a magistrate, an attorney (who had to represent the applicant), and a clerk of the courts. Securing a protection order depended on one's ability to afford an attorney (though one could go through the lengthy procedures for securing legal aid), and depended on the availability of the many people specified (many of whom were only available during typical working hours, from Monday to Friday, excluding public holidays).

Quite apart from legislative inadequacies, other problems negatively impacted on the 1999 Act. The police, for example, continued to maintain that they did not have the necessary manpower and, in many cases, vehicles to allow them to respond to the many domestic violence cases, including instances of breach of a protection order. In addition, while the Act allowed for the continued payment of rent by the spouse of the victim, it did not mandate that such payment be made. A broader issue was that the Act did not take into account the economic capacity of women to support themselves and their children during and subsequent to court processes aimed at reducing domestic abuse. As was the case with the earlier 1991 Act, there continued to be a lack of state-run shelters and services for victims of domestic violence. Bissessar (2000) adds to the debate by making the point that the risk factors for domestic violence in Trinidad and Tobago differ from that of other countries. She indicates that Trinidad and Tobago has 'borrowed' legislation from elsewhere and applied it without critically evaluating its applicability and without altering it to suit the cultural and other peculiarities which apply. It is no surprise then that a number of authors have argued that the legislative provisions for dealing with the issue of domestic violence in Trinidad and Tobago are inadequate (Bissessar 2000; Phillips 2000; Zellerer 2000).

In order for the criminal justice system to be effective in the fight against domestic violence, judges, prosecutors, probation officers and the police need a clear sense of what behaviours constitute domestic abuse, who the perpetrators are, who the victims of domestic violence are, and how they may appear in the criminal justice system. Given that domestic violence is a crime perpetrated against a vulnerable population, the state has an obligation to intervene in personal relationships to protect victims from their abusive partners. Where appropriate, the state can and should remove violent partners from their homes to protect victims (Dobash and Dobash 1979; Schechter 1982). Contemporary women's movements no doubt have triumphed in gaining recognition and public acknowledgement that the state has the obligation to render full protection to abused persons (Pleck 1989). The transformation of domestic violence laws in Trinidad and Tobago has had a powerful effect in raising awareness of victims' rights and security and protection by the law; perhaps even more than regulating behaviour, they are symbolic of the changing values and norms in Trinidad and Tobago's society. In forcing governments to enact these laws, women's organizations have brought about recognition that violence against women is a political issue, not a cultural or private one (Clarke 1997).

Despite the progress made by women's movements in relation to the acknowledgement of the criminality of domestic violence, not much has been accomplished by the criminal justice system in redressing the problems associated with domestic violence and the prosecution of perpetrators. A large part of the problem here has to do with the weight of culture and tradition, and its effect on the criminal justice system. For a long period of time, culture as well as law gave the husband an affirmative endorsement to beat his wife in order to provide her with what was seen as appropriate chastisement and instruction (Coughlin 1994; McConnell 1992). Because the wife was viewed as belonging to her husband, what happened between them was regarded as a private matter and was not a concern to the criminal justice system (Dobash and Dobash 1979). Although wife beating is no longer sanctioned, the abuse of women by husbands and intimate partners still remains prevalent and aggressors are rarely arrested and prosecuted (Black et al. 2011; Dobash and Dobash 1992). Critics of police behaviour have long argued that leniency in the criminal justice system legitimates domestic violence in the minds of many potential aggressors (Ferraro 1989). A criminal justice response to domestic violence is indeed important since this may serve as a catalyst to raise awareness and change cultural values which legitimize violence in the home. The failure of the criminal justice system to respond, in contrast, will indicate that abused persons are not seen as victims, and will serve to reinforce cultural norms that fail to discourage spousal abuse.

Despite the advocacy of a response from the criminal justice system, this is only a partial solution. Many males, for example, may not be deterred by arrests, and instead, this option, if utilized by the courts, could result in increased violence and abuse of their partners (Buzawa and Buzawa 1993). Indeed, arrest is only one among other options which may be available to the criminal justice system in Trinidad and Tobago. What may matter is that a response is made, regardless of whether or not that response involves arrest. The response and the consistency of the response reinforce the idea that domestic violence is unacceptable. Feminist-inspired studies argue that arrest alone is ineffective in halting the long-term expected progression of domestic violence (Ferraro and Pope 1993). Merely adopting a pro-arrest policy alone may signal a primary focus on law enforcement, rather than community involvement and empowerment of battered persons. As previously cited data indicate, economic equality and the resultant lack of dependency of women on men may prove to be an important step in the fight against domestic violence. In this respect, as figure 2.13 indicates, the unemployment rates for females have been decreasing over time though, as also indicated, the disparity in unemployment rates between males and females has not decreased over time. With greater access to education, coupled with increased access to employment, women in Trinidad and Tobago are poised to extricate themselves from abusive relationships. Despite this, the increased cost of living and the fact that gender inequality does not appear to be diminishing over time, may work against the economic independence of women in Trinidad and Tobago.

A number of government initiatives in Trinidad and Tobago reflect cognizance of the fact that, in addition to a legal approach, a social, community-based approach is also required in the fight against domestic violence. In 1996, for example, the Community Policing Unit was instituted and mandated to engage in preventative policing, including dealing with cases of domestic violence.

Figure 2.13: Percentage of Unemployed People over Age 15 in Trinidad and Tobago, 1985–2005

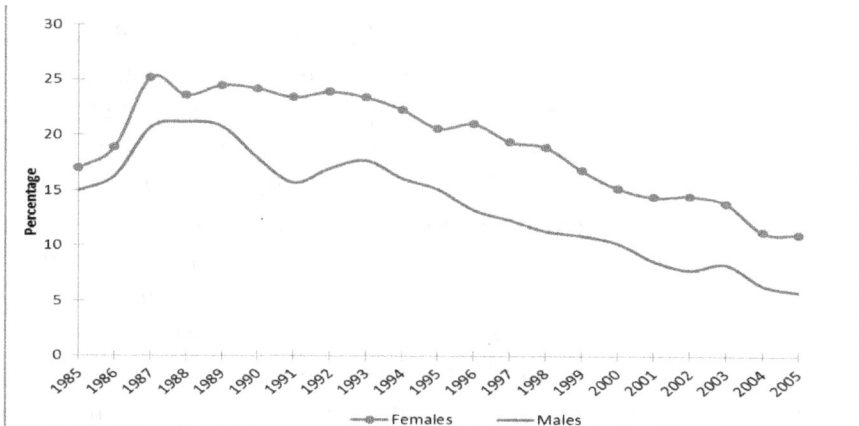

Source: ILO KILM Database (2007)

Among other things, they were required to maintain a domestic violence hotline (800-SAVE), which operates on a 24-hour, seven days per week basis. In addition, the Gender Affairs Division of the Ministry of Youth Gender and Child Development, in collaboration with a number of non-governmental organizations initiated a number of educational exercises which targeted police, shelter workers and other stakeholders. These workshops aimed to raise awareness of the issue of domestic violence and attempted to encourage attitudinal change and an examination of cultural values which condoned violence against women. The Gender Affairs Division also initiated a male support group and a community-based drop-in information centre project. Through this project, members of the public could access assistance on matters related to domestic violence, rape, sexual abuse and family conflict (Phillips 2000).

Domestic violence is an intractable problem which requires a very carefully formulated approach. Such an approach must recognize the utility of the criminal justice system in preventing and reducing the incidence of such violence, but must also recognize that social awareness and a change in cultural beliefs and values are also required in the long run. The cultural dimension of the problem requires a change in thinking about gender equality and a concomitant change in practices which reduce inequality, both in the workplace, and within the home. This change alone is not sufficient as efforts against domestic violence also require changes in the cultural values which encourage the silencing and stigmatization of victims and witnesses, and which discourage law enforcement personnel from intervening even though domestic violence is a criminal offence. Public awareness campaigns may be utilized to alter societal values that currently result in a society which operates as if domestic violence will go away by being ignored.

Where police officers are concerned, police training should include a specific component geared to assist officers in decision-making where such difficult issues are concerned. In addition, the capacity of the police to investigate alleged cases of domestic violence should be assessed. Where there is a limited number of officers, and where there are no officers mandated to deal with domestic violence, decisions may be made that place emphasis on crimes which are perceived to be more serious, and domestic violence incidents may be neglected, more because of its lack of perceived seriousness, than because of its actual seriousness.

In the case of protection orders, effort is required to streamline and simplify the process which is required in the granting of such orders. Women who are victims of domestic violence often are in vulnerable and helpless states, and do not have the personal capacity or the social, or even the financial support which may be required to navigate through the cumbersome processes presently required to get a such orders.

The impact of domestic violence on children also requires careful consideration, and resources need to be devoted to the support and care of children who may need protection. It is the case that policies which deal with domestic violence may focus only on the person who is directly victimized and may neglect other vulnerable people, including children, who may be affected by such violence. Indeed, in Trinidad and Tobago, children who reside in homes where domestic violence against spouses occurs may also become victims of physical, emotional and psychological abuse (Phillips 2000). Research should assess the extent of this phenomenon, and measures should be put in place to cater to the needs of the children so affected.

Notes

1. Statistics for major crimes are available in Appendix 1 while statistics for minor crimes are available in Appendix 2.
2. Average annual increase is calculated as the average of the differences in the number of murders in each year less the number of murders in the previous year for all years of the time period for which data are available. Average percentage increase is calculated as the average of the percentage increase in murders from one year to the next for all years over the time period for which data are available. The same procedure is applied to other crimes.
3. The sex of 0.5 per cent of the victims, the ethnicities of 3.3 per cent of the victims and the ages of 5.4 per cent of the victims were unknown. These were excluded from the computations.
4. These data derive from both convicted and accused persons who were arrested and charged with a murder. The available data do not allow for disaggregation into those who were convicted and those who were charged but not convicted.
5. This includes rapes, incest and other sexual offences but excludes serious indecency and indecent assault.
6. Crime rates were computed using a population of 1,267,145 for Trinidad and 60,874 for Tobago (Central Statistical Office of Trinidad and Tobago 2011 Census).
7. Note that while some of the older age groups appear to have a higher incidence of physical harm than the younger age groups, the age ranges for the older age groups are wider (a span of ten years) than those of the younger age groups (a span of five years). When the older age groups are disaggregated into five-year time spans to ensure comparability with the younger age groups, the data indicate that older people are less likely to be physically harmed than younger people.

8. This comparison is based on victimization data and official crime data for 2009 since 'past year' in the survey refers to 2009.
9. The use of "/" indicates that different terms were used to describe the crimes committed in official crime data vs. victimization survey data. Wherever "/" occurs, the first phrase comes from the victimization survey while the second phrase is used in official crime data.
10. Vulnerability is here defined in terms of susceptibility to injury or harm due to an actual or perceived weakness.

Juvenile Justice

Youth violence, as well as the victimization of youths, represents a special area of concern with respect to citizen security. Media reports, often based on isolated events, give the impression that youth crime is spiralling out of control in the Caribbean, and in Trinidad and Tobago specifically. One of the dangers of this is that the media may affect public perceptions, which in turn may fuel governmental strategies to deal with the issue of youth violence. Such strategies, almost invariably, call for increasing levels of punitiveness. Evidence gathered in this chapter indicates that youth violence is the exception rather than the rule, even among institutionalized youths in Trinidad and Tobago. Despite this, the headlines that appear in the news media attest that the public's perception of youth violence may be at odds with the reality. For example, a headline in the *Trinidad Express* on December 9, 2010 stated 'Gang violence in school' while another in the *Guardian* on April 24, 2011 proclaimed: 'Two choices: Educate or incarcerate them'. Yet another headline in the *Guardian* on February 18, 2011 stated: 'Form one student beats his teacher'. While such captions may improve readership, and while such events are newsworthy, youth violence is not as commonplace in Trinidad and Tobago as the public is led to believe.

This chapter will draw upon available empirical evidence to assess the nature of youth crime and violence in Trinidad and Tobago and, among other things, will assess whether or not public perception is in line with the evidence. This chapter hopes to alter the narratives about youth violence and provides a platform upon which reasonable interventions may be developed and utilized where necessary. It will be argued, consistent with the empirical data presented, that a preventative as opposed to a reactive approach to reducing youth violence may be the most cost-effective and appropriate approach for Trinidad and Tobago. It will be further argued that, even where preventative approaches fail, policymakers must use incapacitative strategies only in the most extreme of cases, and only as a last resort where youths are concerned. Indeed, much criminological and psychological evidence indicates that many youths are amenable to rehabilitation, and more so than adult offending populations (Moffitt 1993). Inappropriate labelling of youthful offenders reduces available alternatives and encourages adaptations which may force youths into a criminogenic lifestyle.

Data from Trinidad and Tobago indicate that youth delinquency may start even while children are in primary school. Vidya Lall (2007) conducted a study in which she interviewed 589 standard three students between the ages of 9 and 11. Data were collected in March 2006. This study was motivated by the recognition that internationally and locally, it appears that children are engaging in delinquent and even illegal action at decreasing ages. Indeed, Lall (2007, 157) writes:

> In Trinidad and Tobago and the Caribbean generally from the data gathered thus far, combined with media coverage and official police statistics, we are witnessing increasing acts of sexual deviance, substance use and abuse (that is, use of illegal drugs, smoking, drinking alcohol), students going to school armed with weapons (e.g., guns, knives, cutlasses), wounding/physical assaults/stabbing with intent – many now ending in death in and outside many of our formal school settings.

Lall (2007) assessed delinquency using a 12-item self-report scale. Respondents were asked to indicate the extent to which they had engaged in each of the specified delinquent acts within the previous six months. The most prevalent acts were being in a fistfight (64 per cent) and disobeying and answering back a teacher (66 per cent). Forty-five per cent of the students said that they drank alcohol, while two per cent admitted to using illegal drugs, and seven per cent admitted to smoking cigarettes. Seventeen per cent said that they stole something, 19 per cent skipped school or class, 26 per cent fought using a weapon, while 27 per cent said that they used force to get something. Forty-four per cent indicated that they got into trouble for not doing their homework. A summary of these findings appears in figure 3.1.

Lall (2007) examined gender differences in the prevalence of delinquency and found that, while boys were on average more delinquent than girls, the girls were not very far behind the boys for some categories of delinquency. Seventy-two per cent of the boys and 66 per cent of the girls disobeyed their teachers, while 74 per cent of boys and 64 per cent of girls were involved in fistfights; 54 per cent of boys and 46 per cent of girls threatened to hit someone; 53 per cent of boys and 45 per cent of girls drank alcohol; 33 per cent of boys and 27 per cent of girls used force to get something; 35 per cent of boys and 26 per cent of girls fought using a weapon; 22 per cent of boys and ten per cent of girls stole something; and three per cent of boys and one per cent of girls used illegal drugs. These data are graphed in figure 3.2. The findings of Lall (2007) are indeed troubling, given the young age at which the respondents engaged in a wide range of delinquent acts, many of them being quite serious. The measures used captured delinquency 'within the last six months'.

Figure 3.1:   Delinquent Acts Committed by 9–11 Year Olds

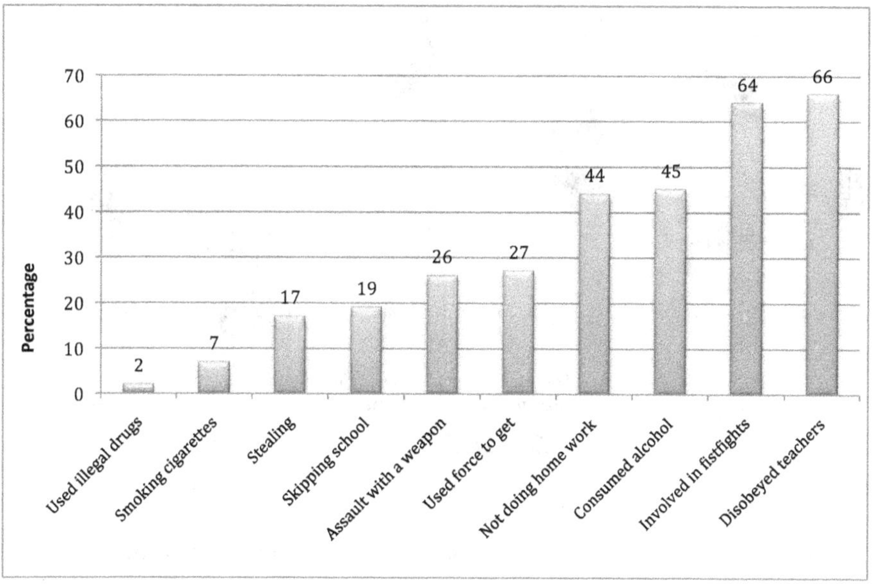

Source: Lall (2007)

Figure 3.2:   Percentage of Boys and Girls Involved in Delinquency

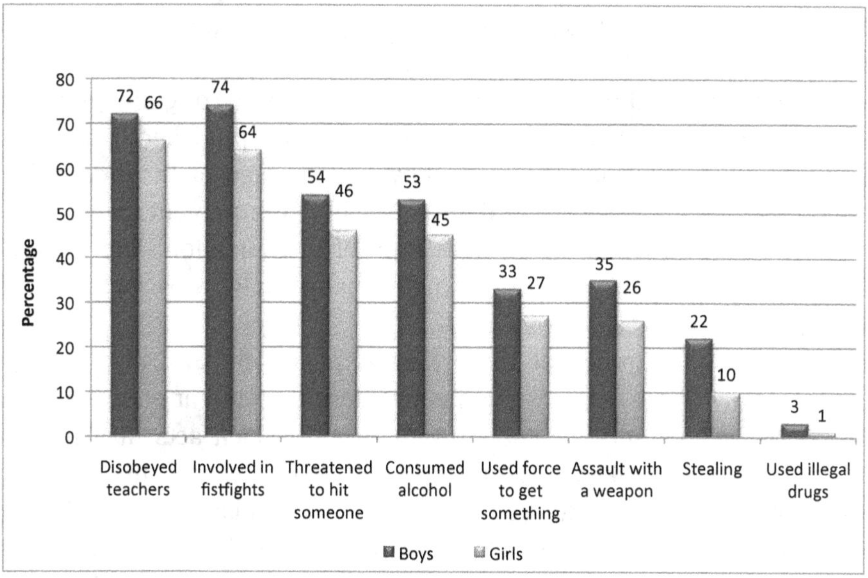

Source: Lall (2007)

Figure 3.3:   Percentage of Students who were Victimized

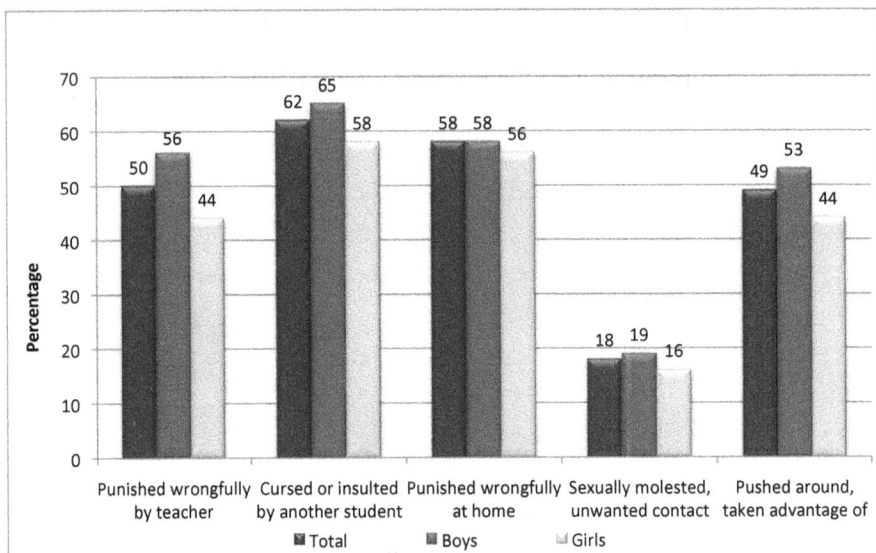

Source: Lall (2007)

The short time period used ensures that the estimates of delinquency are not inflated merely by capturing incidents of delinquency which occurred over an extended time period.

Lall (2007) also collected data on self-reported victimization using a five-item measure. She discovered that when the sample was considered as a whole, 18 per cent said that they were sexually molested (fondled, interfered with, etc.), 49 per cent said they were pushed around/taken advantage of/picked on, 50 per cent said they were wrongfully punished by a teacher, 58 per cent said they were wrongfully punished by a parent or guardian, and 62 per cent said they were cursed or insulted for no reason. Figure 3.3 graphs this data and shows the percentage of males and females who experienced each type of victimization. The findings indicate that a larger proportion of males than females were victims of all the types of victimization examined.

There are a number of important implications of Lall's findings (2007). Many of the acts of delinquency were directed at other children within the school setting. The consequences of such acts may include subsequent involvement in crime and delinquency as students get older, even progressing into adulthood. Such behaviour also affects children's ability to maintain positive relationships, both with peers and within the family. Students who are victimized are afraid to attend school and may have high rates of truancy, which subsequently affect their level of academic achievement and the development of other skills. Even when such students attend school, they may have difficulty concentrating, may be fearful, and remain isolated and withdrawn. Indeed, Lall (2007) found that 20 per cent of her sample did not feel safe for fear of being bullied or victimized at school. Quite apart from the victims of such acts of delinquency, we must also consider the perpetrators. International research has suggested that there is a strong link between delinquency in the early years and later acts of criminality. In addition, researchers have found a link between substance abuse, delinquency, and crime and violence (Farrington 1987; Loeber and Dishion 1983). Substance abuse early in life may also be related to the use of more potent illegal substances later in life, these being associated with several other forms of deviant behaviour, including gang involvement, drug dealing, and a range of property as well as violent crime (Spivak and Cianci 1987).

Randy Seepersad (2014) collected data on victimization and self-reported delinquency from a sample of 1,248 students in ten primary schools in north Trinidad. Students who participated in the survey ranged in age from 8 to 14, with an average age of 10.3. There were slightly more males (55.7 per cent) than females (44.3 per cent). Table 3.1 shows the percentage of students who were victims of specified acts within the last term. The most prevalent acts were children laughing at each other (81.7 per cent of respondents indicated that this happened to them), children calling each other names (81.1 per cent), children hitting each other (78.6 per cent), children saying bad things about each other (78.1 per cent), children pushing each other (76.9 per cent), and children saying hurtful things to each other (71.5 per cent).

Table 3.1 also shows the percentage of males and females who were victims of specific acts within the last term. Of the 21 types of victimization listed, the rates were higher for males in 14 and higher for females in 7. The most pronounced gender differences where male victimization rates exceeded that of females occurred with children punching other children (71.6 per cent of males indicated that this happened to them within the last term compared to 46.6 per cent of females), children kicking each other (75.2 per cent of males vs. 55.4 per cent of females), children trying to take each other's money (46.6 per cent of males vs. 33.4 per cent of females), children saying bad things about each other's families (76.8 per cent of males vs. 64.4 per cent of females), children using something (e.g., a stick) to hurt each other (58.8 per cent of males vs. 53 per cent of females), and children ganging up on each other (51.7 per cent of males vs. 46.5 per cent of females). The most notable gender differences where female victimization rates exceeded that of males occurred with children making other children cry (62.4 per cent of females vs. 50.2 per cent of males), children not wanting to play with each other (59.5 per cent of females vs. 51.2 per cent of males), children saying hurtful things to each other (76.4 per cent of females vs. 70.5 per cent of males), and children laughing at each other (84.7 per cent of females vs. 81 per cent of males).

Table 3.1: **Percentage of Students Who Were Victims of Specific Acts within the Last Term**

	Total Percentage Who Were Victims	Percentage of Males Who Were Victims	Percentage of Females Who Were Victims
A child laughed at me	81.7	81.0	84.7
A child called me names	81.1	81.6	82.5
A child hit me	78.6	82.5	78.0
A child said something bad about me	78.1	80.9	79.5
A child pushed me	76.9	79.6	76.7
A child said something hurtful to me	71.5	70.5	76.4
A child was unkind to me	71.3	71.3	73.4
A child said something bad about my family	69.0	76.8	64.4
A child kicked me	65.2	75.2	55.4
A child stole something from me	61.6	64.5	59.9
A child punched me	59.5	71.6	46.6
Other students left me out of their games	57.7	58.0	60.5
A child damaged my property	57.1	60.2	55.9
Other students picked on me	56.6	58.3	57.0
A child used something to hurt me (e.g., a stick)	55.2	58.8	53.0
Other children made me cry	54.8	50.2	62.4
Other children did not want to play with me	53.9	51.2	59.5
Other children ganged up on me	48.3	51.7	46.5
A child made me frightened	47.8	48.4	47.9
A child took something from me by force	46.9	48.3	46.6
A child tried to take my money	40.4	46.6	33.4
Sample Size	1,248	695	553

Source: Seepersad (2014)

Table 3.2:   **Percentage of Students Who Self-reported That They Victimized Others**

Physical Victimization	I get into physical fights	19.2
	I fight with students who I can easily beat up	10.7
	I threaten to hit or hurt other students	11.3
	I encourage other people to fight	9.6
	I get into a physical fight when I am angry	20.2
	I pick on other students	8.2
	I gang up on other students	7.5
Verbal Victimization	In a group I tease other students	8.8
	I spread rumours about other students	8.4
	I curse other students when I get angry	16.1
	I call other students names	16.3
	I make fun of other students	15.4
Social Victimization	I stop other students from joining my group of friends	11.5
	I make other students cry	10.3
	I ignore other students on purpose	18.4
	I make other students feel sad on purpose	9.0
	I am mean to others when I get angry	19.6
Property-related	I damage other students' property	7.1
	I take things from other students without their permission	6.2
	I force other students to give me their things	4.2
	I force other students to give me their money	4.0

Source: Seepersad (2014)

When the overall pattern of victimization by gender is examined, the data indicate that where males are victims, the act more often than not is one that involves physical force, for example, children taking something by force, pushing, property damage, hitting, stealing, ganging up on each other, hurting each other with sticks and other objects, kicking, punching, etc. Where females are victims, in contrast, the acts typically are non-physical in nature, such as making each other cry, not wanting to play with each other, saying hurtful things, laughing at each other, being unkind to each other, calling each other names, etc. These findings indicate that intervention strategies that target males should focus on physical forms of aggression, whereas those that target females should place emphasis on verbal and psychological elements. This is not to imply that the bullying situation in the participating schools was more of a male than a female problem. Indeed, psychological and social forms of bullying can be just as harmful as physical forms of bullying. The data collected indicate that physical forms of bullying do occur among females, while verbal and psychological forms also occur among males.

Seepersad (2014) also asked students to indicate for the 21 different types of victimization the extent to which they engaged in each, that is, the extent to which they victimized others. Table 3.2 shows the percentage of students who self-reported that they engage often or very often in specified activities. Fully 93.8 per cent of students indicated that they victimized other students. Students who had victimized other students had perpetrated an average of 8.4 acts of victimization each within the last term.

The findings indicate that the most prevalent type of victimization involves students getting into fights when they are angry (20.2 per cent indicated that this happens to them often or very often). This was followed by being mean to others when they got angry (19.6 per cent), getting into physical fights (19.2 per cent), ignoring other students on purpose (18.4 per cent), calling other students names (16.3 per cent), cursing other students when they got angry (16.1 per cent), and making fun of other students (15.4 per cent). When the top ten forms of self-reported bullying are considered, four were forms of physical bullying, three were forms of verbal bullying, and another three were forms of social bullying. In contrast, property-related forms of victimization were the least prevalent. More specifically, the four types of property-related victimization had lower prevalence rates than all other types of victimization.

Other research has attempted to assess the level of violence among secondary school students. The World Health Organization's Global Student-Based Health Surveys in Trinidad and Tobago in 2007 and 2011 collected data from school-aged youths between the ages of 11 and 16. In 2007, data were collected from a sample of 2,969 students with a mean age of 14.2 years, and with 49.8 per cent of the sample being male. In 2011, data were collected from 2,811 youths with a mean age of 13.6 years, and with 54.6 per cent of the sample being male.

In 2007, 39.8 per cent of respondents indicated that they were physically attacked by someone and 42 per cent indicated that they were involved in physical fights. In 2011, in contrast, 33 per cent reported being physically attacked by someone and 36.2 per cent said they were involved in physical fights. When asked whether they were seriously injured within the last 12 months, 47.9 per cent of the students in 2007 and 40.9 per cent in 2011 responded in the affirmative. In 2007, 5.1 per cent of respondents were seriously injured because they were involved in fights or were attacked, assaulted, or abused by someone. In 2011, this figure declined to 2.7 per cent. In 2007, 9.2 per cent of respondents sustained a cut, puncture, or stab wound when they were seriously injured, while 1.6 per cent were injured by a gunshot wound. In 2011, these figures declined to 7.8 per cent and 0.9 per cent, respectively.

The surveys also asked about bullying within the last 30 days. In 2007, 20.8 per cent of students said they were bullied within the last month, while in 2011 that figure declined to 14.8 per cent. The survey asked about six specific kinds of bullying, and in all cases, there was a decline in the proportion of students bullied from 2007 to 2011. In 2007, 3.6 per cent of respondents were kicked, pushed, shoved around, or locked indoors, compared to 2.4 per cent in 2011. In 2007, 1.9 per cent of students were made fun of because of their race or colour, compared to 1.6 per cent in 2011. Similarly, in 2007, 2.1 per cent were made fun of with sexual jokes, comments, or gestures, but this figure declined to 1.5 per cent in 2011.

Ramesh Deosaran and Derek Chadee (1997) offer a rare glimpse into the characteristics of youthful offenders in Trinidad and Tobago. They interviewed the entire population (n = 486) of youths incarcerated in three youth institutions in Trinidad and Tobago. These institutions were the Youth Training Centre (males 16–18 years of age; n = 232), St Michael's School for Boys (males less than 16 years of age; n = 134), and St Jude's School for Girls (females less than 16 years of age; n = 120). Interviews with the youths in these juvenile facilities gathered data in five areas. These were 1) the offences committed, 2) the social and demographic characteristics of the youths, 3) psychological characteristics of the youths, 4) feelings of remorse, self-responsibility and the potential for rehabilitation, and 5) risk factors for delinquency.

When the total population of youths was considered, 37.9 per cent were institutionalized for robbery or robbery-related crimes, 6.1 per cent for drug-related crimes, 2.9 per cent for assault, 1.9 per cent for murder or attempted murder/manslaughter, 3.3 per cent for possession of arms and ammunition, 0.4 per cent for rape, 0.4 per cent for kidnapping, and 0.4 per cent for larceny. Fully 44.5 per cent of the youths in the three institutions, however, were there because of 'offences' which were not illegal but which are considered not acceptable for youths, or because they were in need of protection. For example, when the total population was considered, 27.3 per cent of the youths were institutionalized because they were 'beyond control', 2.6 per cent because they were victims of abuse, 0.4 per cent because there was no one willing to take care of them, and 13.6 per cent because they ran away from home. As will be elaborated upon later in this chapter, fully 58.5 per cent of the youths in St Michael's School for Boys and 92.8 per cent of the youths in St Jude's School for Girls were institutionalized for such status offences, or because they were in need of protection. The public is often of the view that youths from such homes are dangerous and a threat to society. These data are contrary to such opinions.

Table 3.3 shows the number of crimes committed by youths between the ages of 11 and 17 in Trinidad and Tobago for the period 2007–12. On average, for this period, male youths committed an average of 6.8 murders per year while females committed an average of 0.2. Male youths committed an average of 7.3 woundings and shootings per annum, while females committed an average of 0.8. In addition, male youths committed an average of 21.2 rapes and sexual offences per annum compared to an average of zero for females. Data for other crimes are shown in table 3.3. Table 3.4 shows the proportion of crimes committed by youths for the period 2007–10. Invariably, youths commit only a very small proportion of crimes in Trinidad and Tobago. For example, for the period under consideration, on average 479.3 murders were committed per year. Of these, youths committed an average of seven murders per year, or 1.5 per cent of the national total. For the same period, an average of 690.8 woundings and shootings were committed per year in Trinidad and Tobago. Youths committed an average of 8.2 shootings per year during this period, or 1.2 per cent of the national total. In a similar manner, youths were responsible for 2.8 per cent of all rapes and sexual offences, 2.2 per cent of all kidnappings, 1.1 per cent of all burglaries, 1.6 per cent of all robberies, 0.5 per cent of all general larcenies and 5.2 per cent of all narcotic offences. When compared to other countries such as Jamaica, the proportion of crimes committed by youths in Trinidad and Tobago pales in comparison. Crime data for Jamaica for the period 1996–2005 indicate that 20 per cent of all murders, 23.9 per cent of all shootings, 22.5 per cent of all robberies and 32.2 per cent of all burglaries were committed by persons under the age of 20 (Seepersad 2007). The data cited thus far in this chapter indicate that while youths in Trinidad and Tobago are involved in delinquent as well as illegal activities, media portrayals of youths as violent and dangerous are exaggerations, which misinform public opinion and which have the potential to lead to policy prescriptions that may not be consistent with the reality.

Table 3.3: Serious Crimes Committed by Persons Aged 11–17 Years Old in Trinidad and Tobago

Year	Murder		Woundings and Shootings		Rape and Sexual Offences		Kidnappings		Burglaries		Robberies		General Larceny		Narcotic Offences	
	M	F	M	F	M	F	M	F	M	F	M	F	M	F	M	F
2007	9	0	14	0	18	0	4	0	73	5	110	1	26	4	34	5
2008	7	0	10	0	14	0	3	0	47	1	94	2	21	1	29	4
2009	12	0	9	3	24	0	8	0	68	2	103	1	27	0	18	4
2010	9	0	3	0	22	0	2	1	64	1	93	0	27	1	34	4
2011	3	0	6	2	38	0	0	1	54	0	81	2	17	1	25	6
2012[1]	1	1	2	0	11	0	1	0	15	2	23	1	4	0	7	1
Avg.	6.8	0.2	7.3	0.8	21.2	0.0	3.0	0.3	53.5	1.8	84.0	1.2	20.3	1.2	24.5	4.0

Source: Crime and Problem Analysis Branch of the Trinidad and Tobago Police Service

Table 3.4: Average Annual Number of Crimes Committed in Trinidad and Tobago for the Period 2007–10

	Murder	Wounding and Shooting	Rape and Sexual Offences	Kidnapping	Burglaries	Robberies	General Larceny	Narcotic Offences
All crimes	479.3	690.8	751.3	151.8	5191.0	5280.8	3951.8	547.8
Youth crimes (11–17 years)	7.0	8.2	21.2	3.3	55.3	85.2	21.5	28.5
Percentage of crimes committed by youths	1.5	1.2	2.8	2.2	1.1	1.6	0.5	5.2

Source: Crime and Problem Analysis Branch of the Trinidad and Tobago Police Service

Understanding and Dealing with Juvenile Delinquency and Crime

The term 'delinquency' is controversial and fraught with definitional inconsistencies. One of the main factors leading to this lack of precision is that a wide range of non-criminal acts – behaviours which are proscribed for youths, but not for adults – can be used to classify a juvenile as delinquent. In this context Leonard Savitz (1967, 15–16) writes:

> If *crime* and *criminal* seem tortuous concepts, they assume pristine clarity next to the extraordinarily elusive terms *delinquency* and *delinquent*. Delinquencies are all actions legally proscribed for a child above the age of culpability and below a certain maximum age (16, 17, or 18). If a child engages in proscribed behaviour, the state, acting in place of the parent (in loco parentis), is obliged to treat (not punish) the child. Thus all crimes for which adults are liable, plus many other acts which are prohibited only to juveniles until they reach adulthood, are subsumed under 'delinquency'. Purely juvenile delinquencies (as opposed to juvenile crime) include such offenses as truancy, incorrigibility, and running away from home, as well as some rather trivial offenses such as the use of obscene language, street-corner lounging, visiting 'gaming places' and smoking cigarettes.

As was seen from the data gathered by Deosaran and Chadee (1997), many youths were incarcerated in youth institutions in Trinidad and Tobago for 'offences' such as running away from home or because no one was available to take care of them. The flexibility in defining juvenile delinquency opens up the possibility that many youths, who for the most part are law abiding and live within the accepted norms of society, could be drawn into the youth correctional system or other related systems which may initiate the labelling process, and thereby channel such youths into a life of delinquency and later criminality. The labelling process is one which operates at both the individual and social levels. The society at large and particularly people in the youth's immediate social environment re-evaluate the person who is labelled as delinquent, and retrospectively reinterpret the person's past actions and life within the context of the new label. Acts which might have been previously perceived as merely pranks would now be seen as evidence that the person has a maladjusted personality or other such factors which the public may associate with delinquency. Importantly also, people in the social environment alter the way they interact with and behave toward the labelled youth. Acting on stereotypes of what delinquent youths are like, people in the social environment may withdraw social support, informational support, their level of communication, and other such factors which collectively serve to reduce the legitimate opportunities for social advancement. Faced with such reduced opportunities, labelled youths may be forced to make use of illegal opportunities for social advancement.

Perhaps even more insidious is the fact that many youths may internalize the delinquent label, and where they previously did not see themselves as delinquent, may come to re-evaluate their self-status and see themselves as delinquent. Charles Horton Cooley pointed out, in developing the concept of the 'looking glass self', that the actions and beliefs of others have a powerful impact on how we evaluate ourselves. The labelled youth is bombarded by messages and signals from his environment which indicate that he or she is a delinquent. Over time, he or she internalizes the label of delinquent. At this point, it may become extremely difficult to extricate the youth from a life of delinquency since 'delinquent' is now a part of the youth's self-concept. In conjunction with an alteration of the youth's self-concept, youth facilities may serve the unintended function of socializing youths into a life of delinquency. In such institutions, many youths who otherwise would not have led a life of delinquency are exposed to a range of values and attitudes which encourage, or at the very least, facilitate criminal offending. Youths who are more experienced in committing illegal acts may train inexperienced youths in the techniques and skills required for a 'successful' life of crime. Such social systems also serve to reinforce and reward counter-normative values and behaviours. The labelling perspective in criminology warns us, especially with youths but also with adults, that we must be careful to distinguish between offenders who are merely petty criminals or non-criminals and those who are 'hardened criminals' who are highly likely to recidivate. The former class of persons should be given non-custodial dispositions or other dispositions which channel them out of the criminal justice system and which circumvent the labelling process, since inadvertently, if labelled, these otherwise non-criminal individuals may be forced into lives of criminality.

Recent theorizing on the genesis of youth delinquency is supportive of the idea that there are different types of delinquency and that all delinquents should not be channelled into youth facilities or other custodial dispositions which initiate the labelling process. Terrie Moffitt (1993) distinguishes between life-course persistent delinquency and adolescence-limited delinquency. The term 'life course persistent offenders' refers to a small minority of people who have inherited or acquired neuropsychological deficits which lead to antisocial behaviour and other personality traits which predispose them to engaging in counter-normative actions. It is important to clarify here that Moffitt, in referring to neuropsychological deficits, does not restrict her definition to major mental or other diagnosable disorders, but uses the term in a broader sense to include personality and other trait dispositions which may lead to antisocial and other counter-normative actions. Such traits could be acquired through difficult environments, including, but not limited to exposure to teratogens and parenting styles which expose children to excessive punishment, abuse, neglect, and other such factors. The life course persistent offender engages in antisocial and counter-normative actions throughout the life course, with desistence from such behaviour occurring very late in life, by some estimates, when such persons are well into their 50s (Loeber and Farrington 1997; Moffitt 2006). The antisocial behaviours of such persons will change over the life course, and depend very much on the types of opportunities available, and extent of social control applied. As children and youths, such persons may have limited opportunities to engage in serious acts of criminality, but as the life course persistent offender gets older, such opportunities increase, and so too do the range and severity of acts in which they engage. The life course persistent offender represents a small proportion of persons who engage in delinquent and illegal actions, though they engage in such actions with a high frequency. Interventions, except if they are applied early in the life course, tend to be ineffective.

Adolescent limited offenders, in contrast, represent 'normal' youths who grow up in households which do not predispose them to neuropsychological deficits. Moffitt (1993) argues that when such youths reach adolescence, they experience what she calls a 'maturity gap'; that is, they feel that they are physically mature and should be accorded an equivalent social status, but feel that adults restrict them from achieving such status. At the same time, the adolescent limited youth observes the life course persistent youth who, by the evaluation of their peers, have achieved a social status similar to that of adults. Life course persistent youths may have more financial resources (gained from delinquent or illegal actions) and may appear to have more autonomy and are accorded a relatively higher status than the average adolescent limited youth. Adolescent limited youths, therefore, attempt to imitate the life course persistent youth during adolescence and likewise may engage in a range of delinquent or even illegal actions. By the time adolescent limited youths enter young adulthood, however, they become socially mature and no longer feel the need to engage in delinquent actions as a means of social advancement. Accordingly, the adolescent limited youth will desist from delinquent actions without any interventions being necessary.

Moffitt's (1993) theory is consistent with much criminological data which show an increase in offending/delinquency during the adolescent years, and which show a decline in criminal behaviour once people get older. This theory is also consistent with the findings of other researchers (e.g., Wolfgang, Figlio and Sellin 1972 and Shannon 1991) who found that a very large proportion of all offences were committed by a small number of high rate offenders. The data gathered by Deosaran and Chadee (1997), as well as other data cited, appear to be consistent with Moffitt's theory. In the case of Deosaran and Chadee, for example, it was found that only 5.4 per cent of the youths were repeat offenders. This percentage of persistent offenders is consistent with estimates discovered by other researchers such as Moffitt (1993), Marvin Wolfgang, Robert Figlio and Thorsten Sellin (1972), and Lyle Shannon (1991). These recidivists may be the life course persistent offenders who Moffitt describes. Such offenders may not be amenable to rehabilitation and should be separated from other less serious offenders to circumvent the possibility that social learning or socialization processes might foster increased rates of offending for less serious youth offenders.

There are a number of important implications of Moffitt's theory which may be applicable to dealing with delinquency and youth offending in Trinidad and Tobago. Moffitt's theory indicates that adolescent limited youths will desist from delinquency on their own, and warns that interventions by the criminal justice system which initiate the labelling process may ensnare such youth into a life of delinquency and later criminality. Such ensnarement affects youths' legitimate opportunities thus making the return to a normative law-abiding life difficult. Instead of the natural process of desistence occurring, such youths are forced to continue with a delinquent lifestyle since the opportunities for a 'normal' lifestyle become blocked. Moffitt's theory thus implies that in dealing with youth delinquency a distinction must be made between the life course persistent and adolescent limited offender and each should be treated differently. The practical difficulty, however, lies in distinguishing the life course persistent from the adolescent limited offender. There is always the danger that social class and poverty (which in some countries like the US correlate with race) may overlap with family structures which predispose the development of neurological deficits. If this is the case, then class (and race) biases may be implicated in distinguishing between life course persistent and adolescent limited offenders. If it is possible within the Trinidad and Tobago context to develop an unbiased assessment instrument, then it may become feasible and ethically defensible to divert adolescent limited youths away from custodial dispositions and into alternative dispositions, which avoid the consequences of labelling. In contrast, given that life course persistent offenders are highly recidivistic, custodial sentences may be more appropriate and institutional confinement, along with appropriate rehabilitation programming, may be justified. In this context, however, for the life course persistent offender, interventions which occur earlier in life have a greater chance of success and especially so when they compensate for the conditions which lead to acquired neuropsychological deficits. As such, interventions that occur in early childhood have a much better chance of reversing the life course of a potential life course persistent offender, as opposed to interventions that occur during adolescence or later.

An examination of the 'offences' committed by youths in the Deosaran and Chadee (1997) study is supportive of the above-mentioned strategy for dealing with juvenile delinquency in Trinidad and Tobago. These 'offences' could be classified into two major groupings; things which are illegal, and things which may be counter-normative, but which cannot necessarily be used to indicate that the youths concerned would 'graduate' into more serious types of offending. This latter category includes acts such as running away from home, attempting suicide, being beyond control, promiscuity, having no adult who is willing to take care of them, being a victim of abuse, and vandalism. These categories of 'offences' accounted for fully 44.5 per cent of the youths in the three institutions studied by Deosaran and Chadee (1997). The most prevalent of these offences was being beyond control (27.3 per cent of all youths) with this factor being more important for youths at the St Michael's School for Boys (32 per cent) and St Jude's School for Girls (60.7 per cent) than for persons at the Youth Training Centre (6.9 per cent). Almost 14 per cent (13.6 per cent) of all youths were incarcerated because they ran away from home, with this being more important for the boys at St Michael's (24.1 per cent) and the girls at St Jude's (20.5 per cent) than for the youths at the Youth Training Centre (3.7 per cent). Almost three per cent (2.6 per cent) of all incarcerated youths were in the institutions because they were victims of abuse. This was more important for girls at St Jude's (8.9 per cent) than for the boys at St Michael's (1.6 per cent) or boys at the Youth Training Centre (zero per cent). Arguably, many of these 'offences' are not offences at all, and call for care and counselling instead of incarceration. These include cases where youths ran away from home, are victims of abuse, and have no one who is willing to take care of them.

The data uncovered by Deosaran and Chadee (1997) are consistent with the findings of Hazel Thompson-Ahye (1999) who analysed all offences for which juveniles were charged before the courts of Trinidad and Tobago for the period January 1–December 31, 1994. While youth were charged with 42 different types of offences, Thompson-Ahye found that 'The offence for which delinquents were most frequently brought before the court was being beyond control; that outstripped by far, the next prevalent offence, having no parent or guardian' (1999, 189). A very strong argument can be made that youths who commit non-illegal acts should not be incarcerated and that such incarceration may lead to a range of negative consequences, including increasing the propensity for subsequent delinquency and criminality. These findings are consistent with the larger trends of juvenile 'offences' in Trinidad and Tobago. Court data examined by Deosaran and Chadee (1997) indicate that for the period 1986–95, a total of 2,989 juvenile offences were committed (i.e., by persons 16 years old or younger). Within this ten-year period, 'destitution', that is, having no parent or other fit person to provide for the youth, accounted for 30 per cent of the juvenile 'offences', while being 'beyond control' accounted for another 22.7 per cent.

While a large number of youths in the Deosaran and Chadee (1997) study appeared undeserving of incarceration, a wide range of illegal acts were committed by other youths, indicating the possibility that for such youths, institutionalization *may* have been more deserving. Fully 37.9 per cent of all youths were incarcerated for robbery, with this being more important for boys at the Youth Training Centre (60.7 per cent) and St Michael's (31.3 per cent) than for the girls at St Jude's (1.8 per cent). Other important reasons for the incarceration of persons at the Youth Training Centre included drug offences (10.2 per cent), possession of arms/ammunition (6.9 per cent) and assault (3.7 per cent). For the boys at St Michael's, other important reasons for incarceration included drug offences (3.9 per cent), assault (2.3 per cent), larceny (1.6 per cent), and murder/attempted murder (1.6 per cent). For the girls at St Jude's, the only other important reason for incarceration was assault (1.8 per cent). Overall, 58.5 per cent of the boys at St Michael's were incarcerated for committing acts which were not illegal (being beyond control, attempted suicide, running away from home, promiscuity, being a victim of abuse, vandalism, and having no one willing to take care of them). The other 41.2 per cent were incarcerated for illegal acts (including drug offences, robbery, assault, possession of arms/ammunition, rape and larceny). Overall, 11.1 per cent of the boys at the Youth Training Centre committed non-illegal acts, while the remaining 88.9 per cent were institutionalized for committing illegal acts. Overall, 92.8 per cent of the girls at St Jude's were incarcerated for non-illegal acts, while only 7.2 per cent had committed illegal acts. The percentage of youths who were incarcerated for committing non-illegal and illegal acts is displayed in figure 3.4. More recent information from the Ministry of Justice website indicates that as of February 1, 2013 there were 106 young males at the Youth Training Centre. Of these, nine per cent were there for non-illegal acts. Of the 25 young males at St Michael's, 96 per cent were there for non-illegal acts while of the 38 girls at the St Jude's School for Girls 97 per cent were there for non-illegal acts.

While many of the youths interviewed by Deosaran and Chadee (1997) had committed illegal acts, they exhibited characteristics which indicated a strong potential for rehabilitation and leading a prosocial life. More specifically, a large proportion of the youths had accepted and acknowledged that they had done something wrong; they expressed remorsefulness, they wanted to improve their lives and had worthwhile goals, and family was very important to the majority of youths. Deosaran and Chadee (1997) found that there was a 94 per cent concordance rate between the self-reported reason for incarceration and the reason for incarceration as indicated in the official records of the institutions. This indicated willingness by the youths to accept that they had done something wrong. Important goals for the youths included getting a job (55 per cent), furthering their education (31 per cent), and being with family (32 per cent). When asked what was needed to improve their lives, 25 per cent of the youths indicated that they needed more discipline. Prosocial values were also important to many youths. For example, when asked about what they admired most in their friends, responses included their positive attitude and behaviour (28 per cent), loyalty (12 per cent), kindness and helpfulness (22 per cent), and intelligence and leadership ability (nine per cent).

Figure 3.4:   Percentage of Youths who Committed Illegal and Non-illegal Acts

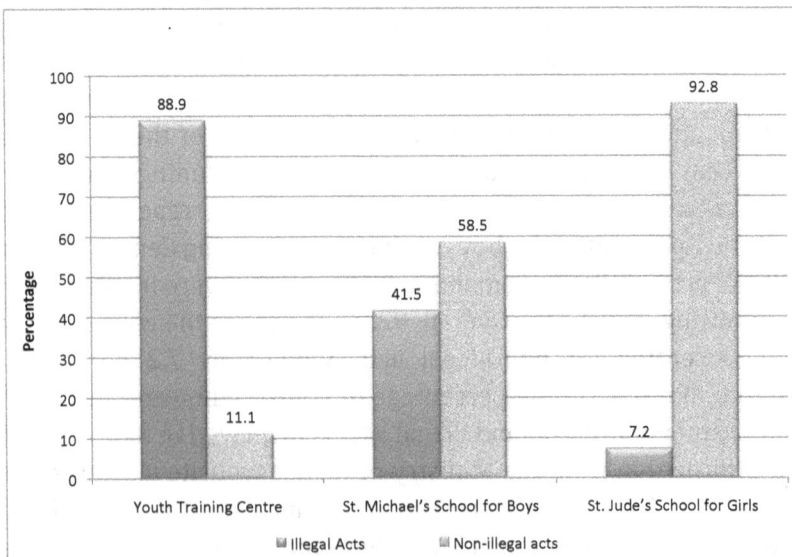

Source: Deosaran and Chadee (1997)

Quite significantly, 68.7 per cent of the youths blamed themselves for being in the institution, while 60 per cent of the youths acknowledged that they had done something wrong which resulted in their institutionalization. Even when we consider the most criminogenic group (those at the Youth Training Centre), fully 77.2 per cent of them blamed themselves for their institutionalization. When asked what they planned to do upon leaving the institution, 45 per cent indicated that they wanted to get a job, 24 per cent wanted to further their education, and 13 per cent wanted to be with family and friends.

While it is possible that incarcerated youths may want to respond in ways which may portray a positive self-image, and while it may be difficult to deny that they had done something wrong by the mere fact of their incarceration, Deosaran and Chadee (1997) report that in their opinion, the responses, including the aspirations and expressions of remorsefulness, were genuine. This intuition, while difficult to quantify and systematically examine, is a judgment which experienced researchers can make, and usually is based on guarantees of confidentiality, anonymity, and the rapport developed between the interviewer and interviewee. This is important, since if genuine, such expressions of remorsefulness provide the basis upon which successful rehabilitation programmes can be developed. It was indicated earlier that labelling and other processes which occur during incarceration may force youths along a path where they have little alternative but to resort to illegal activity. While it is certainly the case that we would want to divert youths who did not commit illegal acts away from an institutional setting for this reason, the data from Deosaran and Chadee suggest that, even for many youths who did commit illegal acts, we would want to think very carefully about the disposition assigned to them. Their expressions of remorsefulness and acknowledgment of guilt indicate that many such youths may not go on to recidivate if proper interventions are applied. The influential and strongly supported ideas of Moffitt (1993) are supportive of the idea that many youths who offend may not necessarily go on to develop criminal careers and will eventually desist from crime and delinquency. To reiterate, according to Moffitt, ensnaring such youths in the criminal justice system interferes with the process of desistance and forces such youths into lives of crime and delinquency. This is not to say that there are not some youths who are dangerous. Indeed, even in the data gathered by Deosaran and Chadee (1997) a small proportion of youths expressed no remorsefulness and indicated that they would return to lives of crime once released. According to Moffitt (1993), very different approaches, including incarceration, may be justified for such youths.

The legislative framework governing the treatment of youthful offenders in Trinidad and Tobago allows room for the approach suggested above since the courts are afforded wide flexibility in the dispositions which they may apply in cases where juvenile offences occur. With respect to youths between the ages of ten and 16, the Children Act (46:01) states:

> Where a youthful offender is charged before the High Court or before a magistrate with an offence punishable in the case of an adult by imprisonment, and in the opinion of the Court... such youthful offender is ten years of age or upwards but less than sixteen years of age, the Court, if satisfied on enquiry that it is expedient so to deal with the youthful offender, may order him to be sent to a certified industrial school. (Section 43)

Section (83) further states:

> Where a child or young person charged with any offence is tried by any court, and the court is satisfied of his guilt, the court shall take into consideration the manner in which, under the provisions of this or any other Act enabling the court to deal with the case, the case should be dealt with, namely, whether –

a.   by dismissing the charge;

b.   by discharging the offender on his entering into a recognisance;

c.   by so discharging the offender and placing him under the supervision of a welfare officer (probation);

d.   by committing the offender to the care of a relative or other fit person;

e.   by sending the offender to an Industrial School;

f.   by sending the offender to an orphanage;

g.   by ordering the offender to be whipped;

h.   by ordering the offender to pay a fine, damages, or costs;

i.   by ordering the parent or guardian of the offender to pay a fine, damages, or costs;

j.   by ordering the parent or guardian of the offender to give security for his good behaviour;

k.   by committing the offender to custody in a place of detention provided under this Part;

l.   where the offender is a young person, by sentencing him to imprisonment; or

m.   by dealing with the case in any other manner in which it may legally be dealt with.

For older youths 16 to 18 years of age, the following laws (Chapter 13:03, Section 7) apply:

1.   Where a person is convicted before the High Court on indictment of any offence other than murder, or before a Court of Summary Jurisdiction

of any offence for which he is liable to be sentenced to imprisonment, and it appears to such Court –

a.   that the person is not less than sixteen nor more than eighteen years of age, and

b.   that by reason of his antecedents or mode of life it is expedient that he should be subject to detention for such term and under such instruction and discipline as appears most conducive to his reformation and the repression of crime, the Court may, in lieu of sentencing him to the punishment provided by law for the offence for which he was convicted, pass a sentence of detention under penal discipline in the Institution for a term of not less than three years nor more than four years.

2.   Before passing such sentence the Court shall be satisfied that the character, state of health, and mental condition of the offender, and the other circumstances of the case, are such that the offender is likely to profit by such instruction and discipline as aforesaid.

3.   No such sentence passed by a Court of Summary Jurisdiction shall be carried into effect until it has been approved by the Minister, for the period fixed by such Court or for some shorter period, and if such sentence is not so approved, the Court may sentence the offender to any punishment provided by law for the offence of which he was convicted.

4.   Where a Court has convicted a person for any offence to which subsection (1) applies, the Court may before passing a sentence of detention as therein provided, in addition to any other powers conferred upon it by any other law, commit the person convicted to prison or to such other safe custody as it thinks fit for such period not exceeding one month as it may deem necessary for the purpose of ascertaining whether it is expedient to pass such a sentence of detention.

5.   Where a Court has committed a person in the manner herein provided, the Court may cause the person so committed to be brought before it at any time prior to the expiration of the period for which he was committed and thereupon to pass sentence according to law.

In the case of offenders between the ages of 10 and 16, and as implied in Chapter 13:03, Section 7, point 2 for offenders between the ages of 16 and 18, the courts of Trinidad and Tobago have the option to enforce non-custodial sentences. The findings from empirical research on youth offending and rehabilitation represent an important consideration when the courts are required to sentence youthful offenders. The work of Moffitt (1993), as well as the data from the other researchers cited in this chapter, indicate that the use of incarceration must be carefully considered and must be used only as a last resort. This point becomes especially forceful given the large amount of international support for Moffitt's theory (for reviews see Moffitt 2003, 2006). Youthful offenders, and especially those who have committed status offences rather than illegal acts, should be diverted away from the criminal justice system and into modes of rehabilitation which avoid the labelling process and which circumvent the possibility that such youths will be put into situations where they may be socialized into lives of crime and delinquency. More than any other population youths are critical to the development process of any nation. As such, youths should be considered to be one of the most critical resources for a country's future. At the same time, improper policies which apply to youths can work against security and development by forcing youths along a path which engenders criminogenic behaviour. No nation can afford to ignore the importance of youths for its future and, as such, where inadequacies with youth policies exist, these should be addressed as a matter of high priority.

Note
1.   January 1–October 31, 2012.

Gangs in Trinidad and Tobago

The Small Arms Survey (2010) indicates that Trinidad and Tobago now rivals Jamaica as one of the most violent countries in the Caribbean, with the annual number of murders rising by over 500 per cent within the past ten years. Indeed, official crime data from the Ministry of National Security of Trinidad and Tobago indicate that there are long-term increases over time for all major crimes except burglary and, that in the case of sexual offences and kidnappings, there have been noted decreases within the last five to six years (see table 2.1 in this book). Very little is known about gangs in Trinidad and Tobago and, thus far, researchers have failed to systematically examine the extent to which gangs contribute to the current crime problem in the country.

This chapter examines the nature and extent of the gang problem in Trinidad and Tobago and assesses the impact of criminal gangs on violent crime. Recommendations to deal with the gang problem in Trinidad and Tobago are also developed. The discussion draws from a range of data sources, including official crime and gang data from the Trinidad and Tobago Police Service, data from the Besson Street Gang Intelligence Criminal History Project,[1] data from Charles Katz and David Choate (2010),[2] and victimization survey data gathered for this study from a nationally representative sample of 1,595 adults in Trinidad and Tobago.

While there are controversies about the definitions of gangs, a distinction must be made between social groupings which may refer to themselves as gangs, but which do not engage in illegal activity, and social groupings which engage in illegal activity. This discussion focuses solely on the latter, and adopts the definition of gangs used by the United Nations Development Programme (UNDP) (2012). The UNDP defines a gang as 'any durable, street-oriented youth group whose involvement in illegal activity is part of their group identity' (67). Here, durability refers to the persistence of the group beyond just a few months, while street-oriented means that the group spends a substantial amount of time on the streets and in public places. The term *youth*, in this context, refers to young adults between the ages of 13 and 25.

Data from the Crime and Problem Analysis branch of the Trinidad and Tobago Police Service and Katz and Choate (2010) concur that there were approximately 95 gangs in Trinidad and Tobago and approximately 1,269 gang members, with the majority of gangs concentrated in Port of Spain and the Western and Northern Police Divisions. More recent data from the TTPS indicate that in 2014 there were approximately 92 gangs and 1,699 gang members. Katz and Choate further indicate that approximately 83 per cent of gang members are of African descent, 13 per cent of East Indian descent and four per cent of other ethnic backgrounds. All of the gangs in Trinidad and Tobago are male dominated, with about 87 per cent comprised of adults. Two thirds of gangs have between six and 50 members while 95 per cent of gangs are comprised of citizens of Trinidad and Tobago. The majority of gangs in Trinidad and Tobago (86 per cent) have a group name, while 61 per cent refer to themselves as a gang, 26 per cent as a crew, and 4.2 per cent as a clip or unit. A large proportion (88 per cent) claim turf while 75 per cent defend their turf. The vast majority (85 per cent) do not have special symbols or identifying clothing and, almost without exception, illegal activity is accepted by all gang members. Twenty-six per cent of gangs in Trinidad and Tobago locate their date of origin prior to 2000, while the remainder originated after 2000. Gangs in Trinidad and Tobago are typically smaller than gangs in Latin America and the United States (US) and typically do not have linkages to gangs in other parts of the region or to gangs in other countries. This contrasts with some of the larger gangs in Latin America which have connections to other gangs within their region and in the US (Katz and Choate 2010; Wells, Katz and Kim 2010).

The Besson Street Gang Intelligence Criminal History Project offers rare insight into the nature and composition of gangs in Trinidad and Tobago. In this project 368 gang members were interviewed with data collected in 2005. The age distribution of the sample gives an indication of the typical age ranges of gang members.[3] The majority of gang members were young adults between the ages of 18 and 45. More specifically, 26.1 per cent were between the ages of 18 and 21, 25.4 per cent between the ages of 22 and 25 and 33.7 per cent between the ages of 26 and 35. Only a small proportion of the sample (5.3 per cent) were 17 or younger at the time of interview, whereas eight per cent of the sample were between the ages of 36 and 45 and 1.5 per cent of the sample were between the ages of 46 and 55. Of the sample used in the Besson Street project, 87.5 per cent were of African descent, 0.8 per cent of East Indian descent and 1.9 per cent of mixed descent, while the ethnicities of 9.5 per cent of the sample were unknown. Gang members were almost exclusively male (95.3 per cent of the sample).

Table 4.1:   Percentage of Gang Members and Non-Gang Members Previously Arrested

	Gang members (n=368)	Non-gang members (n=878)
Ever arrested	51.4	20.2
Arrest by crime type		
Violent offences	31.5	10.4
Firearm-related	25.8	8.7
Drug trafficking	15.2	3.2
Drug use/possession	23.4	8.0
Property offences	13.9	7.6
Sexual offences	2.7	1.8
Other	12.5	5.7

Source: Besson Street Police Station

Given the available data, there is no question that gangs and gang members are engaged in illegal activity in Trinidad and Tobago. Of the gang members surveyed at the Besson Street Police Station, 51.4 per cent had been arrested previously with each member having an average of 2.09 arrests. This compares to a non-gang sample (n=878) where 20.2 per cent had previous arrests, with the mean number of arrests being 0.68. Not surprisingly, arrest data indicate that gang members commit a larger number of crimes than people who are not in gangs. Arrest data in table 4.1 indicate that gang members commit violent offences at approximately three times the rate of people who are not in gangs (31.5 per cent vs. 10.4 per cent). Almost 26 per cent of gang members had been arrested for firearm-related offences compared to 8.7 per cent of non-gang members. Similarly, 15.2 per cent of gang members had been arrested for drug trafficking compared to 3.2 per cent of non-gang members. Similar over-representation in criminal offences for gang members obtains for property offences, sexual offences, and drug use/possession.

Data on the mean number of arrests also support the idea that gang membership is associated with a disproportionately high crime rate (see table 4.2). The average number of arrests for gang members was 2.09, whereas the average number of arrests for non-gang members was 0.68. The mean number of arrests for gang members for violent crimes was 0.81 compared to 0.33 for non-gang members. When only firearm-related offences were considered, gang members had almost twice the average number of arrests (0.45) than non-gang members (0.22). The disparity became much larger when we considered drug trafficking. Gang members had an arrest rate which was almost five times that of non-gang members (0.24 vs. 0.05). In a similar manner, the arrest rates for gang members exceeded that of non-gang members for drug use/possession and property offences. Only in the case of sexual offences were the arrest rates similar for gang and non-gang members. The above findings are consistent with previous research which points to an association between gangs, guns, illegal drugs, and other illegal activities (Katz and Choate 2010; Katz and Fox 2010; Montoute 2010; Wells, Katz and Kim 2010; UNODC and the World Bank 2007).

Trinidad and Tobago Police Service data on the spatial distribution of gangs and on the spatial distribution of crime suggest that gang members may be responsible for a significant proportion of violent crimes in Trinidad and Tobago. Gangs are concentrated in certain areas of Trinidad and Tobago, and the research presented in this chapter indicates that violent crimes tend to be concentrated in the same areas where gangs are located. Data from the Trinidad and Tobago Police Service indicate that the police divisions[4] with the largest number of gangs are the Port of Spain Division, Western Division and the Northern Division. Other areas with a notable gang presence include the Eastern Division and the North Eastern Division. The number of gangs in each police division is shown in table 4.3.

According to Katz and Choate (2010), the five police station districts[5] with the most gangs are, in order of priority, Besson Street, San Juan, Sangre Grande, St Joseph and Belmont. The five police station districts with the highest number of gang members in order of priority are Besson Street, Belmont, San Juan, Carenage and Sangre Grande (see table 4.4).

Table 4.2:   Mean Number of Arrests for Gang Members and Non-Gang Members

	Gang members (n=368)	Non-gang members (n=878)
Number of arrests	2.09	.68
Number of arrests by crime type		
Violent offences	.81	.33
Firearm related	.45	.22
Drug trafficking	.24	.05
Drug use/possession	.32	.12
Property offences	.36	.17
Sexual offences	.03	.03
Other	.20	.16

Source: Besson Street Police Station

Table 4.3:   Number of Gangs in Trinidad and Tobago, by Police Division

Police Division	2009	2012	2014
Port of Spain	16	44	23
Southern	3	04	8
Western	12	16	18
Northern	12	13	13
Central	2	3	4
South Western	1	2	5
Eastern	6	3	2
North Eastern	5	12	10
Tobago	3	5	9
Total	**60**	**102**	**92**

Source: Crime and Problem Analysis Branch of the Trinidad and Tobago Police Service

Table 4.4:   Police Station Districts with the Highest Number of Gangs and Gang Members

Police Station Districts with the Highest Number of Gangs	Number of Gangs	Number of Gang Members
Besson Street	19	385
San Juan	8	130
Sangre Grande	8	90
St Joseph	7	55
Belmont	6	165
Police Station Districts with the Highest Number of Gang Members		
Besson Street	19	385
Belmont	6	165
San Juan	8	130
Carenage	4	100
Sangre Grande	8	90

Source: Katz and Choate (2010).

The spatial distribution of gangs can be compared with the spatial distribution of crime to assess the extent to which areas with higher concentrations of gangs have higher levels of crime. Data for the spatial distribution of gangs are only available for 2009, 2012 and 2014. Table 4.5 provides data on gang-related murders for the period 2001–14, while figures 4.1, 4.2 and 4.3 show the percentage of gangs and the percentage of gang-related murders according to police division for 2009, 2012 and 2014 respectively.

Analysis of the data in table 4.5 shows that the spatial distribution of gang-related murders in Trinidad and Tobago bears a striking similarity to the spatial distribution of gangs. For the period 2001 to 2014, a total of 1,583 gang-related murders occurred in Trinidad and Tobago. Of these, 727 or 45.9 per cent occurred in the Port of Spain Police Division; 272 or 17.2 per cent occurred in the North Eastern Division; 263 or 16.6 per cent occurred in the Western Division while 243 or 15.4 per cent occurred in the Northern Division. These are the same divisions with disproportionately large numbers of gangs. In contrast, divisions with fewer gangs account for a smaller proportion of gang-related murders.

When gang locations and gang-related murders are restricted to 2009, the spatial distribution of these murders closely resembles the spatial distribution of gangs (figure 4.1). In 2009, 49.4 per cent of all gang-related murders took place in the Port of Spain Division, which was also the division with the largest proportion of gangs (26.7 per cent).

Table 4.5: Gang-related Murders by Location

Police Division	Number of Gang-related Murders														Percentage of Gangs by Location		
	2001	2002	2003	2004	2005	2006	2007	2008	2009	2010	2011	2012	2013	2014	2009	2012	2014
Port of Spain	3	10	28	14	33	37	61	116	87	40	59	80	102	57	26.7	43.1	25.0
Southern	0	1	2	1	0	0	4	3	1	4	1	2	3	0	5.0	3.9	8.7
Western	0	0	3	5	27	18	22	47	42	15	13	20	22	29	20.0	15.7	19.6
Northern	0	1	5	1	9	17	55	44	23	5	10	13	37	23	20.0	12.7	14.1
Central	0	0	0	0	0	1	3	10	0	0	2	5	1	1	3.3	2.9	4.3
South Western	0	1	0	0	1	0	1	0	0	0	0	1	1	1	1.7	2.0	5.4
Eastern	0	0	0	0	1	0	6	6	1	3	0	2	3	4	10.0	2.9	2.2
North Eastern	0	4	4	11	10	25	53	52	22	8	8	21	27	27	8.3	11.8	10.9
Tobago	0	0	0	0	0	0	0	0	0	0	0	0	1	0	5.0	4.9	9.8
Total	3	17	42	32	81	98	205	278	176	75	93	144	197	142	60	102	92

Source: Crime and Problem Analysis Branch of the Trinidad and Tobago Police Service

Figure 4.1: Gang Locations (2009) and Gang-related Murders (2009)

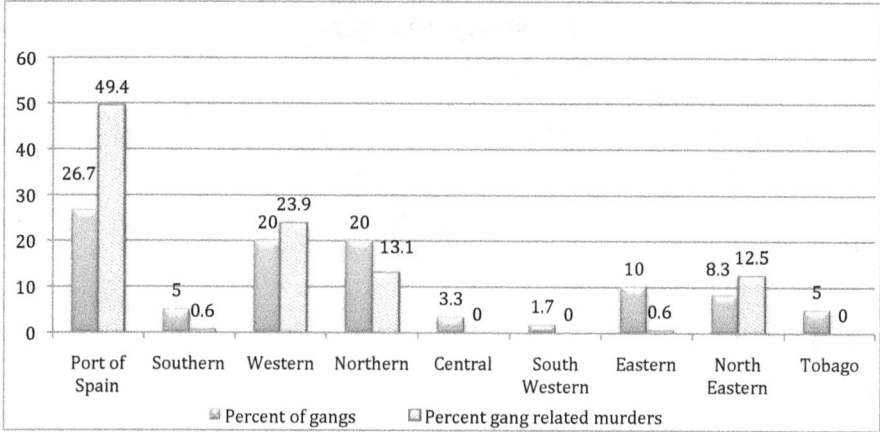

Source: Crime and Problem Analysis Branch of the Trinidad and Tobago Police Service

Figure 4.2: Gang Locations (2012) and Gang-related Murders (2012)

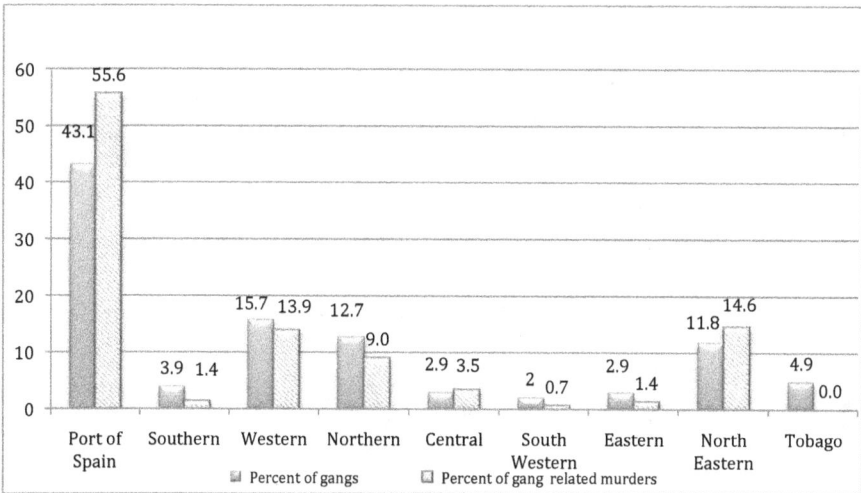

Source: Crime and Problem Analysis Branch of the Trinidad and Tobago Police Service

The Western and Northern police divisions also had disproportionately large numbers of gang-related murders and correspondingly large numbers of gangs. More specifically, in 2009, 20 per cent of all gangs were located in the Western Division; this division accounted for 23.9 per cent of all gang-related murders. The Northern Division accounted for 20 per cent of all gangs and 13.1 per cent of all gang-related murders. As figure 4.1 also illustrates, police divisions with fewer gangs correspondingly had fewer gang-related murders. Data for 2012 also exhibited similar spatial consistency (see figure 4.2). In 2012, the divisions with the largest proportion of gangs (the Port of Spain Division – 43.1 per cent of all gangs; the Western Division – 15.7 per cent of all gangs, and the Northern Division – 12.7 per cent of all gangs) were also the divisions with the highest proportion of gang-related murders. Figure 4.3 shows the percentage of gangs and gang related murders according to police division for 2014. Again, divisions with a large proportion of gangs also have a large proportion of murders.

Figure 4.3: Gang Locations (2014) and Gang-related Murders (2014)

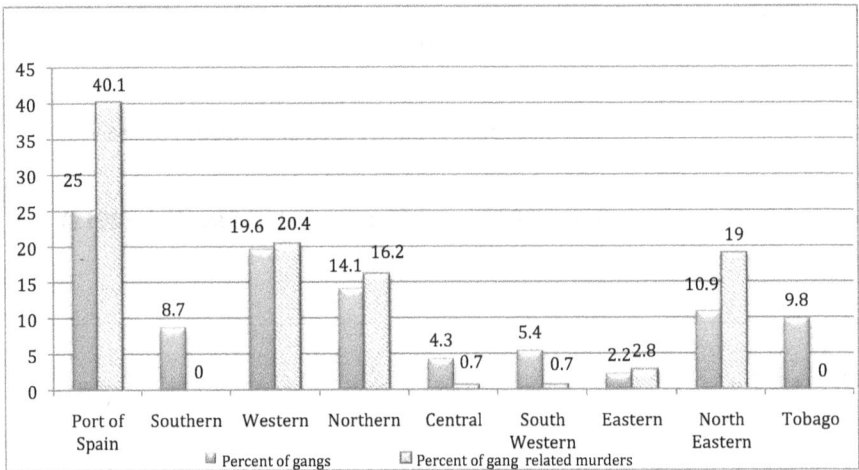

Source: Crime and Problem Analysis branch of the Trinidad and Tobago Police Service

Table 4.6: Spatial Distribution of Gangs (2009) and Crimes (2009)[8]

Police Division	Percentage of Gangs by Location	Murder	Woundings/ Shootings	Sexual Offences	Kidnapping	Robbery	Narcotic Offences	Burglary
Port of Spain	26.7	25.1	22.4	7.0	18.7	17.5	15.0	12.2
Southern	5.0	7.5	10.0	15.8	16.1	14.8	12.5	14.5
Western	20.0	14.6	13.4	6.2	5.8	10.2	4.7	8.6
Northern	20.0	22.5	16.3	13.7	16.1	24.3	24.8	20.4
Central	3.3	8.9	11.8	10.5	11.6	13.7	6.0	14.1
South Western	1.7	3.0	7.1	11.8	12.3	3.5	5.3	6.0
Eastern	10.0	4.7	5.7	13.9	9.0	5.9	16.5	7.2
North Eastern	8.3	10.7	11.3	15.5	4.5	8.4	6.0	9.0
Tobago	5.0	3.0	2.2	5.5	5.8	1.8	9.2	8.0
Total	**60**	**506**	**689**	**760**	**155**	**6,040**	**549**	**5,744**

Source: Crime and Problem Analysis branch of the Trinidad and Tobago Police Service

Figure 4.4: The Spatial Distribution of Gangs and Crime (2009)

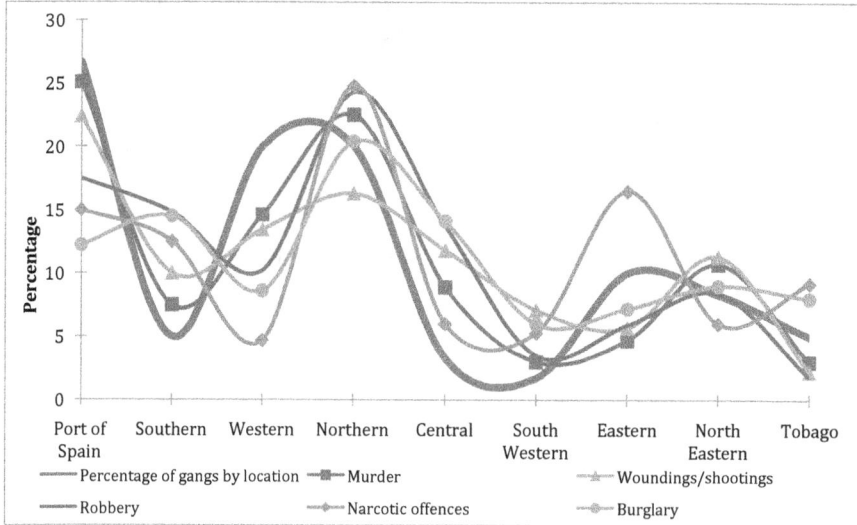

Source: Crime and Problem Analysis branch of the Trinidad and Tobago Police Service

Although a close association between gang presence and gang-related murders should be expected, similar spatial patterns were observed for a range of other crimes, even where no distinction was made between crimes committed by gang members and crimes committed by other persons.[6] The spatial distribution of a range of crimes, compared with the spatial distribution of gangs, supports the possibility that perpetrators may in fact have been gang members, even though official records were unable to verify whether or not these crimes were committed by gang members.   Table 4.6 gives the distribution of gangs in Trinidad and Tobago in 2009, and also indicates the percentage distribution of various crimes, according to police division, for 2009. The spatial distribution of gangs most closely resembles, in priority order, the spatial distribution of murder, woundings and shootings, robbery, narcotic offences and burglary (see figure 4.4). The spatial distribution of gangs was unrelated to the distribution of sexual offences and kidnapping.[7] Table 4.7 gives the spatial distribution of gangs in Trinidad and Tobago in 2012, and also indicates the percentage distribution of various crimes, according to police division, for 2012. The spatial distribution of gangs most closely resembles, in priority order, the spatial distribution of murder, woundings and shootings and robbery (see figure 4.5). The spatial distribution of gangs was unrelated to the distribution of sexual offences, kidnappings, narcotic offences and burglary.

Table 4.8 gives the spatial distribution of gangs in Trinidad and Tobago in 2014, and also indicates the percentage distribution of various crimes, according to police division, for 2014. The spatial distribution of gangs most closely resembles, in priority order, the spatial distribution of murder, woundings and shootings and robbery (see figure 4.6). The spatial distribution of gangs was unrelated to the distribution of sexual offences, kidnappings, narcotic offences and burglary.

Table 4.7: Spatial Distribution of Gangs (2012) and Crime (2012)[9]

Police Division	Percentage of Gangs by Location	Murder	Woundings/ Shootings	Sexual Offences	Kidnapping	Robbery	Narcotic Offences	Burglary
Port of Spain	43.1	27.2	24.0	6.2	5.9	17.6	10.8	9.4
Southern	3.9	10.8	13.5	21.2	17.8	16.8	17.2	16.0
Western	15.7	10.8	10.5	12.0	7.6	7.7	5.9	6.9
Northern	12.7	16.1	15.9	13.3	7.6	21.9	27.7	16.3
Central	2.9	11.1	15.0	10.8	20.5	17.0	8.2	22.5
South Western	2.0	3.7	4.0	7.5	10.8	4.2	11.7	6.3
Eastern	2.9	7.1	5.4	13.5	15.7	3.5	9.8	5.4
North Eastern	11.8	11.9	7.4	9.4	3.8	8.5	4.6	6.5
Tobago	4.9	1.3	4.3	6.0	10.3	2.8	4.1	10.6
Total	**102**	**379**	**579**	**933**	**185**	**4,436**	**437**	**4,321**

Source: Crime and Problem Analysis Branch of the Trinidad and Tobago Police Service

Figure 4.5: Spatial Distribution of Gangs and Crime (2012)

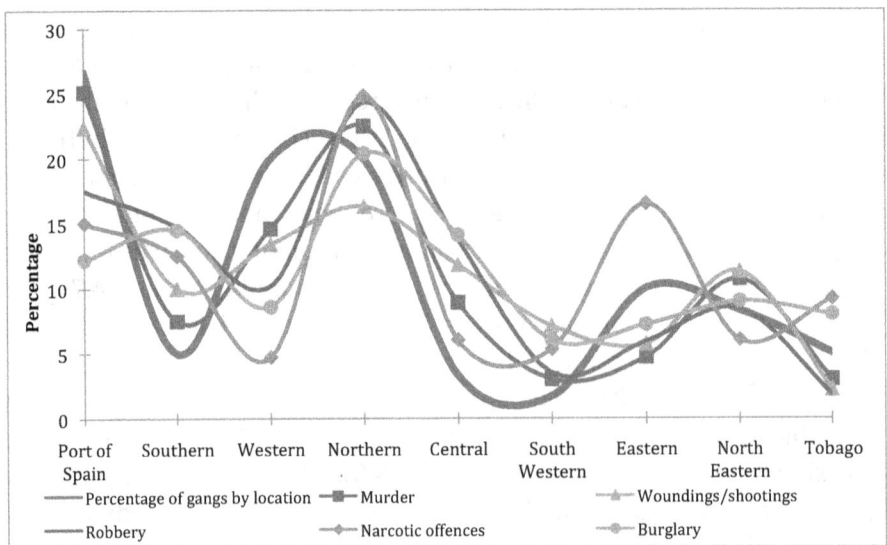

Source: Crime and Problem Analysis Branch of the Trinidad and Tobago Police Service

Table 4.8: Spatial Distribution of Gangs (2014) and Crimes (2014)[10]

Police Division	Percentage of Gangs by Location	Murder	Woundings/ Shootings	Sexual Offences	Kidnapping	Robbery	Narcotic Offences	Burglary
Port of Spain	25.0	20.1	24.9	5.5	16.5	19.8	9.8	10.5
Southern	8.7	9.7	13.4	15.7	19.6	19.4	16.6	14.8
Western	19.6	14.1	12.9	5.8	3.1	7.3	9.3	8.4
Northern	14.1	15.9	11.5	18.2	15.5	15.6	16.4	15.4
Central	4.3	12.4	13.3	12.8	9.3	13.9	9.8	18.1
South Western	5.4	4.5	5.6	9.9	12.4	8.3	10.7	9.2
Eastern	2.2	9.4	5.9	14.4	13.4	3.2	12.1	4.2
North Eastern	10.9	11.9	10.4	7.0	2.1	9.9	6.6	8.1
Tobago	9.8	2.0	2.2	10.7	8.2	2.5	8.7	11.2
Total	**92**	**403**	**558**	**829**	**97**	**2,672**	**439**	**2,592**

Source: Crime and Problem Analysis Branch of the Trinidad and Tobago Police Service

Figure 4.6: Spatial Distribution of Gangs and Crime (2014)

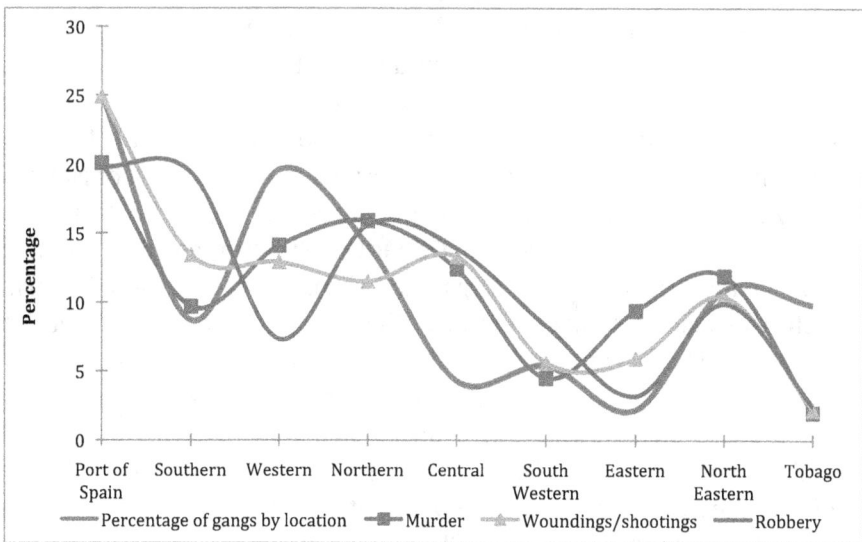

Source: Crime and Problem Analysis Branch of the Trinidad and Tobago Police Service

The above data indicate that locations with higher concentrations of gangs tended to have higher crime rates, particularly for murder, woundings and shootings and robbery, and to some extent, burglary and narcotic offences. In the case of sexual offences, while these might be committed by gang members, the distribution of these offences was not concentrated only in areas with a high gang presence. Similarly, kidnapping was distributed throughout the country. It may be the case, however, that some kidnappings were committed by gang members but that these individuals moved to locations outside of their areas of residence to commit these crimes.

Although the above data are suggestive of the possibility that gangs are responsible for a disproportionate number of crimes and that gangs tend to commit crimes within their areas of residence, caution is warranted in drawing these conclusions. Data on the location of gangs were limited to 2009, 2012 and 2014. Ideally, the distribution of gangs and the distribution of crime should be mapped on a year-to-year basis, both with and without a lag on crime data. Another issue that must be considered is that of causal order. The reasoning above implies that gangs influence crime rates in various places, but it may be the case that gangs gravitate to places with high crime rates for any number of reasons, or it may be that other factors such as the number of illegal opportunities (Cloward and Ohlin 1960) influence both the crime rates and the density of gangs in various places.

Further evidence that gangs in Trinidad and Tobago are responsible for committing illegal acts can be drawn from a survey of experts on gangs in Trinidad and Tobago, conducted by Katz and Choate (2010). The term *experts*, in this context, refer to senior persons in the Ministry of National Security and in the Trinidad and Tobago Police Service, particularly those officers who were in the Repeat Offenders Programme, the Homicide Bureau of Investigations, the Organized Crime Narcotics and Firearms Branch, the Criminal Investigations Division, and the Citizen Security Programme. These experts indicated that two-thirds of the gangs in Trinidad and Tobago are involved in fights with rival gangs, gang members frequently use alcohol and illegal drugs, and gang members engage in the sale of these drugs. Experts also emphasized that gangs are heavily involved in organized fraud, robbery and other forms of armed violence.

The most recent data on gangs in Trinidad and Tobago come from a UNDP survey of 1,595 adults in Trinidad and Tobago. Respondents were 18 years and older, and data were collected in November 2010. Of the respondents, 14.5% indicated that gang violence occurred in their neighbourhoods in 2009, while 13.9 per cent indicated that there was a criminal gang in their neighbourhoods. Fully 18.4 per cent of respondents indicated that gang violence was a somewhat serious, serious, or very serious problem in their neighbourhoods. When the sample was restricted to persons who indicated that there was a criminal gang in their neighbourhoods, 71.7 per cent indicated that gang violence was a somewhat serious, serious, or very serious problem in their neighbourhoods. When the entire sample was considered, 12 per cent of the respondents indicated that gangs made their neighbourhoods less safe, while only 0.6 per cent indicated that gangs made their neighbourhoods safer. When the sample was restricted to only neighbourhoods with criminal gangs, 82.4 per cent indicated that gangs made their neighbourhoods less safe, while 3.2 per cent indicated that gangs made their neighbourhoods safer.

Overall, 15.2 per cent of the sample indicated that their neighbourhoods experienced a small amount of gang violence, 8.1 per cent lived in neighbourhoods with some gang violence, while 2.3 per cent lived in neighbourhoods with a large amount of gang violence. When the sample was restricted to only neighbourhoods with criminal gangs, 34.2 per cent of the sample indicated that their neighbourhoods experienced a small amount of gang violence, 45.5 per cent indicated that their neighbourhood had some gang violence, while 14.4 per cent indicated that their neighbourhood had a large amount of gang violence. Quite importantly, it was found that 16 per cent of respondents in neighbourhoods with gangs reported some form of criminal victimization, as opposed to 9.6 per cent of respondents in neighbourhoods without gangs. People in neighbourhoods with gangs were also almost three times more likely to be victims of violent crimes than people in neighbourhoods without gangs (10.1 per cent vs. 3.7 per cent). Where property victimization was concerned, 5.3 per cent of people in neighbourhoods with gangs reported such victimization compared to 4.2 per cent of people in neighbourhoods without gangs.

Additional evidence that gangs are responsible for a disproportionate number of violent crimes can be derived from homicide data from the Trinidad and Tobago Police Service. Fully 31.5 per cent of all murders for the period 2001–14 were attributed to gangs. Even more troubling is the finding that the proportion of murders being committed by gang members is increasing over time. Whereas the proportion of murders committed by gang members for the period 2001–03 was 11.3 per cent, the proportion rose dramatically to 37.9 per cent for the period 2007–14. The number of gang murders increased consistently for the period 2001–08, but then declined from 2008 to 2010, and thereafter increased until 2013, but declined slightly in 2014 (table 4.9). The observed increase in gang-related murders could be due to increasing awareness and emphasis on gangs, or to the improved ability to solve murder cases. This argument implies that the proportion of gang-related murders may have been high, even in the past, but is only now coming to light as a result of greater awareness of gang involvement in violent crime. At the same time, given the previously mentioned limitations in assessing whether or not murders are gang-related in Trinidad and Tobago (King 2012), it is quite possible that official data underestimate the proportion of murders which are committed by gangs.

In addition to the fact that gang activity is becoming more violent as evidenced by the increasing number of murders committed by gang members, data from the Trinidad and Tobago Police Service also indicate that firearm usage has increased dramatically where murders are concerned (see figure 4.7). For the period 2000–2013, a total of 4,744 murders were committed, of which 3,445, or 72.6 per cent, were committed with the use of a firearm. Indeed, as table 4.10 indicates, firearms have become the weapon of choice when murders are committed. Prior to 2000, firearms were used in less than one third of all homicides in Trinidad and Tobago, whereas after 2000, firearm usage in homicides consistently increased to the point where firearms represent the predominant weapon used in homicides.

Table 4.9: Total Murders and Gang-related Murders (2001–13)

Year	Total Murders	Gang Related	Per cent Gang-related
2001	151	3	2.0
2002	171	17	9.9
2003	229	42	18.3
2004	261	32	12.3
2005	386	81	21.0
2006	371	98	26.4
2007	391	205	52.4
2008	547	278	50.8
2009	506	176	34.8
2010	472	75	15.9
2011	352	93	26.4
2012	379	144	38.0
2013	407	197	48.4
2014	403	142	35.2
Total	5,026	1,583	31.5

Source: Crime and Problem Analysis Branch of the Trinidad and Tobago Police Service

Figure 4.7: Trends in Homicides by Weapon Type (2000–2013)[11]

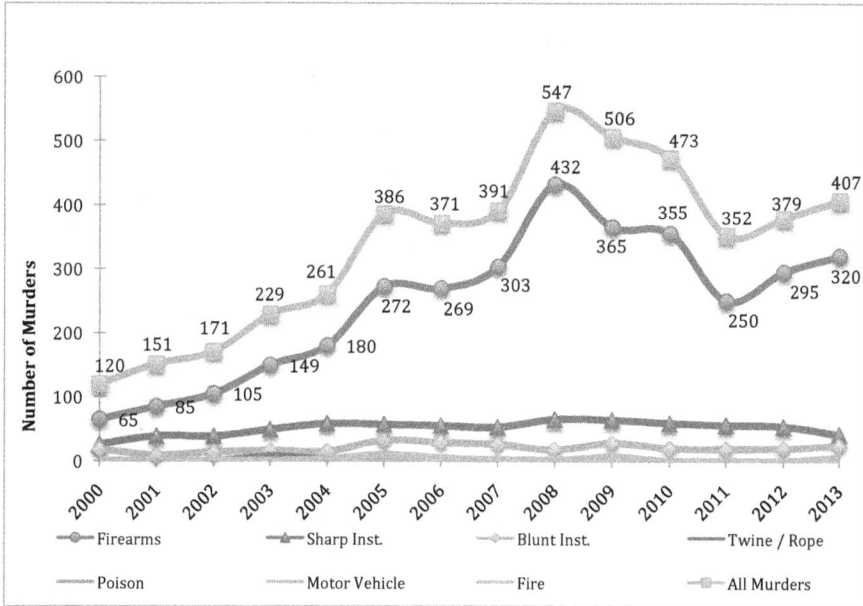

Source: Crime and Problem Analysis Branch of the Trinidad and Tobago Police Service

Firearm usage has increased over time for a range of other crimes, including wounding with intent and shooting with intent (see table 4.10). For the period 2002–10, a total of 2,164 woundings with intent were committed, with an annual average of 240. For this period, wounding with intent increased by an annual average of 13.4 per cent. Shooting with intent exhibited similar upward trends. For the period for which data are available, there were a total of 1,204 such shootings, with an annual average of 134. Shootings with intent increased at an average of 5.4 per cent per annum. The only crimes in which firearms were used, and in which there were decreases, were robbery with aggravation (an annual average decrease of 2.7 per cent) and robbery with violence (an annual average decrease of 0.3 per cent). While there were observed decreases in these crimes, the quantum of such crimes nevertheless is cause for concern. With respect to robbery with aggravation, the annual average number of such crimes occurring is 1,637 while the annual average number of robberies with violence is 455. To the extent that gang members are involved in violent crimes, the data cited here imply that gang members routinely utilize firearms in the commission of such offences.

Table 4.10: Crimes Committed with the Use of Firearms

	Murder	Robbery with Aggravation	Robbery with Violence	Wounding with Intent	Shooting with Intent	Total
2002	105	2026	572	229	122	3054
2003	149	2286	786	198	236	3655
2004	195	1426	347	125	112	2205
2005	272	1634	407	299	121	2733
2006	269	2039	490	510	144	3452
2007	302	1219	333	164	122	2140
2008	432	1419	376	282	126	2635
2009	365	1448	424	212	111	2560
2010	332	1235	359	145	110	2181
Total	2421	14732	4094	2164	1204	24615
Annual average	269	1637	455	240	134	2735
Percentage increase	17.7	-2.7	-0.3	13.4	5.4	

Source: Crime and Problem Analysis Branch of the Trinidad and Tobago Police Service

Consequences of the Presence of Gangs in Trinidad and Tobago

The presence of gangs and gang violence has a number of negative consequences in Trinidad and Tobago. Homicides, as well as other acts of violence, contribute to a reduction in the workforce and to lowered productivity, and are also associated with an increased burden on the health care system since victims must seek medical attention. The increased number of gangs, as well as the associated increase in crime, also results in a diversion of the country's resources from development initiatives toward fighting crime. National security expenditure consumes a large proportion of the total annual budget. This reduces the availability of resources for expenditure in other sectors, including health care, the provision of social services, education, infrastructure development, and economic development initiatives. Indeed, the Economic Commission for Latin America and the Caribbean (ECLAC) (2008) found that the percentage of Gross Domestic Product (GDP) spent on national security in Trinidad and Tobago has increased steadily while welfare expenditure has remained relatively constant. The prevalence of gangs in some areas is also related to a decrease in investment in those areas and in reduced opportunities for employment. In neighbourhoods such as Laventille, for example, there are no businesses except small shops owned and operated by local residents. An added consequence of gang presence in such neighbourhoods is the devaluation of property and land value. Quite apart from internal community issues, linkages with other parts of the society may be reduced or severed. People from known gang areas may be refused employment by people from other neighbourhoods. Indeed, as has happened in the past in Laventille, even public services such as garbage collection and electricity services may be withdrawn. In the past, public service workers have refused to venture into these areas without police escort.

Gang presence also encourages the relocation of law-abiding citizens, as well as law enforcement personnel who reside in these areas (Montoute 2010). This results in a concentration of people who are either more accepting of gangs or a criminal lifestyle, as well as people who have no other alternative but to live in such neighbourhoods. This implies that any benefits of the informal social controls that may be derived from having law-abiding people residing in these neighbourhoods will be lost or continuously weakened. Informal social controls have been consistently found to be important buffers in preventing criminal offending (Hirschi 2002). Compounding this problem is the fact that there is a reduction or withdrawal of corporate sponsorship for community events or programmes in neighbourhoods with gangs. Community events provide another means of social control through building social solidarity and trust among residents.

An even more troubling phenomenon is that communities may actually develop bonds with gangs and gang leaders, especially in situations where gang leaders provide assistance to community members. In practice, however, in situations where community members appear to support or even protect gang leaders or members, it may be difficult to determine whether such support is based on genuine commitment or on fear. Community members may demonstrate support for gangs because of fear, or because of social expectations which dictate that gangs should be supported. A study by Roy McCree (1998) examined public perceptions of gangs in Laventille and assessed the knowledge of gangs in a sample of 400 randomly selected households in this community. Fully 83.8 per cent of people surveyed indicated that they had no knowledge of gangs in Laventille. While there were no gender differences in terms of knowledge of gangs, younger people (aged 15–24 in the study) were somewhat more aware of the existence of gangs in their community than their older counterparts. The apparent lack of knowledge about gangs may be a result of fear of gangs or of community solidarity with gangs. The latter explanation is supported by one informant who indicated that:

Although you may regard the gang leader as a bad person, in the area he is seen as a good person. You go into the area and see a fellow who is known as a gang leader. While you are there, a little child might come to him and say, 'daddy, I don't have any money to buy food'. And he will say: 'well go in the shop and tell them to give it to you; I will deal with it.' Or he might take money from his pocket; he will help the people in the area. The people in the area might even know that he is dealing roughly with their daughters, or that he beat up a woman the other day, but really and truly, he is regarded as the man providing for the village. So the village will protect him (McCree 1998, 167).

Interestingly enough, research in Trinidad and Tobago has indicated that gangs may even provide a law enforcement function for communities (Katz 2009). Charles Katz, in examining data gathered from residents in the community of Gonzales, found that residents believed that gangs reduced crime levels in their community. Katz discovered that gangs in Gonzales had instituted a community court which met weekly and in which community matters, including the disciplining of young males for transgressions against the community, were attended to. Indeed one resident of Gonzales went as far as to say that 'Gangs are the first ones to respond to crime. The police are incompetent; they take too long and never finish the work. If you go to the gang leader you know they will take care of you' (Katz 2009, 26).

Martin Sánchez Jankowski (1991) indicated that gang-community relationships may be of three types: 1) antagonistic/hostile/non-supportive, 2) apathetic – community ignores gangs, or 3) mutual/cooperation/supportive. Jankowski noted that gangs depend more on communities for their survival than communities depend on gangs and, where communities are not in support of gangs (even if only covertly), this may be used to encourage a withdrawal of community support from gangs, leading to the eventual weakening or disbandment of such gangs. Jankowski argued that the gang is dependent on the community for its survival since ultimately the community provides new recruits, offers protection from the police, and provides information on rival gangs and on police activity. Jankowski (1991, 179) summed up the idea as follows:

The gang and community strike up a working relationship, which lasts as long as the two mutually aid and respect each other. If either breaks the code, the pact is terminated and both lose to some degree. However, the gang will experience the greatest loss because it is in more consistent need of the community rather than vice versa. For this reason, gangs make a concerted and aggressive effort to aid the community. If a gang violates the code and is not successful in re-establishing a reciprocal relationship with the community, it will become isolated, which will seriously weaken its ability to operate effectively. This more often than not marks the beginning of the end of such a gang.

Strategies for Addressing the Gang Issue

While 'gangs and gang-related violence are at epidemic proportions in Trinidad and Tobago', Charles Katz, David Choate and Andrew Fox (2010) found, in interviewing key stakeholders and officials in the Trinidad and Tobago Ministry of National Security, the police service, and other bodies, that 'there is almost no attention to primary gang prevention programming and that there is strong resistance to its implementation within some ministries' (20). The data analysed in this study support the idea that gangs in Trinidad and Tobago are engaged in violent offending and, as such, it is imperative that comprehensive intervention strategies be employed. Suppressive strategies are limited in their effectiveness and must be complemented with preventative mechanisms (Katz, Choate and Fox 2010). A comprehensive policy for dealing with gangs must include primary and secondary prevention strategies (Brantingham and Faust 1976) and must focus on proximal as well as distal risk factors which are at various levels of analysis, including the individual, peer group, family, community, economy, and society. Such strategies must be based on empirical evidence that indicates which factors are the most important, such that the factors which are eventually focused on are the ones which have a demonstrated link to the reduction of gang membership and violence.

Primary prevention refers to those strategies which target the general population and are designed to reduce the likelihood of criminal offending. In the context of the present chapter, such strategies should be focused on reducing the likelihood that people will join gangs, should focus on neighbourhood and school social life and safety, and should build a sense of community cohesiveness and develop informal systems of social control. An example of a primary prevention programme which can be adapted for use in Trinidad and Tobago is the revised Gang Resistance Education and Training (G.R.E.A.T.) programme. This is a gang and violence prevention programme built around school-based, law enforcement officer-instructed classroom curricula. The programme is intended to provide immunization against delinquency, youth violence, and gang membership for children in the years immediately preceding the prime age for introduction into gangs and delinquent behaviour.[12] The revised G.R.E.A.T. programme has three primary goals: teaching youths to avoid gang membership, preventing violence and criminal activity, and assisting youths to develop positive relationships with law enforcement.[13] The curriculum emphasizes changes in attitude and behaviour through behaviour rehearsal, cooperative and interactive learning techniques, and extended teacher activities. The programme is comprised of 13 one-hour lessons taught by a trained professional. Evaluation of the programme indicates that youths who participated in the programme were more positive about the police, were less positive about gangs, less likely to join gangs, less likely to self-report committing crime, and were better able to resist peer pressure (National Youth Gang Center 2010).

In Trinidad and Tobago, suppressive and law enforcement strategies are given priority over preventative measures. As the data in table 2.1 indicate, such strategies have met with little success in the fight against crime and violence. There is an absence of coordination between those bodies responsible for crime reduction and other institutions that may provide mechanisms for primary prevention. Establishing such linkages can be used to provide opportunities for preventative measures without substantially increasing the financial burden on the Ministry of National Security and other law enforcement agencies. As an example, while education may increase levels of civility in the population and, by extension, reduce crime and violence, it does so only as a by-product, since there is no purposive strategy whereby the education system is used as a mechanism to reduce crime and violence. Criminological and other relevant knowledge can be used to devise purposeful strategies which are implemented in the education system such that youths develop attitudes, values, and skills, which make them less predisposed to using violence and engaging in criminal activity. The same applies to other systems which are capable of reaching families and communities. Utilizing such institutions will enhance the effectiveness of the Ministry of National Security and other similar agencies, and allow them to capitalize on the strengths, reach, and resources of these institutions in the fight against gangs and violence.

Secondary prevention strategies should focus on communities with a high gang presence and with high rates of criminal offending. The spatial distribution of crime in Trinidad and Tobago indicates a high degree of stability and available data quickly point to those communities which are high crime areas. Table 4.8, for example, shows the distribution of serious crimes across police divisions for 2014. The data which are utilized to compile divisional statistics contain the addresses where each offence was committed. Such datasets can be used to determine which police station districts, and which communities in each district are responsible for a disproportionate number of violent offences. An examination of the addresses for all murders for the period January 1, 2009–October 31, 2011, for example, indicates that the police station districts with the highest number of murders were Besson Street (243 murders or 19 per cent of the national total for that period),[14] Arima (99 murders), West End (78) and Morvant (68). The communities with the highest number of murders were Laventille (172 murders or 13.4 per cent of the national total for that period), Diego Martin (66), and Morvant (53). Statistics from the range of serious crimes can also be employed to identify those communities which should be targeted for sustained intervention. This should be used in conjunction with data on the prevalence of gangs in various communities.

There is, unfortunately, no systematic attempt to determine the number and location of gangs and their members in Trinidad and Tobago. The only official data which exist are shown in table 4.3 of this chapter. The most recent data that can be used to ascertain the location of gangs were derived from a nationally representative sample of people who were interviewed by the UNDP in November 2010. Of the people who responded 'yes' to the question 'is there a criminal gang (or gangs) in your neighbourhood?' (n = 222 or 13.9 per cent of the sample), the majority of them were located in the communities of Port of Spain, Bonaire, San Fernando, and Arima.

Interventions in these communities should be based on their needs and should target those risk factors which are the most relevant in each community. There is only one study which examined the risk factors associated with gang membership in Trinidad and Tobago. Katz and Fox (2010) attempted to determine which risk and protective factors were predictors of gang membership. Their sample consisted of 2,206 students with a mean age of 15 years. The sample was drawn from 22 high-risk schools in Trinidad and Tobago.[15] Almost 60 per cent of the sample were females, while 41 per cent were of African descent, 23 per cent of East Indian descent, and 15 per cent were mixed (one parent of African and the other of East Indian descent). The majority of respondents (79.4 per cent) reported never having been in a gang, while 6.2 per cent were current gang members, 6.8 per cent were former gang members, and 7.7 per cent were gang associates. Katz and Fox assessed the relationship between 30 risk factors and 13 protective factors and gang membership. These factors belonged to the peer-individual, family, school, and community domains. Risk factors which were important at the peer-individual domain were having antisocial peers, having peers who use illegal drugs and alcohol, early initiation into antisocial behaviour, and the intention to use drugs. In the community domain, residential mobility and the availability of guns were important predictors. In the school domain, low commitment to school was an important predictor, while in the family domain, parental attitudes favourable to antisocial behaviour were important. A number of protective factors were also found to be important predictors of gang membership. At the peer-individual level, gang members were less likely to report high levels of social skills or prosocial values and attitudes. Katz and Fox also found that exposure to a greater number of risk factors increased the likelihood of gang membership while exposure to a larger number of protective factors reduced the likelihood of gang membership.

Data collected by the UNDP (n = 1,595 adults in Trinidad and Tobago) also allow for an assessment of risk factors. These data indicated that important risk factors included income, community cohesion, societal cohesion and informal social control. Dependent variables were the presence of gangs, gang problems in the neighbourhood, and the level of gang violence. These were assessed by asking the following questions: 'Is there a criminal gang (or gangs) in your neighbourhood?'; 'To what extent is there a criminal gang problem in your neighbourhood?', and 'To what extent has your neighbourhood experienced gang violence?' It was found that lower income was related to a higher likelihood of gang presence in neighbourhoods. Income was, however, not related to gang problems and gang violence. Community cohesion as well as societal cohesion suppressed gang problems and gang violence in neighbourhoods. More specifically, high levels of each type of cohesion were related to lower levels of gang problems and gang violence. Notably, each type of cohesion exhibited independent influence on gang problems and violence. Informal social control was also found to exhibit a suppressive effect on gang violence. This may indicate that informal systems of control are effective in reducing gang violence, but could also indicate that higher levels of gang violence may exert a suppressive effect on informal systems of behaviour regulation.

Secondary prevention strategies should focus on eliminating the social conditions which encourage the formation of gangs and which encourage youths to feel that they have no alternative but to join gangs. In the case of Trinidad and Tobago, being born into some communities automatically reduces one's life chances since this immediately comes with stigmatization and labelling by the wider society. Social development initiatives should seek to encourage the integration of such communities into the wider society so that stereotypes may be broken. This may be done, for example, by highlighting the successes of such communities, by showcasing the talents in such communities, or by facilitating the participation of residents from such communities in wider social events. Ultimately, young males who feel alienated from mainstream society and the legitimate opportunities which it provides will turn to their communities and the illegitimate opportunities which are provided by gangs or other similar entities. The Citizen Security Programme in the Ministry of National Security targets high-risk communities and engages in secondary prevention interventions. With effect from June 2015, the Citizen Security Programme will implement the Chicago Cease Fire model in East Port of Spain. This is an example of an important secondary prevention initiative.

Data from the UNDP survey of 1,595 residents in Trinidad and Tobago indicate that, of the people who reported that there were criminal gangs in their neighbourhood, 3.2 per cent indicated that the gangs made their neighbourhood safer. This supports findings by McCree (1998) and Katz (2009) who discovered that there were community members in Laventille and Gonzales who were in support of gangs and their leaders. In the case of Laventille, some community members asserted that gangs offered physical protection and financial support. These respondents also felt that their community was alienated and isolated from the rest of Trinidadian society. In the case of Gonzales, some residents believed that gangs provided a necessary law enforcement function where the protective services had failed so to do. In such communities, it may be difficult to encourage residents to relinquish their association with and support for gangs in their area.

This is an extremely difficult situation since it makes the eradication of gangs much more complicated. Nonetheless, only a minority of people are in support of gangs in their neighbourhood. It is also entirely possible that community members may express support for gangs because of fear of reprisals. This assertion is plausible in Trinidad and Tobago. The Gonzales IMPACT Fact Sheet 2006, for example, stated that 71 per cent of residents strongly agreed that people who report crimes committed by gangs to the police were likely to experience retaliation by gang members (Johnson 2007). Secondary prevention strategies should, therefore, attempt to weaken the linkages between gangs and community members. Such linkages, as in the case of Jamaica, may represent one of the biggest obstacles to the eradication of gangs if they are not addressed in the early stages of their development.

Many of the risk factors, indicated in the previous discussion on secondary prevention, are distal causes – often referred to as root causes of violence and gang membership. Addressing these root causes is important as they are related to long-term reductions in gang membership and violence. It is, however, also important to address proximate causes in the fight against gangs. 'Proximate causes are explanatory factors that are much closer in time and space to a violent event' (Maguire 2012, 8). Addressing proximate causes can generate quick reductions in gang violence and requires less time and expenditure compared to other approaches. Important proximate causes in Trinidad and Tobago include perceived disrespect, territory, disputes over money, retaliation, internal power struggles, and functioning as an informant to the police (Maguire 2012). In this context, it is also useful to examine the reasons that people give for joining gangs. In Trinidad and Tobago, Katz, Choate and Fox (2010) found in interviewing 2,292 youths, that 29.4 per cent joined gangs for reasons of protection and safety, 42 per cent joined for friendship, 8 per cent joined to make money, 5.9 per cent joined because either their parent or a sibling was in the gang, and 14.7 per cent joined for other reasons. Further research is required to determine which proximate causes are important in areas with high concentrations of gangs. Intervention strategies can then be designed to address these factors.

While preventative approaches may inhibit the formation of new gangs, this may not hinder the continuance of already established gangs. Suppressive approaches may be more relevant in this context. Suppressive strategies are reactive in nature and rely on criminal law and the weight of legal sanctions to be effective. Suppressive mechanisms can include arrests, prosecution, fines, imprisonment, seizure of property and other such strategies. Suppressive strategies may serve to incapacitate gang members, deter gang members who have been convicted (specific deterrence), and deter people who may become involved in gangs (general deterrence). Suppressive strategies will not be successful without the simultaneous use of preventative strategies. For example, if imprisoned gang members are subsequently released and go back into a community where there are no economic and other legitimate opportunities, and where the social and environmental conditions encourage gang membership, then it is unlikely that such persons will desist from future offending.

Suppressive strategies should increase police presence in communities with gangs. Policing should be visible in such communities with frequent patrols and with mobile units allocated to such communities. Where necessary, police should be equipped with suitable protective gear such as bulletproof vests and additional arms and ammunition, police vehicles, communication equipment, and other necessary equipment. At the same time, officers should be mandated to facilitate communication and dialogue with community members. Communication may provide deeper insight into the gang problem and may point to meaningful solutions. Prosecution of crimes committed by gang members should employ appropriate forensic and other technologies, including the use of the services and information provided by the Regional Integrated Ballistics Information Network (RIBIN). The use of intelligence, both locally and regionally (for example, the Strategic Services Agency and the Regional Intelligence Fusion Centre) may be profitably employed in the struggle against gang violence. This should be complemented by information sharing among police stations and divisions, and should attempt to incorporate a systematic data-collection strategy aimed at uncovering more information about the evolving gang situation. Suppressive strategies should also attempt to cut off the funding available to gangs. In Trinidad and Tobago, state funding is channelled to gangs through legitimate projects such as the Community-Based Environmental Protection and Enhancement Programme and the Unemployment Relief Programme (UNDP 2012). Such funding aids in the legitimization of gangs and contributes to the continuance of such gangs. Where gang members are successfully prosecuted, incapacitation should be coupled with rehabilitative strategies, and there should be a simultaneous emphasis on reducing the social, economic and other conditions which predispose gang formation and criminal offending.

One measure which may stem the increasing rate of gang violence relates to removing access to illegal weapons. While the government of Trinidad and Tobago ensures that very strict criteria are observed in the granting of licences for legal firearms, the majority of offences are committed with the use of illegal firearms (UNODC and World Bank 2007). A promising initiative in the fight against illegal firearms has been undertaken by the United Nations Regional Centre for Peace, Disarmament and Development in Latin America and the Caribbean (UN-LiREC). This initiative relates to the destruction of stockpiled weapons. More specifically, illegal firearms, which are seized as evidence or otherwise gathered, are typically stored for indefinite periods and often end up back in the hands of criminals. UN-LiREC officials estimate that internationally, as much as 40 per cent of all weapons in the hands of criminals are sourced from weapons which are legally stockpiled by law enforcement agencies. With respect to Trinidad and Tobago, UN-LiREC found that there was:

> No regular destruction of surplus, obsolete or confiscated firearms and ammunition... *the* latest destruction had been undertaken in 2003. *There also were* no destruction protocols or procedures *and* no written standard operating procedures. *While some weapons destruction occurs,*

there is limited weapons destruction capability (using disc cutters and industrial smelting) which is logistically inefficient for the number of surplus weapons potentially available for destruction. *UN-LiREC further found that there were* an estimated 5,000 surplus, obsolete and confiscated firearms *and* 10 tons of small arms ammunition in the Trinidad and Tobago Police Service which are in need of destruction (UN-LiREC Annex 2 – country profiles).[16]

UN-LiREC offered a number of recommendations for the security and destruction of arms and ammunition. This initiative also made assessments and recommendations in the areas of firearms and ammunition stockpile management, training, and legislation and policy. CARICOM IMPACS' implementation of the RIBIN represents yet another related initiative. This system allows users to identify weapons used in the commission of crimes from ballistic information and will facilitate tracing the movement of weapons throughout the Caribbean region. This, together with better gun registries, marking of seized firearms, and better detection procedures at ports of entry, as well as better coastal surveillance, will contribute to a reduction in the availability of illegal firearms.

While it is important to attempt to block the entry of illegal firearms, it is also critical that measures be put in place to stem the supply of such weapons. The UNODC and World Bank (2007) indicate that lax regulations govern the purchase of firearms in South and Central America, and as a consequence 'straw purchasers' are able to legally procure weapons from manufacturers. These weapons may then be resold to be used illegally. Gun registries and better tracking methods, including marking guns at the point of manufacture for identification and tracing purposes, as well as closer regulation of gun purchases and scrutiny of purchasers, including conducting background checks in the receiving country to ensure that the buyers are authorized to purchase and import weapons, will contribute to a reduction in the availability of firearms. A number of international treaties and conventions also represent important initiatives aimed at regulating the flow of firearms. These include the United Nations' Protocol on the Illicit Trafficking in Firearms and the Organization of American States' Inter-American Convention against the Illicit Manufacturing of and Trafficking in Firearms, Ammunition, Explosives and other Related Materials.

Current weaknesses in the criminal justice system of Trinidad and Tobago must also be addressed if suppressive strategies are to be effective. The most recent example, which highlights the inability of the criminal justice system to control gangs, was the state of emergency that was imposed from August 21 to December 5, 2011. During this time,

242 people were arrested under the Anti-Gang Act (2011) of Trinidad and Tobago. The Act, which defines a gang as 'a combination of two or more persons, whether formally or informally organized, that, through its membership or through an agent, engages in any gang related activity' makes it illegal to belong to a gang (2011, 3). All the individuals detained under this Act were subsequently released, either because there was insufficient evidence or no evidence at all. Quite apart from the circularity of the definition, law enforcement and intelligence capabilities are limited, such that the capacity to deal with crime generally, and gangs specifically, is severely curtailed. Where murder is concerned, for example, detection rates, measured by arrests, indicate severe weaknesses. Between 1990 and 2000, detection rates in Trinidad and Tobago ranged between 50 and 70 per cent, but exhibited a continuous decline after 2000. For the period 2000–2014, the average detection rate for murder stood at 24 per cent. For the same period, the average detection rate for woundings and shootings was 33.7 per cent, for robberies 14.9 per cent, and for burglaries and break-ins 13.3 per cent.

While specialist units in the Trinidad and Tobago Police Service may be used in the fight against gangs and violence, past experience has shown that there are problems here as well. In Trinidad and Tobago, the Gang/Repeat Offender Task Force was established in May 2006. This was initially staffed with 40 police officers who were trained by specialist officers from the US. The unit was responsible for arresting wanted persons, for gathering intelligence on gangs, conducting patrols in areas with gangs, and for disseminating information to various other units in the police service. This specialized unit was, however, disbanded as a result of allegations of police misconduct, which included accusations of kidnapping, passing information to criminals, and participating in extrajudicial killings. The Special Anti-Crime Unit of Trinidad and Tobago (SAUTT) was a similar specialist police unit which was disbanded on October 31, 2010. Specialist training and personnel, as well as the use of intelligence, are important in the fight against gangs and violence. The provision of such services should be governed by carefully formulated regulations, and officers in specialist units must be aware of the regulations which govern their functioning. There must also be clear guidelines and procedures for discipline in the event of the breach of these regulations.

Katz (2012) indicated that part of the inefficiency in Trinidad and Tobago is related to the lack of experience of homicide detectives. In interviewing 462 police officers, he discovered that the majority (224) had investigated only one homicide, while a large number (85) had investigated only two homicides, while 42 officers had investigated only three homicides in their careers. Very few officers had investigated four or more homicides. Katz also discovered that there was a large backlog of firearms cases to be processed at the Forensic Science Centre in Trinidad and Tobago. In 2005, the number of backlogged cases stood at slightly over 2,000. Each case involved one or more pieces of evidence (referred to as exhibits), which required analysis. Inefficiencies in processing are even more strongly highlighted when the number of unanalysed exhibits is considered. In 2004 alone, while almost 500 exhibits were processed, slightly more than 3,500 exhibits went unprocessed. King (2012) added to the list of inefficiencies in the Trinidad and Tobago criminal justice system by assessing police procedures and techniques. He found that 'basic policing and investigation tasks were poorly performed' while ancillary organizations such as the crime lab, prosecutors, the judiciary, and community groups complained about the police, and contributed to the inefficiency of investigations (7). William King advised that all components of the criminal justice system, including ancillary organizations, should be examined, since training and technology in policing and other restricted areas would not have the desired effect without considering and remedying inefficiencies in other areas.

The existence of gangs is an extremely challenging problem in Trinidad and Tobago. Available data indicate that gang violence is increasing and is associated with the increased usage of firearms. Gangs also appear to be integrated into some communities, creating additional challenges for their eradication. The gang issue is one which must not be ignored since this increases the risk that the problem may escalate to the point where gangs cannot be eradicated. This chapter argues that the use of suppressive strategies should be complemented by preventative strategies in the fight against gangs in Trinidad and Tobago. Preventative strategies should be focused at the individual, community and national levels, while suppressive strategies should target the availability of firearms and should ensure that legal action against gangs and their members utilizes appropriate technologies and evidence to ensure successful prosecution.

Notes

1. This project collected data from 368 gang members and 878 non-gang members in 2005. Data were collected by the Besson Street Police Station, situated in Port of Spain, Trinidad.
2. Data from Katz and Choate were obtained from a range of sources including a survey of gang experts (n =52) in all police districts in Trinidad and Tobago. This expert survey was patterned after the Eurogang Research Program

Expert Survey. Data employed by Katz and Choate were also obtained from the Trinidad Arrestee Project Survey (n = 421 recently booked adult arrestees), the Trinidad Detention Survey (n = 60 adult detainees) and the Trinidad and Tobago Youth Survey (n = 4000 secondary school students).

3. These data derive from n = 264 respondents for whom ages were known.
4. Trinidad and Tobago is divided into nine police divisions. There are approximately 78 police stations in these divisions.
5. Police station districts refer to the area of jurisdiction of each police station.
6. Data which indicate whether or not other major crimes are gang-related are not available from the TTPS.
7. Comparison of the ranking of gangs and crimes according to police division was used to determine which crimes were most closely associated with the location of gangs.
8   Crime figures indicate the percentage of crimes that occurred in each police division.
9. Crime figures indicate the percentage of crimes that occurred in each police division.
10. Crime figures indicate the percentage of crimes that occurred in each police division.
11. 'Other' weapons and 'unknown' weapons are omitted from this graph.
12. Katz and Choate (2006) report that in Trinidad and Tobago, youths who reported gang membership indicated that on average, they became involved with gangs when they were 12 years old.
13. National Gang Center (2010) G.R.E.A.T. Programme http://www. nationalgangcenter.gov/About/Related-Web-Sites.
14. As of March 2012, there were 77 police station districts in the nine police divisions in Trinidad and Tobago. A total of 1,281 murders occurred in Trinidad and Tobago during the period January 1, 2009–October 31, 2011.
15. In this study, 'high-risk schools' were defined as those identified by the Trinidad and Tobago Ministry of Education as having disproportionate numbers of students living in high-crime areas, or schools with a large number of incidents of delinquency.
16. United Nations Caribbean Regional Workshop on Firearms Destruction and Stockpile Management: Moving from Assessment to Action, Trinidad Hilton Conference Centre, December 8–9, 2010.

Risk Factors and Determinants of Crime and Insecurity in Trinidad and Tobago

This chapter will examine some of the main risk factors which have been identified by past criminological research and theorizing as important for understanding criminal offending and insecurity. This will be followed by an assessment of research in Trinidad and Tobago which has focused on risk factors, and will conclude with an examination of the findings of existing primary data.

Human insecurity in the Caribbean region has not declined despite the commitment of a vast amount of resources and the implementation of a range of policies to address crime and violence. It is a fundamental assumption of this chapter that crime policy must be data driven, and must be informed by a systematic understanding of the root causes of crime. Failure to do so will result in the continued implementation of populist policies; those which help ruling parties gain political mileage, but which may be based on public opinion rather than on empirical data. Too often governments tailor their crime reduction policies to fit popular notions of what works. These popular notions may be based on media headlines and 'pop psychology' which have very little, if any, grounding in criminological theory and research. All too often, short-term policies which promise quick fixes are preferred to long-term efforts to fight crime. This same tendency to prefer quick fixes and to bend to public will also serves to distort those crime-fighting efforts which are grounded in empirical research. Policy as it is formulated and policy as it is implemented, may be two very different things. Crime trends in the Caribbean region speak volumes about the failure of such approaches. Indeed, for the most part, in the case of Trinidad and Tobago, serious crimes have risen over the last 20 years, though there have been modest declines within recent times. Any government which is serious about addressing the crime situation has to be willing to move away from citing short-term fluctuations in crime as evidence that crime has decreased. Such governments need to be willing to acknowledge that past efforts have failed, and must be willing to make policy decisions which are not always consistent with popular sentiment.

This chapter contends that, in order to effectively fight crime and insecurity in the Caribbean, at least two conditions must be met. Firstly, a thorough examination of criminological literature must be conducted to identify the major causes of crime and insecurity and secondly, empirical data from the Caribbean must be examined to determine which of the main causal factors are applicable to the Caribbean region generally, and to Trinidad and Tobago specifically. Not all of the factors indicated by the international literature may be applicable to the Caribbean and indeed, it may be the case that different factors may be applicable to different countries within the Caribbean. Knowledge of these factors will indicate where emphasis must be placed in order to reduce human insecurity.

In examining the causes of crime and insecurity, researchers distinguish between the levels of aggregation at which the causal variables are operative. Some researchers argue that effective crime reduction policies must be focused at the aggregate level (for example, nation, state, city or community) while others argue that interventions must be focused at the level of the individual, or on smaller units such as the family. An example which illustrates the issue with the level of aggregation relates to poverty reduction as a means of reducing crime. While there is some debate about whether or not poverty causes crime, a number of researchers have found a relationship between poverty and crime rates. This relationship has been found at the aggregate level for cities (Bailey 1984; Flango and Sherbanou 1976), standard metropolitan statistical areas (Blau and Golden 1986; DeFonzo 1983; Fowles and Merva 1996), and countries (Gartner 1990; Sigelman and Simpson 1977). These studies suggest that poverty interventions should be aimed at the aggregate level, though the researchers disagree on which level of aggregation may be most appropriate. In contrast, other researchers have looked at variations among people in their level of poverty and level of self-reported criminal offending (Krahn and Harrison 1992; Stiles et al. 2000). These latter studies suggest that interventions should be directed at the individual level. As such, while it is typically agreed that poverty reduction should reduce crime and insecurity, researchers disagree on the most appropriate level at which interventions should be applied. The main idea being brought out here is that policymakers must be aware that some causal factors may operate at one level of analysis while other causal factors may operate at another level of analysis. To be effective, interventions must be aimed at the appropriate level of analysis which is relevant to each causal factor. Where there are disagreements on the most appropriate level of analysis, an examination of empirical data should provide the best indication of the level at which interventions may be most cost-effectively applied.

Economic Deprivation

A number of researchers have found that economic deprivation is causally linked to criminal offending. This is not to say that all economically deprived people will commit crime, nor does it imply that all types of crime are driven by economic deprivation. The literature on economic deprivation and crime has conceptualized economic deprivation as poverty, inequality, or relative deprivation. Poverty refers to the non-attainment of basic nutritional and other non-nutritional requirements which are considered essential to a healthy productive life. The poverty line is specific to particular locations, and is defined according to the cost required to meet these basic needs in that specific location. The nutritional threshold below which a person is likely to suffer ill health varies from place to place, depending on climate and other such factors. The World Bank defines this threshold for the Caribbean region as a daily intake of 2,400 calories per adult. People who do not earn enough income to meet their basic nutritional requirements are termed indigent.

Inequality, typically assessed at the aggregate level of analysis (for example, inequality between countries, states, cities, neighbourhoods, etc.), is often measured by the Gini coefficient which computes the disparity in average incomes among a distribution of incomes among the relevant units of analysis. High levels of inequality indicate that there are large disparities between the incomes of the rich and the poor. Relative deprivation refers to the perception of inequality. Perceptual measures are restricted to the individual level of analysis, though some authors argue that perceptions can be inferred from structural indicators (see, for example, Davies 1962; Gurr 1970; Rosenfeld 1986). Relative deprivation researchers argue that the perception of inequality may be very much at odds with measures of inequality based on objective data such as income since, typically, people are unaware of such objective data for others and are thus not in a position to make accurate comparisons. These researchers contend that people's perceptions of economic deprivation impact upon their behaviour and that such measures form an important complement to measures based on objective data.

Researchers have typically argued in favour of either poverty, inequality or relative deprivation as important causes of crime. In defending the utility of the preferred measure, researchers typically try to explain why the chosen measure is causally linked to crime and why the other measures are not causally linked. This controversy is fuelled in part by the fact that each measure has received some level of empirical support. For example, Beverly Stiles et al. (2000) and William Bailey (1984) found that poverty was a significant predictor of property crime and homicide respectively, while James Davies (1969) and Richard Rosenfeld (1986) found that relative deprivation was a significant predictor of political violence and violent crime respectively. Leslie Kennedy et al. (1991) and Leo Carroll and Pamela Jackson (1983), in contrast, found that inequality was a significant predictor of homicide and property crimes respectively.

Recent research has argued, however, that the compartmentalization of economic deprivation into 'pure' subscales such as poverty or inequality may be misguided. This research argues that economic deprivation is a complex experience that cannot be captured by a single measure, and instead must be assessed using multiple simultaneous measures. The approach typically taken is that a range of potential indicators of economic deprivation are analysed to determine which subscales tap the latent construct of economic deprivation. Factor scores, as well as weighted sums of applicable subscales, are typically used to represent this more complex conceptualization of economic deprivation. These multifaceted measures of economic deprivation have been found to be strong predictors of both property and violent crime (Land, McCall and Cohen 1990).

Economic deprivation may lead to crime and insecurity for a number of reasons. One of the most frequently cited explanations relates to the frustration-aggression hypothesis (Dollard et al. 1939). This hypothesis states that the occurrence of aggressive behaviour always presupposes the existence of frustration and that the existence of frustration always leads to some form of aggression. Frustration refers to interference with goal-directed behaviour and in the case of economic deprivation it refers to one not having adequate economic means to achieve one's goals. Other researchers have argued that economic deprivation creates an 'unbalanced' or 'uncomfortable' mental state, not unlike Leon Festinger's (1957) cognitive dissonance or Jean Piaget's (1953) disequilibrium. Denton Morrison (1973) writes that 'dissonance is a psychologically upsetting state that generates attempts to reduce this dissonance' (159). One means of dissonance reduction involves engaging in criminal or violent activities which will allow one to gain that which is lacking.

Economic deprivation may also serve as a 'technique of neutralization' (Sykes and Matza 1957), reducing inhibitions against proscribed behaviours and facilitating the victimization of others (Agnew 1999; Agnew et al. 1996). Economic deprivation may also reduce social trust and the commitment to the conventional social order if others are perceived to be the cause of one's deprivation (Kawachi et al. 1997, 1999). Ichiro Kawachi et al. (1997) argue that 'belief in the goodwill and benign intent of others facilitates collective action and mutual cooperation...Collective action, in turn, further reinforces community norms of reciprocity' (1,492). 'Visibly high inequalities in material assets tend to produce resentment that in turn disrupts the social fabric' (Kawachi et al. 1999, 721). This disruption of the social fabric interferes with informal systems of social control which normally operate at the community level, and which suppress criminal activity.

Social Disorganization

The classic work of Clifford Shaw and Henry McKay (1942) represents one of the first examples of criminological theorizing which sought to locate the explanation for criminal offending at a social level, rather than within the individual. Shaw and McKay, in studying Chicago's juvenile court records realized that crime rates were stable in different parts of the city, regardless of who entered or left these areas. This suggested that ecological factors, rather than the characteristics of the people themselves, influenced the crime rates in various parts of the city. The important task for Shaw and McKay was to discover which ecological characteristics influenced criminal activity.

Shaw and McKay (1942) recognized that a number of characteristics were consistently associated with high crime rates. Areas with these characteristics were described as 'socially disorganized' and were characterized by racial heterogeneity, high rates of residential mobility, and low average socio-economic status. In such neighbourhoods, the conventional institutions of social control, such as community organizations, schools and churches, were unable to regulate the behaviour of youths within their communities. In addition to the lack of informal social controls, socially disorganized neighbourhoods tended to produce 'criminal traditions' or accept counter-normative patterns of behaviour which could be passed on to successive generations through the process of socialization.

The three factors identified by Shaw and McKay work against social cohesion and the mechanisms of informal social control. High levels of residential mobility in various neighbourhoods could occur for a number of reasons. If people feel unsafe in particular places or if they do not feel a sense of belonging to, and pride for, their neighbourhood, they may be inclined to relocate as soon as it becomes feasible. In addition, many residents may choose to leave poorer neighbourhoods once they are economically able to do so. The high rate of population turnover works against the development of bonds which tie people to each other, and which help to build a sense of trust and commitment to others in the neighbourhood. Racial heterogeneity, especially where there is distrust among people of different races, also hinders the development of community cohesion. Where there is a lack of social trust and a breakdown of community cohesion, people become unwilling to intervene in each other's affairs. As functionalist theorizing suggests, informal mechanisms of behaviour regulation are far more important in ensuring normative behaviour than the responses of the legal system. More often than not, it is the case that the majority of people in a given population choose to be law-abiding, not because they fear repercussions from law enforcement agencies, but because they are committed to adhering to the norms of society. Socialization, as well as informal means of social control, ensures such behaviour regulation. Social disorganization, by affecting socialization and social solidarity, weakens informal controls, which in turn leads to increased rates of criminal offending.

Strain Theory

While social disorganization theory assumes, among other things, that the rejection of conventional middle-class values may increase rates of criminal offending, Robert Merton (1968) believed that adherence to certain middle-class values could serve to increase criminal offending. Writing about the American obsession with economic success, Merton argued that at all levels in the social strata, Americans believed that they could achieve the 'American dream' and that they could become rich and successful. This belief, according to Merton, created a powerful motivational force to achieve economic success. Despite the widespread belief in the possibility of upward social mobility, however, the American social structure limits individuals' access to the means to achieve such mobility. That is, everyone does not share equally in terms of the means to achieve success via legitimate channels. While there is normative emphasis on the ends, the same level of consensus about the means to achieve these ends does not exist. Where opportunities are blocked, people may use illegitimate or illegal means to achieve socially prescribed success goals. Messner and Rosenfeld, in their 1997 publication, *Crime and the American Dream*, refine and extend the work of Merton. While Merton argues that the American stratification system restricts access to legitimate opportunities for upward social mobility, Steven Messner and Richard Rosenfeld, in contrast, recognize that 'the American dream promotes and sustains an institutional structure in which one institution – the economy – assumes dominance over all others' (1997, xi). That is, the pursuit and commitment to achieving economic wealth creates 'institutional imbalance' where other institution such as the family and education have limited ability to reduce crime rates by insulating members of the society from the criminogenic pressures of the American dream.

Merton's theorizing may be applicable to the Caribbean to the extent that regional societies share similar cultural values and strive to achieve similar success goals, and to the extent that access to achieve material success may not be equitably distributed. One of the problems in assessing the applicability of the work of Merton (1968) and that of Messner and Rosenfeld (1997) is that aggregate level measures which represent cultural values or institutional structure are lacking in the Caribbean context. A number of aggregate-level studies using American data, however, are supportive of strain theory (e.g., Chamlin and Cochran 1995; Messner and Rosenfeld 1997; Piquero and Leaper Piquero 1998).

Robert Agnew (1985, 1992), in contrast to Merton (1968), examines the impact of strain at the individual as opposed to the structural level of analysis. Agnew's (1985, 1992) general strain theory posits that strain leads to negative emotions which may lead to a number of outcomes, including crime and delinquency. The specific strains discussed in the theory include the failure to achieve positively valued goals (e.g., money or status), the removal of positively valued stimuli (e.g., loss of valued possessions), and the presentation of negatively valued stimuli (e.g., physical abuse). While many specific types of strain may fall into these categories, Agnew specifies the conditions under which strain is likely to lead to crime. Strains which are 1) seen as unjust, 2) high in magnitude, 3) associated with low social control, and 4) create some incentive to engage in criminal coping are most likely to lead to violence and delinquency.

According to general strain theory, individuals experiencing strain may develop negative emotions, including anger when they see adversity as imposed by others, resentment when they perceive unjust treatment by others, and depression or anxiety when they blame themselves for the stressful consequence. These negative emotions in turn necessitate coping responses as a way to relieve internal pressure. Responses to strain may be behavioural, cognitive or emotional, and not all responses are delinquent. General strain theory, however, is particularly interested in delinquent adaptations. General strain theory identifies various types of delinquent adaptations, including escapist (e.g., drug use), instrumental (e.g., property offences), and retaliatory outcomes (e.g., violent offences). Delinquent adaptations to strain become more likely when strain leads to anger. This is the case because anger 'increases the individual's level of felt injury, creates a desire for retaliation/revenge, energizes the individual for action, and lowers inhibitions' (Agnew 1992, 60). Coping via illegal behaviour and violence may be especially true for adolescents because of their limited legitimate coping resources, greater influence from peers, and inability to escape many stressful and frustrating environments.

General strain theory has attempted to specify the factors which increase the likelihood that individuals will cope with strain by committing crime. Agnew contends that crime becomes a likely outcome when individuals have a low tolerance for strain, when they have poor coping skills and resources, have few conventional social supports, when they perceive that the costs of committing crime is low, and when they are disposed to committing crime because of factors such as low self-control, negative emotionality, or their learning history.

Routine Activities Theory

Routine activities theory, developed by Lawrence Cohen and Marcus Felson (1979), instead of attempting to explain why offenders may be motivated to commit crime assumes that there will always be a pool of motivated offenders and attempts to explain how the basic elements of time, location, and people may either increase or decrease the likelihood of criminal victimization. The routine activities approach recognizes the interdependence between people and the environment in which they operate. Cohen and Felson argue that once there is the convergence of three factors, victimization will occur. These factors are 1) motivated offenders, 2) the existence of suitable targets, which include people or property, and 3) the absence of capable guardianship. Routine activities theory thus indicates how people's actions and the environments they occupy may be crime producing. A number of tests of routine activities theory have found that the variables it suggests are significant predictors of crime. Examples of research which provide empirical support include work done by Matthew Robinson and Christine Robinson (1997) who use burglary as their dependent measure, and Leslie Kennedy and Robert Silverman (1990) and Steven Messner and Kenneth Tardiff (1985), who use homicide as their dependent measure.

While the routine activities approach highlights the importance of the environment in criminal offending, one of its shortcomings is that it does not attempt to explain offender motivation. This is an important component, especially where crime reduction is the objective. Indeed, Kevin Bryant and J. Mitchell Miller (1997) sought to compensate for this weakness and found, using 1990 data, that adding a measure to represent motivated offenders improved the predictive ability of routine activities variables.

The Social Support/Altruism Approach

Social support approaches in criminology have attempted to explain how social support and altruistic actions insulate people from engaging in crime. This approach draws from a range of studies and concepts, including John Braithwaite's (1989) theory of reintegrative shaming, Francis Cullen's (1994) development of social support as an important construct for criminology, Mitchell Chamlin and John Cochran's (1997) social altruism theory, and Steven Messner and Richard Rosenfeld's (1994, 1997) institutional anomic theory. While there are important differences among these approaches, a central proposition which runs through each approach is that social aggregates vary in their degree of cohesiveness, support and shared values, as well as their willingness to assist others, and importantly, this variation is assumed to be predictive of crime rates.

Nan Lin (1986, 18) defines social support as 'the perceived or actual instrumental and/or expressive provisions supplied by community social networks and confiding partners.' Cullen (1994) argues that 'whether social support is delivered through governmental social programs, communities, social networks, families, interpersonal relations, or agents of the criminal justice system, it reduces criminal involvement' (527). The closely related construct of social altruism is also inversely related to crime and refers to 'the willingness of communities to commit scarce resources to the aid and comfort of their members' (Chamlin and Cochran 1997, 204).

In an empirical test of the social support/altruism approach, Chamlin and Cochran (1997) collected data from a sample of 279 US cities. They operationalized social altruism as the amount of United Way contributions in each city. Controls in their analyses included poverty, inequality, population size and age structure, racial heterogeneity, residential mobility, and family disruption. Net of the effect of controls, Chamlin and Cochran found that their measure of social altruism was inversely related to both property and personal crimes. While their findings tend to imply that communities in which people are more supportive tend to have lower crime rates, it is also possible to reverse the causal order in explaining the relationship between both variables. That is, in communities with lower crime rates, people tend to be more supportive. In all likelihood, there is a reciprocal relationship between both variables where social support affects crime, but where crime also affects social support. An important intervening variable in the latter causal sequence may be social trust. Where crime rates are high, people may become more distrustful of their neighbours and, because of fear or the belief that their neighbours do not deserve altruistic behaviour, people may reduce the amount of social support they offer. Here, while social support may insulate people against crime, crime may work against social support.

Subcultural Theories

Unlike social support/altruism approaches which assume that structural factors can insulate individuals from committing crime, subcultural theories attempt to outline the social and cultural conditions which can increase the predisposition to commit crime. The main idea behind this approach is that certain cultural conventions can be criminogenic. One of the earliest attempts to use this approach was based on the observation that on average, places in the southern United States had higher crime rates than in the north (Huff-Corzine, Corzine, and Moore 1986). Researchers have argued that cultural norms in the South may predispose individuals to engage in acts of violence, and such norms may also serve to foster approval of such actions when committed by others in the community. Researchers, however, disagree on which norms specifically are responsible for increased rates of violence in the South. A range of factors have been proposed, including a tradition of chivalry (Hackney 1969), increased defensiveness (Erlanger 1975), willingness to resort to violence if someone's good name is sullied (Brearley 1932) and family and community socialization (Gastil 1971).

More recent researchers have argued that urbanization creates conditions which encourage subcultural adaptations which foster a criminogenic lifestyle. According to Claude Fischer (1975), large urban populations produce deviant subcultures through a three-step process. Firstly, larger urban populations imply that there is a greater likelihood that people with unconventional interests and lifestyles will come into contact with conventional others. Secondly, urban contexts provide environments where unconventional people can make linkages with each other and establish subcultures within the larger culture. Finally, limited space and resources result in competition between various subcultural groupings and the dominant culture, resulting in an 'intensification' of subcultural values. Here, members of subcultural groups adhere more closely to their values and belief systems as a means of increasing group cohesion to improve their chances of survival. The result, according to Fischer, is an increase in unconventional behaviour, including crime and deviance. Through the process of socialization, these values which are supportive of unconventional behaviour may be diffused across generations.

In the Caribbean setting, the social and spatial isolation of various groups, especially where these groups perceive themselves to be marginalized, may lead to the development of subcultures which oppose the dominant normative culture and its values. In areas such as Laventille and Beetham in Trinidad, or Don controlled areas of Kingston, Jamaica, opposition to mainstream culture and values may develop since residents perceive that the state does not support them or look after their welfare. Further, people from such areas may feel ostracized by mainstream society. These factors encourage two outcomes. Firstly, people may feel that the state has no jurisdiction over them since there is the perception that the state does not care about them and does nothing to help them. This erodes the legitimacy of the criminal justice system and reduces or eliminates its ability to regulate behaviour in such locations. Secondly, lack of a sense of belonging to mainstream society results in opposition to a law-abiding lifestyle. This is not to say that such people are inherently criminogenic, but rather, in recognizing their social isolation and in affirming their selfhood in response to such isolation, they necessarily perceive themselves as being in opposition to mainstream society, and therefore must reject its culture and value system. Ironically, this sets up a self-fulfilling prophecy where members of mainstream society take the behaviour of such people as a justification for their social exclusion. Such persons must live and function within their own communities, and reinforce their own counter-normative culture and lifestyle if they are to be respected in their environments.

Empirical Research on Root Causes of Crime in Trinidad and Tobago

While the theoretical literature has proposed a number of potentially useful variables which should be considered in attempting to understand the causes of crime and insecurity, for the most part such research has been validated in North America. Policymakers must be guided by the findings of local research when designing interventions. While empirical research in North America or elsewhere may validate various theoretical approaches and explanatory variables, it cannot be assumed that those findings may generalize to the Caribbean, generally, and to Trinidad and Tobago specifically. The historical and sociocultural context of Trinidad and Tobago is different from that of other countries and, as such, empirical research conducted locally provides the most solid grounding in terms of the directions which policymakers should take. The remainder of this chapter will examine such research and includes an analysis of primary data collected from a sample of 1,595 adults in Trinidad and Tobago.

Charles Katz and Andrew Fox (2010) offer one of the most recent assessments of the prevalence of gangs in Trinidad and Tobago and, importantly, assess the relationship between a number of risk and protective factors and gang involvement. Katz and Fox attempt to determine which risk factors are important predictors of gang membership and also examine the cumulative effect of multiple risk and protective factors as they relate to gang membership. Katz and Fox (2010) examine data from the Trinidad and Tobago youth survey. This survey, funded by the Trinidad and Tobago Ministry of National Security, was conducted to provide insight into the nation's crime problem. The target population was third and fifth-form students in high-risk urban public schools. High-risk schools were those with high proportions of students living in high crime areas, or schools in which there was a high incidence of delinquency. The final sample consisted of 22 schools which represented 24 per cent of all public schools in Trinidad and Tobago and 33 per cent of all public schools located in urban areas. Usable data were collected from a total of 2,206 students in 2006. Respondents were 11 to 19 years of age with a mean age of 15 years. Almost 60 per cent of the sample were females, while 41 per cent were of African descent, 23 per cent of East Indian descent, and 15 per cent were mixed. People of other ethnicities made up the rest of the sample. A comparison with Trinidad and Tobago's population statistics (Central Statistical Office 2000 census) indicated that East Indians were underrepresented in this sample. This may have occurred since many of them may attend rural schools, schools in low-risk areas, or private schools.

Katz and Fox (2010) distinguish between current gang members, former gang members, gang associates (having two or more friends in a gang), and people who have never been in a gang and do not know people from a gang. Items measuring these typologies include 'Have you ever belonged to a gang?' and 'Think of your four best friends. In the past year, how many of your best friends have been a member of a gang?' The majority of respondents (79.4 per cent) reported never having been in a gang, while 6.2 per cent were current gang members, 6.8 per cent were former gang members, and 7.7 per cent were gang associates. Males were more likely than females to be current gang members (8.9 per cent vs. 4.4 per cent), former gang members (10.1 per cent vs. 4.5 per cent) and gang associates (10.4 per cent vs. 5.8 per cent). With respect to ethnicity, 7.6 per cent of youths classified as 'other', 6.4 per cent of the youths of African descent, 5.8 per cent of the youths of East Indian descent, and 4.5 per cent of youths of mixed descent reported that they were current gang members. Almost ten per cent of the youths of mixed descent reported being former gang members, while 6.8 per cent of 'other' descent, 5.6 per cent of African descent, and 6.4 per cent of East Indian descent reported former gang membership. Nine per cent of youths classified as 'other' reported being gang associates, while eight per cent of African descent, 7.4 per cent of mixed descent, and 5.8 per cent of East Indian descent similarly reported having two or more friends who were gang members.

It is important to ascertain whether or not Katz and Fox's (2010) estimates of youth involvement with gangs represent a true reflection of the situation as it exists in Trinidad and Tobago. While a number of factors appear to indicate that the findings may overestimate the prevalence of youth involvement with gangs, other factors which may reduce the estimates compensate for this possibility. Katz and Fox restrict their focus to students from high-crime at-risk areas and do not examine data from rural areas, low-crime areas, and from private schools. In addition, while Katz and Fox ask questions about the organizational structure of gangs (gang name, territory/turf, having a gang leader, having meetings, rules, consequences/punishment for breaking gang rules, colours/signs/ symbols/clothing, drug sale/use, and engaging in other illegal activities) they do not use this data to distinguish between criminal gangs and non- criminal gangs. Failure to restrict the focus to criminal gangs and to include rural low-risk areas may serve to inflate the estimates of youth involvement with gangs. A number of other factors, however, counteract this tendency. The data utilized by Katz and Fox were collected during school time. Prior research has shown that gang members tend to have high absenteeism rates (Hardwick 1995). If this applies to Trinidad and Tobago, many youths may have been excluded from the study. This study also excludes youths who may have been in detention or who were suspended from school due to disruptive behaviour. In addition, since the study was based on self-report data, responding in a socially desirable/acceptable way was possible. If this occurred, some respondents would have failed to disclose their membership in, and association with, gangs. To the extent that the countervailing factors identified above counterbalance each other, the estimates of youth involvement in gangs in Trinidad and Tobago may represent a true picture of the present situation. While it is difficult to speculate on the relative impact of each factor on the estimates provided by Katz and Fox, the large sample gathered supports the argument that the estimates provided may be reliable.

In addition to assessing gang membership, 30 risk factors and 13 protective factors were measured; these factors belonged to four domains: the community, school, family, and peers-individuals. With respect to risk factors at the community level, measures included low neighbourhood attachment, community disorganization, social mobility and perceived availability of handguns. School-level risk factors included academic failure and low commitment to schools. Family risk factors included a family history of antisocial behaviour, family conflict, poor family management, permissive attitudes towards the use of alcohol and drugs, and parental attitudes favourable toward antisocial behaviour. At the peer-individual level, risk factors included rebelliousness, early initiation into antisocial behaviour, early initiation of drug and alcohol use, attitudes favourable toward antisocial behaviour, having antisocial peers, and sensation seeking. Community, school and family-level protective factors included opportunities for prosocial involvement and rewards for prosocial involvement relevant to each context. Peer-individual level protective factors included religiosity, social skills, prosocial attitudes/values, prosocial involvement, and interaction with prosocial peers.

Katz and Fox (2010) employ multinomial logistic regression to examine the relationship between the risk and protective factors and the specified outcome variables. Prior to analysis, collinearity diagnostics were employed, which indicated that there were no multicollinearity problems with the predictors. Risk factors in the peer-individual domain were more important as predictors of gang involvement than predictors from the other domains. Despite this, there were a number of significant predictors in the school, family, and community domains. With respect to the peer-individual domain, it was found that people who were associated with gang members were more likely to report having antisocial peers and having peers who used illegal drugs and alcohol. Early initiation of antisocial behaviour as well as the intention to use drugs predicted former gang membership. Current gang members reported having more antisocial peers, peers who used illegal drugs, early initiation into antisocial behaviour, and the intention to use drugs. In the community domain, the availability of handguns and residential mobility were important predictors of gang membership. Former gang members were more likely to report higher levels of residential mobility, while the availability of handguns predicted former as well as current gang membership. In the school domain, it was found that former gang members reported lower commitment to school. In the family domain it was found that parental attitudes favourable toward antisocial behaviour predicted association with gang members.

Katz and Fox (2010) discovered that a number of protective factors were related to gang membership. In the individual domain it was found that current gang members were less likely to report high levels of social skills or prosocial values and attitudes. Former gang members reported less interaction with prosocial peers as well as having fewer social skills. Contrary to expectations, however, opportunities and rewards for prosocial involvement predicted gang membership. More specifically, it was found that reporting rewards for prosocial involvement increased one's odds of being a former gang member or a gang associate. In the school domain, current gang members were more likely to report opportunities for prosocial involvement, while former gang members reported more opportunities for prosocial involvement in the family domain. Katz and Fox speculate that rewards for prosocial involvement, as well as actual prosocial involvement, may serve to increase gang involvement since such involvement may bring current gang members into contact with at-risk youths, as well as youths who are not currently in gangs. Socialization effects and peer influence processes may serve to encourage youths in the latter two categories into pro-criminal lifestyles. Alternatively, it may be the case that opportunities for prosocial interaction may be created in communities which are perceived to be at risk. If both processes are operative, this ironically may indicate that social programmes which aim to provide prosocial opportunities for at-risk youths may inadvertently create opportunities for socialization into pro-criminal values and attitudes. This suggests that, in designing intervention strategies, care should be taken to minimize the opportunities whereby at-risk youths are socialized into a culture of deviance by gang-involved youths. One possibility here may be to focus on those interventions which target factors in the community, school, family, and which focus on the individual, but which do not facilitate interaction between at-risk youths and gang members. That said, further research is needed in Trinidad and Tobago to fully clarify the relationship between gang involvement and opportunities for prosocial involvement.

Katz and Fox (2010) conducted analyses to assess the cumulative effect of multiple risk and protective factors. Respondents who were exposed to a greater number of risk factors were more likely to be gang involved than those exposed to fewer risk factors. As expected, respondents who were exposed to a greater number of protective factors were less likely to be gang involved than those who were exposed to fewer protective factors. It was found, for example, that 'current gang members were disproportionately in the highest cumulative risk category, next were former gang members, followed by gang associates, and those never in a gang' (Katz and Fox 2010, 194). Importantly, Katz and Fox also found that a number of youths who were exposed to multiple risk factors, but simultaneously exposed to multiple protective factors, were not likely to be gang involved. This suggests that protective factors may counteract the effect of risk factors and may be used as interventions for at-risk youth. Unfortunately, however, many youths who are in at-risk communities, schools and families, are not simultaneously exposed to protective factors. The identification of at-risk youths should be followed by intervention programmes aimed at developing a protective environment to buffer the effect of risk factors. Simultaneously, important risk factors must be addressed. This approach suggests that intervention strategies should be two tiered, and focus on both risk and protective factors in multiple environments such as the community, school and family. The findings of Katz and Fox (2010) indicate the critical importance of personal factors and peer influence, vis-à-vis predictors at other levels of analysis such as the community, school, and family. This implies that interventions which target the individual-peer level of analysis may have stronger impacts on the reduction of delinquency and gang involvement than interventions which target other levels of analysis. It is nevertheless the case that these various contexts are interrelated, and the importance of not neglecting each context must be stressed.

The finding that the perceived availability of handguns is linked to gang association warrants closer attention. This association suggests that people who live in communities where there are many handguns may join gangs for protection (Decker and Winkle 1996; Klein and Maxon 2006; Peterson et al. 2004). If this is the case, feelings of fear and a lack of perceived community solidarity and safety may be driving forces for joining gangs. This suggests that emphasis should be placed on removing firearms from communities while building a sense of social cohesion and trust, such that community members, and youths particularly, do not feel the need to join gangs for protection. The finding that residential mobility was linked to gang involvement further supports the need for interventions to build community solidarity. Communities characterized by high rates of residential mobility tend to have lower levels of informal social control due to a lack of cohesion and trust among community members. In such fragmented communities, people feel isolated and lack a sense that others in the community care about and are interested in their well-being. As such, there is the need to seek protection from alternate sources such as gangs. Providing other sources of control and security may reduce the need to seek such security from within gang structures. Quite ironically, residential mobility and the fragmented communities this creates may engender a lack of stability with respect to value systems, norms, roles and the like in various communities. Gang structures, while they may be counter-normative, may nevertheless exhibit stability in terms of the expected norms of behaviour and codes of conduct which are upheld. It may be the case that some people may join gangs for the sense of stability and belonging which such structures provide. Social cohesion within neighbourhoods, as well as harmonious family relationships may act as buffers under such circumstances.

That the family is an important element to consider comes from the finding that youths who are more likely to be associated with gangs come from families which favour antisocial behaviour. This idea points specifically to the socialization role of the family but implicates the family as a critical institution in the life of young adults. In this respect, parental ability to adequately supervise and socialize children may be an important factor in building resilience and resistance against gang involvement. Parental skills development is something which does not exist in Trinidad and Tobago, but can be established indirectly through inclusion of relevant content in the high school curricula, or through parental classes for expectant parents. While the study by Katz and Fox (2010) provides important insights into the risk and protective factors at the community, school, family, and peer-individual levels of analyses, research is also required on larger social processes and structures. Such research may suggest additional intervention strategies.

Randy Seepersad (2009) examined the relationship between economic relative deprivation and crime and counter-normative actions in a sample of 950 males drawn from 71 randomly selected communities in Trinidad and Tobago. Respondents were between the ages of 16 and 30 at the time of interview. Relative deprivation occurs when one compares oneself (egoistic) or one's in-group (fraternal) to a comparison referent and discovers that one or one's in-group is economically deprived relative to the comparison referent. Outcome measures in this study included past year self-reported criminal offending, lifetime self-reported criminal offending, willingness to participate in counter-normative political actions, actual participation in counter-normative political actions, willingness to participate in counter-normative non-political actions, and actual participation in counter-normative non-political actions. Seepersad (2009) found that cognitive relative deprivation (the recognition of deprivation) led to affective relative deprivation (feelings associated with deprivation, e.g., anger, frustration, resentment) which in turn led to crime and counter-normative actions. This finding applied to both personal (egoistic) and group (fraternal) relative deprivation. It was further discovered that a number of additional variables conditioned or moderated this causal pathway. More specifically, personal deprivation was found to lead to stronger emotional responses if people were pessimistic about their deprivation being relieved in the future, while at the group level, higher levels of optimism about future economic improvements were related to stronger emotional responses. Both types of deprivation also led to stronger emotional responses when people believed that financial success and wealth were important. It was also discovered that, where respondents had criminal peers, relative deprivation was more likely to lead to crime and counter-normative actions than if respondents did not have criminal peers. It was also found that the recognition of personal deprivation was more likely to lead to depression and lower self-esteem if people blamed themselves for their deprivation than if they did not. People who were not optimistic that their deprivation would be relieved in the future were more depressed than people who were optimistic. While this study focused on relative deprivation, a number of additional variables were included in the analyses. Other important predictors of crime and counter-normative actions were criminal values and attitudes, having criminal peers, the availability of illegal opportunities and low self-control.

Primary data gathered from a sample of 1,595 adults in Trinidad and Tobago measured a number of indicators of crime and insecurity. Measures included crime in the community, victimization within the past year and within the past ten years, domestic violence, gang presence and gang violence, self-reported criminal offending and fear of crime. A number of important predictor variables were also measured. These included a range of demographic variables, community cohesion, societal cohesion, and informal social control. Each outcome measure was regressed on the range of predictor variables indicated above (see table 5.2 for a summary of the findings of these analyses).

Three measures assessed the level of criminogenic behaviour.[1] The first was the level of crime in the community, in which respondents indicated whether or not each of 13 specified crimes had occurred in their community within the last year. The responses to these items were summed to create the measure of crime in the community. Significant predictors of crime in the community were age, the level of education, community cohesion and informal social control. The two other measures which were used to assess criminogenic behaviour were the level of criminal victimization experienced within the last ten years and within the last year. In each case, respondents were presented with a list of 18 specified crimes and asked to indicate the frequency with which they had been victimized in the respective time periods. Overall measures were created as the sum of responses in each time period. For both measures, significant predictors were gender, education and societal cohesion. Ethnicity and income were also significant predictors of victimization within the last ten years, while informal social control was a significant predictor of victimization within the last year.

A number of consistencies exist with respect to the predictors of the three measures of criminogenic behaviour. With respect to ethnicity it was found that people of East Indian and mixed descent were more likely than people of African descent to be victimized within the last ten years. It was further discovered that education was significantly and positively related to all outcome measures. This indicates that people who are more educated are more likely to be victimized and, at the community level, that victimization occurs more frequently in communities with higher average levels of education. This is not surprising since, on average, education tends to be positively correlated with income so that people with higher educational levels tend to have more material possessions or, at least, are perceived to do so. Having more possessions increases the number of opportunities for criminal victimization, at least where property crimes are concerned. If actual or threatened violence is used in the acquisition of such property, then such crimes will be classified as violent crimes, indicating the possibility that such people could also be the victims of violent crimes. This was confirmed by supplemental analysis (not shown in table 5.2) in which education was positively and significantly related to both property and violent victimization within the last ten years and property crime within the last year.

Community cohesion, societal cohesion and informal social control were significantly negatively related to the three measures of criminogenic behaviour. More specifically, community cohesion was a significant predictor of crime in the community (β = -.143, p < .001), while societal cohesion was a significant predictor of victimization within the last ten years (β = -.059, p < .05). Societal cohesion (β = -.089, p < .004) and informal social control were significant predictors of crime in the community (β = -.065, p < .016) as well as past year victimization (β = -.056, p < .04). These findings are not surprising, as much criminological literature has indicated that tightly knit communities are better able to regulate behaviour through informal systems of control. In such communities, members have a stake in the community and feel a sense of kinship and responsibility to their fellow men and, as a consequence, are willing to intervene when prosocial norms are broken. What is interesting about the findings is that the cohesion measures exhibit independent influences on criminogenic behaviour net of the effect of informal social control (at least in the case of crime in the community and past year victimization). This indicates that, while societal or community cohesion may exert an influence on criminogenic behaviour through its effect on informal systems of control, such cohesion results in behaviour regulation through other means quite apart from its influence on informal social control. This implies that, in Trinidad and Tobago, interventions which seek to reduce crime and insecurity can focus both on developing cohesion and on enhancing systems of social control.

Significant predictors of domestic violence were age, gender, and societal cohesion (table 5.2). Age was significantly related to domestic violence (β = .057, p < .027). In this case, older people were more likely to be victims of domestic violence than younger people. This may be the case simply because older people have spent greater lengths of time in relationships or have had more relationships than younger people, thus increasing the number of opportunities available for incidents of abuse to occur. The data also indicate that females are more likely to be victims of domestic violence than males (β = .15, p < .001). This finding is consistent with much international literature. Quite importantly, it was found that societal cohesion was inversely related to domestic violence (β = -.083, p < .006).

The above is consistent with the argument in chapter 2 that societal conditions can either encourage or discourage domestic violence. In this case, higher levels of societal cohesion can reduce the incidence of domestic violence. Societal cohesion could result in greater support for victims and could even increase the provision of advice and counselling to abusers or potential abusers. In addition, people who feel more closely integrated into their society may experience a greater sense of belonging and well-being, and may thus be better adjusted than people who are not as closely integrated. It may be the case that better adjusted people have better skills at resolving relational conflicts when they occur, or that better adjusted people simply have fewer conflicts in their relationships. It is also possible that societal cohesion can reduce domestic violence by exerting an influence through informal systems of social control. In this respect, supplemental analyses, not shown in table 5.2, indicate that once the domestic violence regression equation was recomputed but with the societal cohesion measure omitted, community cohesion became significant (β = -.089, p < .001), while informal social control almost became significant (β = -.048, p < .076). When community cohesion was removed from this equation, informal social control became significant (β = -.079, p < .002). This seems to suggest that, in addition to exerting an effect on domestic violence through informal social control, societal cohesion is also capable of reducing domestic violence through its effect on community cohesion. That is, societies which are more closely integrated result in more closely integrated communities, which in turn serve as a buffer against domestic violence.

With respect to gangs, 13.9 per cent of the respondents indicated that there were criminal gangs in their neighbourhood. Of these, 49.5 per cent indicated that gangs posed a slight problem, while 41.9 per cent indicated that gangs posed a serious problem for their neighbourhood. Slightly over 11 per cent of the respondents indicated that criminal gangs had become a problem in their neighbourhood within the last year, while 18.5 per cent indicated that the time frame was between one and three years, 24.3 per cent indicated that the time frame was between three and five years, and 36 per cent indicated that gangs had become a problem more than five years before. Of those who indicated that there were criminal gangs in their neighbourhoods, 82.4 per cent indicated that gangs had made their neighbourhoods less safe, while a small minority (3.2 per cent) indicated that gangs had made their neighbourhoods safer. Slightly more than 14 per cent of the respondents in neighbourhoods with gangs indicated that there was a large amount of gang violence in their neighbourhoods, while 45.5 per cent indicated that there was some violence, 34.2 per cent indicated that there was only a little violence, while five per cent indicated that there was no violence. These findings are summarized in table 5.1.

Table 5.1:   Survey Findings: Gangs in Trinidad and Tobago

	Percentage
There are criminal gangs in my neighbourhood	13.9
Gangs pose a serious problem	41.9
Gangs pose a slight problem	49.5
Gangs make the neighbourhood a less safe place	82.4
Gangs make the neighbourhood a safer place	3.2
Large amount of gang violence in neighbourhood	14.4
Some gang violence in neighbourhood	45.5
Little gang violence in neighbourhood	34.2
No gang violence in neighbourhood	5.0

Data Source: Victimization Survey of 1,595 Adults in Trinidad and Tobago

Regression analyses indicated that age, income, community cohesion, societal cohesion and informal social control were significant predictors of gang presence, gang problems and gang violence (see columns five to seven in table 5.2). More specifically, lower levels of income were related to a higher likelihood of gang presence in neighbourhoods. This indicates that gangs are more likely to be located in poorer areas. Age was positively related to gang violence. This may simply indicate that older people are more sensitive to incidents of violence (or that younger people are more desensitized to violence), and as such, older people may perceive that there are greater levels of violence than younger people. Community cohesion as well as societal cohesion suppressed gang problems and gang violence in neighbourhoods.[2] More specifically, high levels of each type of cohesion were related to lower levels of gang problems and gang violence. Notably, each type of cohesion exhibited independent influence on gang problems and violence. Informal social control was also found to exhibit a suppressive effect on gang violence.[3] This may indicate that informal systems of control are effective in reducing gang violence, but could also indicate that higher levels of gang violence may exert a suppressive effect on informal systems of behaviour regulation.

Self-reported criminal offending represents a measure of personal offending.[4] Significant predictors of self-reported criminal offending were age, gender, education, community cohesion, and societal cohesion. Age was significantly negatively related to personal offending (β = -.087, p < .001) where older people were less likely to be involved in criminal offending. Education was similarly negatively related to personal offending (β = -.091, p < .001) where more educated people were less likely to offend. Not surprisingly, males were more likely to commit offences than females (β = -.199, p < .001). While lower levels of societal cohesion were related to higher levels of personal offending (β = -.095, p < .002), contrary to expectations it was found that higher levels of community cohesion were related to higher levels of personal offending (β = .066, p < .034). This finding may be explained if we consider the simultaneous effects of low societal cohesion and high community cohesion. Low levels of societal cohesion may indicate the isolation of various communities, where the members of such communities may feel excluded from the institutions and opportunities provided by the wider society. This may encourage the development of community cohesion for isolated communities. Such internal cohesion may serve as a means of protecting the members of such communities from the wider society which may be perceived to be antagonistic to the members of isolated communities. Higher levels of community cohesion in turn may facilitate interaction between people who do and people who do not commit criminal offences. Since this occurs in the context of socially isolated communities, such communities may develop norms and values which go against those of the wider society, that is, such communities could develop norms which value criminal offending. If this is the case, then people who do not normally commit criminal offences may potentially be socialized into criminal offending. This is consistent with the research of Katz and Fox (2010) who found that more opportunities for prosocial involvement were related to a greater likelihood of becoming involved with gangs. It will be recalled that Katz and Fox speculated that prosocial involvement may serve to increase gang involvement since such involvement may bring current gang members into contact with at-risk youths, as well as youths who are not currently in gangs. Socialization effects and peer influence processes may serve to encourage youths in the latter two categories into pro-criminal lifestyles. Given that data from Katz and Fox (2010) and the primary data used for this study derive from Trinidad and Tobago and have consistent findings in this respect, this indicates that policymakers and practitioners must be aware of the potential negative effects of socialization processes when criminogenic and non-criminogenic people interact. Policymakers should also be aware of the potential negative effects which could occur when communities are socially isolated from the wider society.

The final measure of insecurity which was employed was fear of crime. Two sub-measures (worry and safety) were employed.[5] The findings across the two measures are almost perfectly consistent. Significant predictors of both measures are age, ethnicity, education, community cohesion and societal cohesion. Additionally, income and informal social control were significant predictors of the safety measure of fear of crime. With respect to ethnicity, people of African descent worried less about crime and felt safer than people of other ethnicities, while people of Indian and mixed descent worried more about their safety. In addition, people of mixed descent felt more fearful for their safety than people of other ethnicities. Where income was concerned, people with higher income levels felt more fearful for their safety than people with lower incomes. Education was positively related to both worry and safety. More specifically, people who were more educated experienced greater levels of worry and felt more fearful for their safety. Community cohesion and societal cohesion were inversely related to both measures of fear of crime.

Table 5.2: Predictors of Crime and Insecurity[8]

Predictors	Dependent Variables									
	Crime in the community	Victimization (past 10 years)	Victimization (past year)	Domestic violence	Gang presence	Gang problems	Gang violence	Self-reported offending	Fear of crime (worry)	Fear of crime (safety)
Age	**-.066			*-.057			***.106	***-.087	-.044[9]	*-.057
Gender		**-.072	**-.072	***.15				***-.199	*.051	
Ethnicity		[10]							[11]	[12]
Income		-.046[13]			*-.059					*-.051
Education	*.063	***.114	**.070						***.120	***.119
Community cohesion	***-.143				**.080	**-.083	*.064	*.066	**-.087	**-.094
Societal cohesion		*-.059	**-.089	**-.083	***.127	***-.112	***.129	**-.095	*-.073	**-.081
Informal social control	*-.065		*-.056				**.082			**-.124

*p < .05, **p < .01, ***p < .001

Source: Victimization Survey of 1,1595 adults in Trinidad and Tobago

That is, fear was higher where there were lower levels of community and societal cohesion. Informal social control was negatively related to the safety measure of fear of crime. This indicates that, where there were high levels of informal social control, people felt safer than where there were low levels of social control.

When the pattern of findings is considered as a whole, the most important predictors of crime and insecurity are societal and community cohesion (significant predictors of nine and seven outcome measures respectively). Education and age are each a significant predictor of six of the ten outcome measures employed. Gender is a significant predictor in five of the ten equations computed, while informal social control is significant in four equations. Ethnicity and income are each significant predictors of three of the outcome measures examined.

These findings indicate that interventions to reduce crime and insecurity should focus on community and societal cohesion. Both variables are related measures, though one operates at the community level while the other operates at the national level. Despite the similarity in both constructs, each has distinct implications and can exist without the other. For example, we can have communities with a high amount of internal cohesion, yet at same time, such communities can be ostracized by and isolated from the rest of society. While the data indicate that, on average, higher levels of community cohesion reduces crime and insecurity, it is entirely possible that if such communities feel a sense of isolation from the larger society (that is, if there is low societal cohesion), then such communities can develop and reinforce norms which are at odds with those of the wider society. People who feel a sense of isolation from the wider society may not feel compelled to conform to prosocial norms of behaviour, especially if such norms are perceived to be products of the wider society. Where pro-criminal norms develop in socially isolated communities, residents and indeed youths may feel that they need to defend such norms as a form of defiance against the wider society. In such situations, it may be difficult or impossible for the average person, and more so for youths, to transcend such counter-normative systems and adhere to the prosocial norms which are expected of the wider society. This reasoning indicates that in Trinidad and Tobago we must be careful to avoid situations where entire communities are stereotyped and isolated from the wider society. Such stereotyping immediately sets up barriers to achievement via conventional means since the legitimate opportunity structure normally provided by the wider society may not be accessible to people in such communities. When this occurs, people in such communities may need to 'innovate' to achieve the success goals which are normally expected in the society. Where such success goals include the acquisition of financial wealth, such innovators may resort to illegal means of achieving these success goals. Overall, the findings suggest that policies should aim at building both societal and community cohesion.

The findings further suggest that policymakers should focus on the possibility of using education to reduce crime and insecurity. It was found that education reduced the likelihood of committing criminal offences. These findings suggest that education is an important factor for consideration, especially where marginalized and at-risk youths and communities are concerned. The education system functions as a selection mechanism to allocate people to various roles in society. People who are not successful in the educational system may not be allocated roles where they have opportunities to achieve the level of material wealth or other success goals which they desire. A focus on literacy and on ensuring that at-risk persons have access to the support systems necessary to ensure that they persist with their education and are eventually successful will go a long way to reducing crime and insecurity. If youths are allowed to drop out of the school system, and if there are no mechanisms for monitoring and following up on excessive truancy, then such youths may become vulnerable to joining gangs and other counter-normative groups. Monitoring mechanisms may help to reduce the likelihood that at-risk youths could end up becoming involved in criminal lifestyles. Truancy in schools is something which should not be ignored, and instead should be aggressively pursued by following up with parents or guardians. Frequent absenteeism may be a signal that youths are becoming involved in counter normative and illegal behaviour.

Also within this context, preschool education becomes important. Research has shown that students who are afforded preschool education are more likely to achieve academic success as they progress through the various stages of their education (Schiefelbein 1981). The move toward universal preschool education in Trinidad and Tobago is, therefore, a step in the right direction. In Trinidad and Tobago, this is part of a larger initiative to provide universal education, at least up to the secondary level, and to provide affordable education even at the tertiary level. While such initiatives are important, the provision of education alone is not sufficient. The availability of education does not mean that quality education will be accessed. While educational opportunities may be available, at-risk youths may be the ones least likely to benefit from such opportunities. Measures must be put in place to ensure that these opportunities are utilized to their full potential. While education is an important predictor, a focus on education also comes with disadvantages. While more educated people are less likely to commit criminal offences, they are also more likely to be victimized and are more fearful than people who are less educated. If the benefits of education could be maximized, however, this should reduce the number of offenders and subsequently erode the level of victimization and fear of people with higher levels of education.

Income was related to three of the outcome measures of crime and insecurity; these measures included victimization within the last ten years, gang presence and the safety measure of fear of crime. While these data illustrate that there is a relationship between income at the personal level and measures of crime and insecurity, it is also important to assess the relationship between national indicators of economic well-being and the level of crime and insecurity. Economic indicators for Trinidad and Tobago are available for the period 1990–2008.[6] Correlations were computed using the economic indicators provided by the International Monetary Fund (IMF) and the range of crime measures available from the Crime and Problem Analysis branch of the Trinidad and Tobago Police Service. Measures of property and violent crime were computed from the crime data and were also employed in calculating these correlations.[7] Analyses indicate, almost invariably, that the number of unemployed persons and the unemployment rate are inversely related to violent crimes but are positively related to property crimes and narcotic offences (table 5.3). This indicates that unemployment is related to an increase in property offences and drug usage; whereas lower levels of unemployment (i.e., higher levels of employment) are related to higher levels of violent crime. This can occur where there is a higher level of resource availability and economic well-being, but where such economic resources are not equitably distributed in the population. Visible disparities in income and standards of living can create frustration and anger for those who are deprived in society. Such frustration and anger can translate into increased levels of violence. This is supported by other economic data in Trinidad and Tobago (table 5.3). Both gross domestic product (GDP) and gross national income (GNI) are positively related to a range of violent crimes, including murder, wounding and shooting, rape and sexual offences, kidnapping, robbery, other serious crimes and total violent crime. In contrast, both variables are inversely related to narcotic offences and property crimes, including burglary, fraud, and total property crime. The only exception to this rule is with general larceny which is positively related to GDP and GNI. While data on the distribution of economic resources is not available for the time period under consideration, these findings strongly suggest that increasing wealth and economic well-being, if unaccompanied by an equitable distribution of such wealth, can result in increased levels of violent crime. While national efforts should focus on increasing overall wealth, policymakers should put measures in place which ensure that the poor and dispossessed share in some of the wealth which is generated.

One of the most recent studies which examined risk factors in Trinidad and Tobago was by Randy Seepersad (2014). This study utilized data from a sample of 1,248 students in ten primary schools in north Trinidad. Students who participated in the study had an average age of 10.3 years. There were slightly more males (55.7 per cent) than females (44.3 per cent) in the sample. Table 3.1 shows the percentage of students who were victims of specified acts within the last term while table 3.2 shows the percentage of students who self-reported that they victimized others within the last term. One of the primary aims of this study was to determine which risk factors were the most important predictors of being victimized and victimizing others. Each of these dependent variables included subscales for verbal, physical, social and property forms of victimization.

Table 5.3:   Correlations between Economic Indicators and Crime Measures[14]

	Labour force (thousands)	Employment (thousands)	Unemployment	Unemployment rate (%)	Gross domestic product	Gross national income
Murder	**.815	**.832	**-.884	**-.844	**.966	**.967
Wounding and shooting	*.615	**.655	**-.656	**-.637	**.718	**.707
Sexual offences	**.938	**.953	**-.928	**-.947	**.869	**.864
Serious indecency	-.331	-.132	.222	.139	-.381	-.383
Kidnapping	**.876	**.889	**-.815	**-.861	**.703	**.691
Narcotic offences	**-.742	**-.747	**.756	**.746	**-.724	**-.717
Burglaries	**-.911	**-.924	**.893	**.927	**-.756	**-.747
Robberies	**.624	**.638	**-.632	**-.621	**.706	**.697
Fraud	*-.498	-.340	*.461	.377	*-.542	*-.554
General larceny	**.768	**.821	**-.817	**-.814	**.847	**.846
Other serious crimes	**.840	**.871	**-.826	**-.855	**.770	**.767
Violent crime	**.786	**.813	**-.802	**-.798	**.842	**.833
Property crimes	**-.742	**-.778	**.753	**.789	*-.568	*-.559

*p < .05, ** p < .01*

Source: Crime and Problem Analysis Branch of the Trinidad and Tobago Police Service and the International Monetary Fund International Financial Statistic online database.

Regression analyses were conducted to determine which variables were important predictors of experiencing victimization (table 5.4) and the perpetration of victimization (table 5.5). In each case, the dependent variable was used as a total measure, and was also categorized into components reflecting verbal, physical, social and property forms of victimization. Independent variables which were utilized were alienation from school (peers), alienation from school (teachers), alienation from home, violence at home, self-control, dispositional anger and social support.   Control variables were age, gender, academic performance, depression, locus of control, self-efficacy, self-esteem, peer approval of bullying and teacher response to bullying.

It was found that violence in the home consistently predicted both types of victimization and all subscales within each type of victimization. The findings indicated that students who live in homes with high levels of violence experience higher levels of victimization in school, but at the same time, such students victimize others at higher rates than students who do not experience violence at home. When total measures were used, the correlation between experiencing victimization and perpetrating victimization, though significant, was only moderate in strength ($r = .237$, $p < .001$). This suggests that while there are some students who are victimized to a high degree and who also perpetrate victimization against others to a high degree, there is a larger number of students who either experience victimization or perpetrate victimization, but do not do both. This implies that violence at home may cause some children to be violent against others while in other cases it may increase some children's vulnerability to victimization at school. In all likelihood, different processes may be operational in each case. Supplementary analyses conducted by Seepersad revealed that the relationship between violence in the home and both the perpetration and experience of being victimized was stronger for males than for females.

The study also found that dispositional anger was a consistent predictor of experiencing victimization and perpetrating victimization. The findings indicated that students who have higher levels of anger are more likely to victimize others. Such students were also more likely to be victimized in the school setting. These findings suggest that angry students are more inclined to hurt others, while students who are victimized are more likely to become angry because of their experiences of victimization.

Seepersad (2014) also discovered that alienation from school as a result of peers was a significant predictor of experiencing victimization (table 5.4) while alienation from school as a result of teachers was a significant predictor of perpetrating victimization against others (table 5.5). Both predictors had significant positive coefficients in all five equations in the respective tables. Conversely, alienation from school as a result of teachers was not a significant predictor of experiencing victimization (table 5.4), while alienation from school as a result of other students was not a significant predictor of perpetrating victimization (table 5.5). Alienation from peers may indicate that peers dislike the person who is being alienated, and it is thus not surprising to find that students who are alienated by other students experience higher levels of victimization. The finding that alienation by peers was not related to the perpetration of victimization suggests that either such alienation does not encourage others to become bullies in the school setting, or that persons who victimize others are not ostracized by their peers for doing so. Indeed, it may be the case that persons who victimize others may receive praise and recognition from other students in the school setting. It was also found that alienation in school as a result of teachers was not related to experiencing victimization, but was related to the perpetrating of victimization. It was not surprising to find that students who are victimized more are not alienated by their teachers. Indeed, it would be expected that teachers would be more supportive of such students. The finding that alienation from school as a result of teachers was related to the perpetration of victimization suggests that either such alienation encourages children to become more violent, or that more violent children attract more condemnation from their teachers.

The study also found that social support was significantly related to experiencing victimization in three of five equations, and almost approached statistical significance in a fourth equation (table 5.4). The findings indicated that students who received higher levels of social support experienced higher levels of victimization. This suggests that persons who were victimized more received a higher level of social support in response to that victimization. The equations in table 5.5 indicate that there is no relationship between social support and the perpetration of victimization.

It was also found that self-control was related to the perpetration of victimization, but not to experiencing victimization. More specifically, self-control was a significant predictor of four of the five equations which used the perpetration of victimization as the dependent measure, and in all cases the coefficients were positive (table 5.5) but was non-significant in all equations where the experience of victimization was used as the dependent measure (table 5.4). This indicates that children with low self-control are not necessarily more vulnerable to being victimized, but also indicates that children with low self-control are more likely to victimize others. The latter finding has been well documented in international literature.

The final predictor variable which was focused upon by Seepersad (2014) was alienation from the home. Alienation from the home was non-significant in all ten regression equations. This indicates that such alienation does not have an impact on vulnerability to victimization and also indicates that alienation from the home does not encourage children to become more violent. In the present context it may be that alienation from the home was overshadowed by the importance of violence in the home.

Control variables which were important in Seepersad's study (2014) were gender and depression. Gender was an important predictor of experiencing and perpetrating victimization. Here, males were more likely than females to experience victimization and to perpetrate victimization. Depression was an important predictor of the perpetration of victimization.

Table 5.4:   Predictors of Experiencing Victimization[15]

Predictors	Total Victimization	Verbal	Physical	Social	Property
Age	-.002	***.100	-.032	-.051[16]	.018
Gender	***-.139	***-.106	***-.240	-.026	***-.132
Alienation from school (peers)	***.354	***.255	***.212	***.416	***.238
Alienation from school (teachers)	-.045	-.025	-.032	-.047	-.046
Alienation from home	-.018	-.020	-.011	-.027	.012
Violence at Home	***.153	***.137	***.139	***.127	***.107
Self-Control	-.052	-.054	-.020	-.053	-.047
Dispositional Anger	***.121	***.148	***.111	*.063	***.110
Social Support	*.077	*.081	.052	.059[17]	*.077
Academic Performance	-.002	.024	-.026	-.017	.033
Depression	.037	.041	.031	.036	.010
Locus of Control	-.010	.026	.003	-.034	-.016
Self-efficacy	.024	-.005	.005	.039	.035
Self-esteem	-.026	-.012	.019	-.036	*-.068
Peer approval of bullying	.005	.035	-.042	.009	.027
Teacher response to bullying	.022	.009	.022	.048	-.035
Adjusted R^2	.221	.136	.140	.233	.123

*Source: Seepersad (2014). * p < .05, ** p < .01, *** p < .001*

The significant negative coefficients in four of the five equations (table 5.5) indicated that persons who victimized others were less likely to be depressed.

Overall, the analyses in Seepersad (2014) indicated that important predictors of experiencing victimization were alienation from school caused by peers, violence at home, dispositional anger and social support. Important predictors of perpetrating victimization were alienation from school caused by teachers, violence at home, low self-control and dispositional anger. In addition, gender was a significant control variable for both dependent measures as well as their subscales. Seepersad's findings (2014) can be used to guide the formulation of interventions to reduce victimization since they point to important variables which should be considered in the design of such interventions.

Table 5.5:   Predictors of Perpetrating Acts of Victimization[18]

	Total Victimization	Verbal	Physical	Social	Property
Age	.005	***.097	-.006	-.049[19]	-.039
Gender	***-.186	***-.115	***-.241	***-.118	***-.148
Alienation from school (peers)	.049	.053[20]	.022	*.055	.051
Alienation from school (teachers)	***.152	***.149	***.119	***.156	***.101
Alienation from home	-.003	.001	-.024	.011	.015
Violence at Home	***.226	***.219	***.203	***.173	***.193
Self-Control	***.121	***.110	***.109	***.127	.059
Dispositional Anger	***.207	***.189	***.215	***.181	**.096
Social Support	-.007	.023	-.021	-.031	.017
Academic Performance	-.037	-.021	-.046	-.022	-.038
Depression	*-.071	*-.064	-.041	**-.084	*-.072
Locus of Control	-.031	-.016	-.028	-.026	-.046
Self-efficacy	.047	.011	*.058	.048	.043
Self-esteem	-.011	.005	-.004	-.025	-.021
Peer approval of bullying	.045	*.058	.048[21]	.035	-.001
Teacher response to bullying	-.052[22]	-.039	-.054	-.009	***-.100
Adjusted R²	.310	.252	.295	.237	.155

*Source: Seepersad (2014). * p < .05, ** p < .01, *** p < .001*

The focus of this chapter was risk factors and determinants which facilitate crime and insecurity. Policymakers must be mindful of three key issues if they intend to manipulate risk factors to reduce crime and insecurity. The first has to do with the level of aggregation at which the risk factors and outcomes are situated, the second with the preventative versus reactive distinction, and the third with the amount of variance which each risk factor explains in the outcome measures of interest. The level of aggregation at which risk factors are situated is an important consideration. Risk factors may be situated at the aggregate (social structural) level of analysis or at the individual (personal) level of analysis and can be located anywhere along this continuum. As such, risk factors which are targeted may operate at the level of the society, community, school, family or individual. The manipulation of risk factors at any given level of analysis usually targets specific outcomes at the same level of aggregation, though there are obviously linkages between the different levels of analysis. Knowing that there are different levels of analysis helps in the organization of intervention strategies since multiple levels of analyses can be targeted simultaneously. This also aids in evaluation research since well-specified predictors usually lend themselves to a clear understanding of what outcomes may be expected when such predictors are manipulated.

The second issue relates to the preventative versus reactive distinction. This sensitizes policymakers and researchers to the fact that interventions can be put in place to prevent the escalation of crime and insecurity, but where this does occur, interventions can also be targeted to reduce the likelihood of the reoccurrence of criminal offending. This book previously drew upon the ideas of P. Brantingham and F. Faust (1976) who made the distinction between primary, secondary and tertiary prevention. Primary prevention refers to those intervention strategies which target outcome behaviour before it happens. Examples include preschool education and social skills training for adolescents. Secondary prevention targets at-risk people and communities, while tertiary prevention is a reactive approach which typifies the functioning of the criminal justice systems of many countries. While many populations may prefer reactive-type strategies because of their visibility and perceived short-term effects, preventative strategies are just as important. While these may be long-term in terms of their outcomes, such strategies over the long run reduce the burden of crime and insecurity faced by the criminal justice system, facilitating more manageable and efficient operations. Another advantage of preventative interventions is that their effects tend to be more lasting. Chapter 7 will utilize the ideas of levels of analysis and a preventative versus a reactive approach to crime prevention to develop a conceptual framework for considering risk factors (see table 7.1).

The final issue of importance, when considering intervention strategies, is the amount of variance which each predictor explains in the outcome variables of interest. Simply put, some risk factors have more powerful impacts on crime and insecurity and, where these are manipulable, it makes more sense to tackle these factors since this improves the cost effectiveness of the intervention strategy. Many statistical tools, including multiple regression and analysis of variance can provide estimates of the relative impact of various predictors. These analyses can be used to guide the formulation of intervention strategies.

Notes

1. See the first three data columns in table 5.2.
2. The positive coefficients for community and societal cohesion as predictors of gang violence result from the codings used. A high score represents high levels of cohesion for both measures. Gang problems were coded such that a high score represented a high level of problems whereas gang violence was coded such that a high score represents a low level of violence.
3. The positive coefficient for the effect of informal social control on gang violence occurs for a similar reason as does the positive coefficients of the community and societal control measures in this equation (see the previous footnote).
4. See column 8 in table 5.2.
5. See columns 9 and 10 in table 5.2.
6. Source: International Monetary Fund (IMF) International Financial Statistics (IFS) online database.
7. Violent crime includes murder, wounding and shooting, rape, serious indecency, kidnapping, and robberies. Property crime includes burglaries, fraud and general larceny.
8. Standardized regression coefficients are shown.
9. $p < .083$
10. African descent $\beta = .244^{***}$, East Indian descent $\beta = -.225^{***}$, Mixed descent $\beta = -.161^{**}$
11. African descent $\beta = .285^{***}$, Mixed descent $\beta = -.128^{*}$
12. African descent $\beta = .117^{*}$, East Indian descent $\beta = .104$, $p < .07$
13. $p < .081$
14. Economic measures were sourced from the International Monetary Fund International Financial Statistics online database, while crime data were provided by the TTPS.
15. Standardized regression coefficients are shown.
16. $p < .055$
17. $p < .067$
18. Standardized regression coefficients are shown.
19. $p < .064$
20. $p < .059$
21. $p < .062$
22. $p < .057$

Responses of the Population to Insecurity

In democracies, policy is influenced by the responses of the population to crime. These responses may set the agenda for action and demand greater responsiveness by state agencies and the political administration. They may, however, also instigate negative outcomes. The responses of the public are not always well informed and, even when informed, are not always governed by reason. Violent crimes tend to evoke strong emotions. Reactions may be conditioned by the prejudices and biases of the population. These emotions, biases and prejudices may fuel ineffective responses and even undemocratic ones. Out-groups are easily made scapegoats, instant solutions are demanded, and the underlying causes of the problem and well-designed prevention programmes that are based on these are neglected. If policy is to be influenced in socially constructive and value appropriate ways, then the responses and policy orientation of the population must be better understood.

This trend is not restricted to Trinidad and Tobago. The *Central American Human Development Report* (UNDP 2009), for example, identifies several myths that are generally accepted by sections of the populations of Central American countries. Population orientations of this type must be closely monitored because such myths may, for example, be politically manipulated and used to inform the implementation of hardline policies that support increasingly punitive responses to criminal activity without addressing the root causes of crime. On the other hand, a more strategic approach to improve the provision of services by government institutions to improve and better manage the overloaded security and justice systems may not always find popular support, and policies that do not have popular support are unlikely to be implemented. This trend may reduce the existing system to a simple triangle of police, judges, and jails, and ignore the missing links to civil society and to other state institutions, including those at the local level. In an attempt to come to terms with the impact of the population on crime and security initiatives, this chapter evaluates the opinions of the

Trinidad and Tobago population on crime, violence and insecurity. It also examines other aspects of citizens' subjective responses to insecurity, including levels of confidence in state institutions which are integral to the provision of citizen security. This chapter concludes by arguing that success in the fight against crime must not only rely on the functioning of the criminal justice system, but must employ preventative approaches which go beyond the remit of law-enforcement agencies.

The level of insecurity experienced in any country is tied to the level of development. Insecurity is a broad term and refers, not only to those psychological and other outcomes of crime, but also to the general condition and quality of human life. As such, human development impacts on human security, which in turn has implications for the policy orientation of the population under consideration. The link between human development and security is thus critical. Human development not only refers to the growth of per capita income but is also related to critical factors such as freedom and justice, which are also essential for human beings to lead better lives. The level of human development is also tied to the availability of factors ranging from nutrition and education to income and employment, self-esteem and to freedom of expression. In the final analysis, these factors should all be enjoyed on a peaceful and permanent basis, in a safe and secure way.

The United Nations Development Programme (UNDP) (2009, iii) defines human security as 'the liberation of human beings from those intense, extensive, prolonged, and comprehensive threats to which their lives and freedom are vulnerable'. Human security is reinforced when the state retains the ultimate power of coercion and uses this power to support its commitment to fostering respect for the rights of its citizens. When other groups usurp control of instruments of force or in any way reduce the level of control wielded by the state, whether in real or perceived terms, human security and the perception of such security are negatively impacted. An important component of human security is citizen security. This relates specifically to the risk of becoming a victim of violence or of dispossession. There can be no human development without protection against violent and predatory crime. Citizen security, like the broader construct of human security, is a necessary precondition for human development.

Fear of crime reduces liberties and the ability to live a normal life. Crime causes the state and all citizens to divert their scarce resources to pay for hospitals, jails, police officers, insurance premiums, and other expenses needed to prevent crime or to correct its adverse effects. Additionally, insecurity diverts investment away from the country, hinders its economic growth and produces unemployment. Criminality weakens the social fabric, destroys confidence among people and erodes the credibility of institutions and respect for the rule of law. From the perspective of human development, citizen security has several major implications:

1. Attention should not centre on the crime itself or on the offender – as in conventional criminology – but should focus first on the actual or the potential victims of those crimes. The main interest of human development should, therefore, be the protection of citizens against the violent or predatory actions which negatively impact their basic opportunities or liberties.

2. The very concept of human development would imply a universally accepted definition of ethics.

3. The distinctive mark of the human development paradigm is its recognition that public policies should not be directed towards a single goal – for example, wealth – or to maximize a single value – for example, efficiency. This recognition stems from the fact that there exists a plurality of values which, although not always compatible with one another, are worth pursuing for their own sakes.

From the standpoint of human development, the challenge is to find policies or programmes that would effectively contribute to the simultaneous achievement of the several values. Citizen security is in and of itself a human value which depends directly on elements of freedom and equity. Yet, in order to achieve freedom and equity, sacrifices must be made or negative 'collateral effects' must, by necessity, be expected. With respect to freedom, one civil liberty or another has to be sacrificed or some 'soft' legal provisions will be ignored in order to control crime. With respect to equity, it is difficult to maintain in the face of increasing criminality, and society adopts an 'everyone is to fend for himself' attitude, even though this implies that the weak in society will be unprotected. The challenge then is to single out the strategies which will provide effective security for everybody with freedom and equity for all. 'Effective security' means an actual reduction in crime rates and in the probability of being victimized by criminals.

The Trinidad and Tobago population accords critical importance to issues of citizen security. Indeed, data gathered for this book indicate that crime is one of the most serious concerns of residents in Trinidad and Tobago. Respondents were asked to rate the seriousness of several issues facing the country. The largest proportion of respondents (69.8 per cent) indicated that the cost of living was a very serious concern. This was followed by the level of violent crime which was rated as very serious by 68.8 per cent of the respondents. Other important areas were the cost of food (67.8 per cent), corruption (55.2 per cent) and the level of property crime (40.4 per cent). These findings are illustrated in figure 6.1.

While violent crime is one of the most pressing concerns of the population, the perception of crime does not always mirror the realities of crime. Yet, the ability to properly distinguish between perception and reality as they relate to crime is critical if we are to understand the problem and design effective policies to address the problem. Since the perception of crime may not mirror the reality of crime, it is dangerous to allow the beliefs of average citizens to be tainted by fear, prejudice, false information or manipulation. This only serves to exaggerate or, in some cases, to minimize the actual magnitude of the problem and, in essence, distorts the nature of the real criminal threats facing society. The distortions are often perpetuated by the media who can exaggerate the frequency or the incidence of crime, stereotype the typical criminal to the detriment of certain segments of society, generalize from a few observations and, more importantly, make irresponsible generalizations with respect to the causes of crime, how crime is manifested and possible remedies.

Figure 6.1:   Most Serious Issues Faced By the Country

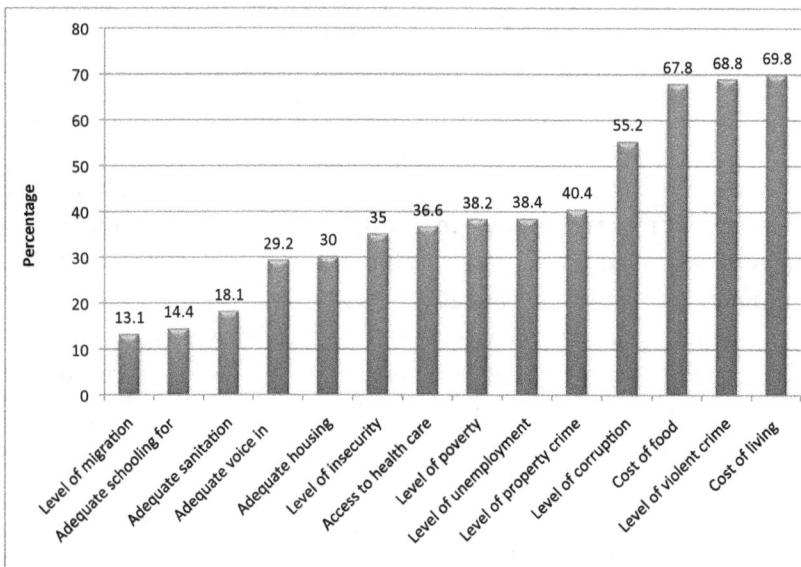

Data source: Victimization Survey of 1,595 Adults in Trinidad and Tobago

There are growing concerns about the level of crime and violence in the English-speaking Caribbean, particularly in Jamaica and Trinidad and Tobago. A March 2007 report by the World Bank and the United Nations Office on Drugs and Crime (UNODC) revealed that the murder rate in the Caribbean was higher than in any other region of the world. While the concern about crime is paramount in the population, the data in figure 6.1 indicate that there are several other pressing concerns, most notably those related to economic well-being (e.g., the cost of food, the cost of living, poverty and unemployment). These represent important issues which must be addressed if human security is to be improved in Trinidad and Tobago.

While the larger issue of human security is an important one, the more specific issue of citizen security also warrants closer scrutiny. As far as Trinidad and Tobago is concerned, the 'popular ideology' about citizen insecurity could be narrowed down to a dozen or so extended, but inexact, beliefs. In attempting to assess these beliefs, respondents who were interviewed were asked to indicate whether they agreed or disagreed with a number of issues which attempted to assess the policy orientation of the population as it relates to citizen security. A number of items attempted to assess the extent to which the population believed that a more punitive approach was required to address the crime situation in Trinidad and Tobago (table 6.1). Fully 89.8 per cent of the population agreed or strongly agreed that criminals should be more harshly punished, while 75.2 per cent supported the death penalty. This is consistent with the overwhelming belief (90.2 per cent agreed or strongly agreed) that criminals represent a threat to the way of life in Trinidad and Tobago.

Despite the above findings, responses indicated that the population did not believe that reactive, punitive-type approaches were the only type required to solve the crime situation. Indeed, a large proportion of the respondents were strongly in support of preventative measures as a means of addressing the crime problem. For example, 89.1 per cent of respondents believed that education was an important initiative in this respect, while 91 per cent supported initiatives for youths. Job creation, the reduction of poverty, as well as investment in poor urban communities were also seen as critical (92 per cent, 90.5 per cent, and 89.1 per cent respectively agreed or strongly agreed). In addition to this, 89 per cent believed that reducing corruption would reduce crime levels.

The support for a preventative orientation was consistent with a lack of support for a number of other policy alternatives. More specifically, only 31.8 per cent of respondents believed that police should be given a free hand to kill criminals, while only 33.7 per cent believed that building more prisons was the solution. In addition, only 17.2 per cent of respondents believed that easier access to firearms by law-abiding citizens represented a viable means to reduce crime. Similarly, only 11.8 per cent believed that only a military government could reduce crime.

Table 6.1:   Percentage Agreed or Strongly Agreed on Issues Related to Citizen Security

Item	Percentage
I feel that my society is fundamentally unjust (unfair)	51.4
I feel that my society is fundamentally law abiding	30.9
Criminals should be more harshly punished	89.8
I support the death penalty	75.2
Criminals are a threat to our way of life	90.2
Human rights are obstacles to more effective crime control	42.0
It is alright for the police to break the law in order to better control violent crimes	17.9
The police should be given a free hand to kill criminal gunmen	31.8
In order to reduce the crime rate the government should invest more in the police force/service	72.5
In order to reduce the crime rate the government should invest more in education	89.1
In order to reduce the crime rate the government should invest more in programmes for young people	91.0
In order to reduce the crime rate the government should invest more in job creation	92.0
In order to reduce the crime rate the government should invest more in reducing corruption	89.2
In order to reduce crime, the government should invest more in the communities of the urban poor	89.1
In order to reduce crime the government should invest more in reducing poverty.	90.5
In order to reduce crime, the government should build more prisons	33.7
In order to reduce crime, the government should rely more on the military	53.0
In order to reduce crime, people should be allowed easier access to firearms.	17.2
In order to reduce crime dons should be used as agents of crime control	11.0
The problem of crime has no remedy	15.7
Only a military government can effectively control crime	11.8
Nothing can be done to control crime in this country	12.1

Data source: Victimization Survey of 1,595 Adults in Trinidad and Tobago

This does not mean, however, that the population was not in support of the use of the military in crime suppression. Almost half of the people surveyed (53 per cent) believed that the government should rely more on the military in order to reduce crime. In a similar manner, the police was also seen as important. A large proportion of respondents (72.5 per cent) believed that the government should invest more in the police service, though only a minority (17.9 per cent) believed that it was acceptable for the police to break the law to control crime. In contrast to this, a sizeable proportion of the respondents (42 per cent) believed that human rights represented an obstacle to effective crime control. While respondents expressed a broad spectrum of views, both within the reactive/punitive and the preventative orientation, a small proportion of the respondents believed that there was no remedy to the crime problem in Trinidad and Tobago (15.7 per cent) and that nothing could be done to control crime (12.1 per cent).

There are several myths that hamper the process of improving citizen security from a policy standpoint. Some of these include the belief that citizen security is an issue which falls only within the remit of the police, that the problem of insecurity can be solved by spending more money, putting minors in jail, expediting trials and extending punishments, and that 'zero tolerance' must be enforced. According to this well-known belief, a maximum of severity should be applied to the majority of crimes.

The problem, however, is more complex than this. Research has supported the idea that severe punishments are not effective deterrents to criminal offending, and that the certainty of punishment is much more important than the severity of punishment (Bailey and Peterson 1999; Doob and Webster 2003). There is no strong statistical relationship, for example, between the increase in the rate of imprisonment and medium or long-term reduction in crime rates (Doob and Webster 2003). As another example, available United States (US) data from 1990 to 2009 indicate that the murder rates in death penalty states are consistently higher than the murder rates in non-death penalty states.[1] Unfortunately, popular sentiment and inaccurate beliefs about the importance of severity drive policy responses in Trinidad and Tobago. Such beliefs are also applied inappropriately to youths. While popular belief is that youth crime is out of control, the data presented in chapter 3 indicate that youth crime and violence is the exception rather than the rule.

The police service specifically, and the criminal justice system generally, rely on a reactive approach and come into effect only after transgressions of the law have occurred. Preventative approaches should be employed in addition to the reactive approaches such that social skills training, parental training, interventions for youths and families and other such measures are put in place to build a citizenry which is less likely to be involved in illegal behaviour. Many factors including poverty, unemployment, inequality and other such things affect crime levels. Preventative approaches should focus on these as well. The fight against crime, therefore, requires a multifaceted approach, which takes both a preventative and a reactive approach. To think that the crime issue is one that can be solved only by the police is to limit the policy options which will be put in place to reduce crime.

In contrast to the level of insecurity caused by street crime in Trinidad and Tobago, there is another major source of insecurity that is seldom considered as such; one that traditional studies typically fail to mention. This source of insecurity is corruption. Corruption is defined by the UNDP (2012) as the undue appropriation of public or collective property; that is, property belonging to each and every citizen. In this context, corruption takes one of three principal modalities:

1. One of inaction in which the failure of authorities to act on behalf of the public interest perpetuates the de facto power of the perpetrators.

2. The acceptance of bribes in cash or in kind, by public officers, sometimes of the highest rank.

3. Small-scale corruption in which many citizens are involved, e.g., requesting an illegal fee in exchange for electoral support or paying bribes for public services, etc.

In addition to the many traditional insecurities of citizens, there are some non-traditional ones that deserve just as much attention. They are typically referred to as the 'invisible' or 'hidden' insecurities. These invisible insecurities revolve around specific social groups that are targets of social discrimination in that they are more likely to be victimized and less likely to receive adequate and relevant protection from society. This social discrimination typically affects four groups of people in Trinidad and Tobago. These include: 1) members of specific ethnic/cultural minorities – in the case of Trinidad and Tobago, young males of African descent; 2) young men and adolescents, especially in poor urban areas such as East Port of Spain; 3) children, particularly those living in low income households; and 4) women exposed to violence from their partners and in their immediate home or work environment.

The above implies that the failure of the current retributive approach to criminal justice in Trinidad and Tobago is in part due to the fact that there is no such thing as citizen *insecurity* but there are citizen *insecurities*. A comprehensive approach against citizen insecurity requires that both visible and 'invisible insecurities' should be recognized and addressed. One of the most important obligations of the state is to guarantee the security of its citizens. In order to effectively carry out this charge, citizen security should be treated as a public issue, and therefore be subject to public scrutiny. Security is not an issue for the police only or for any other specialized agency for that matter. Despite this, all modern societies entrust the core responsibility for crime prevention and public control to the three arms of the criminal justice system; the police, the courts and the prisons. Trinidad and Tobago is no exception and, like all the other states in the region, continues to support and sustain those three institutions, while at the same time neglecting other institutions which could be potentially useful in the fight against crime.

In Trinidad and Tobago, the police service, the judiciary and the prisons are all overwhelmed by the exceptionally high rate of crime. This contributes directly or indirectly to the level of citizen response to crime and violence, and to their opinions about the criminal justice system. Citizens acknowledged several weaknesses in the processes of the criminal justice system which negatively impact upon crime and violence. These include: 1) poor quality of criminal investigation which results, in many cases, in a lack of evidence to identify, detain and sanction offenders; 2) a shortage of competent lawyers to represent detainees who do not have the resources to retain private attorneys. This has resulted in a phenomenon of 'prison for the poor'; and 3) the ineffectiveness of the correctional system, which includes ineffective or non-existent rehabilitation programmes and in which inmates are socialized into values, culture, and skills which encourage them to become 'better' criminals. This, coupled with the less than adequate service provided by the police, bottlenecks in the courts, and overcrowding in the prisons, has caused the average citizen to feel overwhelmed by the apparent state of lawlessness.

Despite the above, many processes have been implemented to improve the quality of the protective services. The Trinidad and Tobago Police Service (TTPS) would argue, for example, that they have reengineered themselves to present a more civilian-friendly face. The results of the victimization survey belie this argument. The TTPS would also argue that they have adopted a degree of professionalism and that they now work in closer tandem with communities. Again, the results of the victimization survey indicate that there is room for continued improvement in this area. Additionally, a growing number of crime prevention programmes have been launched, and new preventive units of the police have been created. The criminal justice system has also been reformed to leave behind the traditional formalism in favour of procedural efficiency, with better qualified personnel and with better equipped offices. These and other innovations have been implemented to improve the provision of citizen security. Unfortunately, it would appear that many of the reforms are more of form rather than of substance and, from a practical perspective, one cannot expect institutions as complex as the police, the judiciary and the prisons to change overnight. In spite of their ongoing reforms, the three institutions are still overwhelmed by the new wave of violence and insecurity that has been plaguing the country. Additionally, social issues such as unemployment, inequality, and the lack of social welfare policies continue to contribute to increased levels of criminality.

Despite these efforts and reforms, the perceived lack of effective police response has contributed to widespread dissatisfaction with the TTPS performance, exacerbating feelings of insecurity and undermining trust in government institutions. Fully 62.3 per cent of the respondents interviewed for this study indicated that, at the national level, the police perform poorly or very poorly with respect to controlling robbery. Almost 60 per cent answered similarly for rape, 60.1 per cent for domestic violence, 62.9 per cent for burglary, 73.5 per cent for the control of drug trafficking, 73.8 per cent for the control of arms trafficking, and 67.6 per cent for crimes of the powerful. It was further found that 49.4 per cent of the sample thought that the police performed poorly or very poorly with regard to demonstrating respect for people's rights, while 49.5 per cent felt similarly with regard to the police having respect for the law, 46.6 per cent with respect to dealing with people, 54.8 per cent with treating people equally, and 48 per cent with respect to demonstrating courtesy to citizens. Overall, at the national level, 19.4 per cent of the respondents felt that the police had become more effective over the last three years with respect to controlling crime while 41.3 per cent felt that their performance was the same, and 38.6 per cent felt that the performance of the police had declined.

Similar findings were obtained when respondents were asked to indicate their level of satisfaction with police performance at the community level. With respect to the control of robbery, 43.4 per cent of respondents felt that the police performed poorly or very poorly, though notably, 38.9 per cent felt that police performance in this area was fair, while 17.2 per cent felt that their performance was good or very good. With the control of rape, 36.7 per cent felt that the performance of the police was poor or very poor, while 39.4 per cent felt that their performance was fair, and 21.7 per cent felt that their performance was good or very good. With respect to the control of domestic violence, 39.9 per cent of the sample felt that police performance was poor or very poor, while 39.2 per cent felt that their performance was fair, and 19.9 per cent felt that their performance was good or very good. With respect to controlling house-breaking, 49.8 per cent of the population felt that police performance was poor or very poor, while 32 per cent felt that their performance was fair, and 17.5 per cent felt that their performance was good or very good. Overall at the community level, 18.6 per cent of the respondents felt that the police had become more effective over the last three years with respect to controlling crime while 50.8 per cent felt that their performance was the same, and 29.8 per cent felt that the performance of the police had declined. Given these findings it is not surprising that confidence in the police is less than would be desired. Indeed, the majority of respondents (an average of 66.4 per cent across all crimes considered) had low or very low confidence in the police.

Similar to the findings for the police, a large proportion of the public is dissatisfied with the court system in Trinidad and Tobago (table 6.3). Almost half (46 per cent) of the respondents felt that the court system was not fair, while 35.9 per cent felt that the court system had not gotten fairer over the last five years. Fully 44.6 per cent of respondents felt that suspects who might be innocent were not sufficiently protected by the courts, while 49 per cent believed that poorer subjects were treated less fairly. Interestingly, a large proportion of the respondents (60.4 per cent) thought that the justice system might yield to political pressure or could be manipulated by politicians. Consistent with this it was found that 70.2 per cent of the sample believed that politically connected criminals were likely to go free. In a similar manner, 61.6 per cent felt that powerful criminals were likely to go free. When asked about corruption, 69.7 per cent felt that there was corruption in the justice system while 58.6 per cent felt that judges were corrupt.

The level of victimization as indicated by official crime statistics indicates that the population is subject to high levels of property and violent crime. Long-term trends indicate that crime rates, particularly for violent crimes, have been increasing, though there were noted decreases within very recent times (table 2.1). Self-reported victimization data utilized in this book also indicate that the population experiences high levels of insecurity, and more so than would be suggested by official crime data (table 2.6). Indeed, comparisons of the findings from the victimization survey indicate that the actual rates of robbery are 4.6 times higher than suggested by official crime statistics, while the incidence of sexual offences is 6.6 times higher, burglaries 4.1 times higher, motor vehicular theft 2.4 times higher, and financial crimes 7.2 times higher. This helps to fuel distrust and dissatisfaction with the performance of the protective services in Trinidad and Tobago.

Table 6.2:   Confidence in the Police

	Low or Very Low	Neutral	High or Very High
	Percentage (%)		
Rape and sexual assault	62.0	28.3	9.7
Burglary	63.2	26.3	10.5
Domestic violence	60.1	29.0	10.9
Robbery	65.0	24.2	10.8
Extortion	53.3	33.0	13.7
Murder	72.2	19.1	8.7
Gang violence	69.0	21.1	9.9
Drug trafficking	73.6	16.0	10.4
Gun trafficking	74.7	15.5	9.8
High level fraud	70.8	20.4	8.8

Data Source: Victimization Survey of 1,595 Adults in Trinidad and Tobago

Table 6.3:   Confidence in the Courts[2]

	Disagree or Strongly Disagree	Agree or Strongly Agree
The courts are fair	46.0	30.8
The courts are more fair today than they were five years ago	35.9	23.1
I am confident that the courts effectively protect suspects who are innocent of the crimes for which they are charged	44.6	21.2
Suspects who are poor are not likely to be treated fairly	26.8	49.0
I am confident that the justice system is not manipulated by politicians/ does not yield to political pressure	60.4	13.1
The judges are not corrupt	58.6	15.3
The justice system is free of corruption	69.7	9.4
The justice system is unable to convict powerful criminals. Powerful criminals are likely to go free	18.4	61.6
Politically connected criminals are likely to go free	14.5	70.2

Data Source: Victimization Survey of 1,595 Adults in Trinidad and Tobago

Despite the widespread dissatisfaction with the criminal justice system, this does not necessarily mean that this system is not functioning. While it is agreed that violent crimes are increasing, what we need to consider is the alternative situation of what would happen in the absence of a functioning criminal justice system. That is, it is quite possible that the increase in violent crimes may be much worse without the presence of the criminal justice system in Trinidad and Tobago. Evidence of this came in the form of increased illegal activity during the 1990 attempted coup in Trinidad and Tobago. This was most likely brought about by a temporary cessation of the functioning of the criminal justice system. As such, the assumption that the criminal justice system is not performing may be a simplification. It may be the case that the criminal justice system is performing, but lacks the resources to fully control the increase in crime rates. The intention here is not to justify inaction by the criminal justice system, or to say that its functioning cannot be improved. Rather, to illustrate that with successful preventative approaches in place, the criminal justice system with its limited resources may be better able to manage the country's crime situation once some of the potential offenders are removed from the equation through preventative interventions.

While crime levels and the opinions of people who were interviewed suggest that the criminal justice system is performing less than adequately, the solution to the crime and insecurity issues in Trinidad and Tobago lies not only within the criminal justice system but also outside of that system. Typically, criminal justice systems come into contact with perpetrators of criminal offences only *after* such offences have occurred. That is, criminal justice systems around the world typically operate in reactive or after-the-fact manners. Reactive approaches must be complemented by proactive or preventative approaches where measures are put in place to reduce the likelihood of criminal offending occurring in the first place. This 'up front' type of approach would reduce the burden on an already strained criminal justice system, which could then be poised to deal with those (much fewer) cases that may occur whenever preventative approaches prove to be less than adequate.

An important area which policymakers can consider for use in the fight against crime, and which is operative outside the boundaries of what normally obtains in the criminal justice system, is informal social control. Much of behaviour regulation takes place via informal social means as opposed to being regulated by the threat of punishment from the criminal justice system. If informal systems of control can be reinforced, this removes some of the burden from the criminal justice system in terms of societal reliance on formal procedures for behaviour regulation. Limited staffing does not afford the police service and other protective services the luxury of monitoring all behaviour in Trinidad and Tobago and, as such, it is imperative that social controls function effectively in regulating behaviour and ensuring that for the most part, citizens operate within the constraints of the law.

Survey data gathered to inform the development of this work speak directly to the policy orientation of the population with respect to informal social control. Respondents were asked to indicate the likelihood that community members would intervene if three specified transgressions of the law occurred. Fully 31.7 per cent of respondents thought that it was unlikely or very unlikely that people in their communities would intervene where domestic violence was occurring, whereas 43.3 per cent thought that it was likely or very likely that community members would intervene. In the case of a fight, many more people (57.9 per cent) thought that it was likely or very likely that community members would intervene, though some people (20.6 per cent) thought that it was unlikely or very unlikely. Where a stranger was suspected of stealing something, 61.6 per cent thought that it was likely or very likely that the community would intervene, whereas 16.7 per cent thought that it was unlikely or very unlikely.

Quite interestingly, the data also reveal that there is a significant positive correlation between measures of societal and community cohesion and the three measures of informal social control mentioned in the previous paragraph. These findings indicate, not surprisingly, that informal social controls are more likely to be operative where communities are more closely knit, and where the society as a whole is more closely integrated. This indicates that strategies which build a sense of community and societal cohesion will act to strengthen informal systems of social control. Given that societal and community cohesion has a demonstrated capacity to reduce crime (UNDP 2012), the building of such cohesion should not be left to chance but should be utilized as a purposeful strategy in the fight against crime and insecurity.

Conclusion

Based on citizens' responses as well as official data gathered from the Crime and Problem Analysis branch of the Trinidad and Tobago Police Service, there appears to be a failure in policies aimed at reducing crime. This has resulted in an increase in various categories of crime as well as mistrust of law enforcement. The lack of a coordinated and collaborative approach to the many dimensions of the problem and failure, until recently, to place sufficient emphasis on prevention, has constrained the ability of the criminal justice system to respond effectively.

An overall transformation is required to be able to satisfy citizens' security needs, which in turn, will be reflected in improved public opinions about the criminal justice system. There must be short-term as well as long-term improvement in the effectiveness of state policies. State agencies will need to design strategies to initiate dialogue, information sharing and collaboration. Respect for citizens' rights must become the rule and not the exception. This should, by necessity, involve promoting respect for the different cultures and norms. To achieve this, the government will need to mobilize regional and international partners to increase capacity and, through this, build advocacy coalitions with state and non-state agencies. This approach would also build the capacity to design, implement and monitor public policies to enhance citizen security while facilitating the implementation of strategies to promote dialogue and information sharing, and to improve cooperation and collaboration.

The most obvious way to reform policies and agendas is to determine what shifts in thinking are required and, if any, which ones best take a citizen security approach. The state must also ask if any new elements need to be added to the policymaking process and, if so, on what principles are they to be based? Strategies must be put in place to strengthen social capital to foster respect for the law as the norm, thus rebuilding citizen confidence and trust and encouraging a reorientation of the population. The long-term implications for these polices would be safer communities and a promotion of citizen participation and community initiatives to reduce violence at the community level and allow for a greater degree of offender reintegration. The state should also evaluate initiatives promoted by private/civil society that have positively impacted, reduced or prevented crime. They must also implement initiatives to increase public trust and confidence in the effectiveness of state policies which deal with citizen security issues.

Any strategy which focuses on human development will, by necessity, require effective and efficient security for all citizens, with a focus on freedom, equity, and respect for civil liberties. The launch of any security strategy that is consistent with a human development focus requires a credible, effective and legitimate set of supporting state institutions. This institutional support can only be provided by a state that fulfils all of its basic functions effectively and without bias. Citizen security in any democratic society strengthens social cohesion. The implementation of effective security measures will result in a reduction of crime rates and the risk of victimization. Security with freedom assumes the protection of all citizens and the absence of unreasonable levels of fear as currently exists in Trinidad and Tobago. Additionally, the alleged perpetrators of crimes should also be free from judicial abuse, and their rights should be fully protected in the event of prosecution and trial. Finally, security with equity should be afforded to all citizens and not just those who are able to pay for it. Human development is based on the widening of life options and the effective liberties of people, independent of their circumstances. Citizen security is therefore a necessary component of any strategy for human development.

Notes

1. Death Penalty Information Center: http://www.deathpenaltyinfo.org/deterrence-states-without-death-penalty-have-had-consistently-lower-murder-rates.
2. Percentages are given. Responses of 'don't know' were omitted from this table.

The Future of Crime and Security in Trinidad and Tobago

The preceding chapters examined various aspects of citizen security in Trinidad and Tobago. Chapter 1 focused on the criminal justice system with coverage of each of the three arms; the police, the courts and corrections. Chapter 2 focused on criminal victimization and examined both official crime data as well as victimization survey data. Domestic violence, which represents a specific case of victimization of a vulnerable group in Trinidad and Tobago, was also examined in chapter 2. Chapter 3 focused on juvenile justice and examined the extent to which youths in Trinidad and Tobago were delinquent and committed acts of violence. This chapter also examined relevant theorizing on youth violence. Chapter 4 assessed the issue of criminal gangs in Trinidad and Tobago with an examination of the extent to which gangs are responsible for violent crime. This chapter also provided a discussion of the consequences of the presence of gangs and offered strategies for reducing gang violence. Chapter 5 offered an empirical basis upon which to design intervention strategies, and examined the risk factors which encourage crime and violence. Chapter 6 looked at the responses of the population and state to insecurity and argued that, if political decisions are based solely on popular sentiment, this could lead to ineffective crime policies. Chapter 6 also argued that, while the opinion of the population is important, it must be understood within the context of the findings of theoretical and empirical work in criminology. Chapter 7 assesses the nature and extent of the problem, drawing on linkages to human development, and offers recommendations for dealing with crime and insecurity in Trinidad and Tobago.

The criminal justice system in Trinidad and Tobago is responsible for dealing with issues of crime and security. Proactive (preventative) as well as reactive (after the crime has occurred) measures are required if the nation is to be successful in its fight against crime. With the exception of general deterrence strategies, it could be argued that much of what is done by 'traditional' criminal justice systems is reactive. A progressive criminal justice system is one which extends its focus to include preventative measures. This is not to say that it is expected that the criminal justice system will have all the resources or personnel necessary to engage in preventative crime control through all or most of the major institutions in Trinidad and Tobago. Rather, there should be a more purposeful and deliberate integration of criminology and criminal justice ideas and strategies in other institutions, such that these institutions have planned strategies to aid in the fight against crime. So, for example, while the education system in Trinidad and Tobago may serve a crime reduction function, this occurs as a by-product of its functioning, rather than as a result of a deliberate strategy. Programmes could be developed for schools which are aimed at developing social skills, civic mindedness, self-control, self-esteem, racial and religious tolerance, the ability to defer gratification, moral values, and other such factors which may help in the development of law abiding youths and young adults.

The use of the education system is but one example. Such ideas could be applied to other institutions of social control such as the community and family. In the United Kingdom (UK), the Crime and Disorder Act (1998) offers a useful template of how legislation may be used to integrate the functioning of a range of governmental and non-governmental agencies where crime control is the issue. Among other things, this Act affords the opportunity for each local authority in England and Wales to formulate and implement strategies to reduce crime and disorder in their area. The Act also requires each local authority to work with the police authority, probation authority, health authority, social landlords, volunteers, and local residents and businesses. A system has been put in place to ensure that there is communication and coordination among the various entities and that there is a sharing of expertise in moving forward with initiatives which are derived from specified goals as they relate to the reduction of crime and insecurity.

While the above argues for a re-conceptualization of the functioning of the criminal justice system in Trinidad and Tobago, it is also important to strengthen the law enforcement function of this system. Inefficiencies and problems within the police service, judiciary, and prisons can reduce the effectiveness of the criminal justice system with regard to controlling crime. A major problem facing the Trinidad and Tobago Police Service (TTPS), for example, is a lack of public confidence. Primary data gathered for this study show that, for a range of performance areas, approximately 60 per cent of the population feel that the police perform poorly or very poorly. It is misleading to think that public opinion is unimportant for the functioning of the police service as the public functions as a system of surveillance for the police and, where the public fails to report incidents of victimization due to a lack of confidence in the police, such illegal activity will go unchecked.

Additionally, where the public believes that the police do not function effectively, they may attempt to take justice into their own hands, possibly resulting in even more serious transgressions of the law. It is also the case that people who feel insecure due to a lack of confidence may migrate. Typically those people who are more educated, or who possess greater financial resources are the ones more likely to migrate, resulting in a removal of intellectual and financial resources from the country. Finally, a sense of confidence, where people feel that the police are there to serve and protect them, will foster a sense of community and partnership with the police and the criminal justice system generally, and facilitate a situation where both the public and police work together to achieve the common goals of reducing crime and building security.

Community policing represents one way whereby partnerships between the police and public may be developed. Chapter 1 examined a number of reasons why community policing in Trinidad and Tobago has met with less success than initially expected. Community policing, as a philosophy and as a new way of policing, should not be abandoned. Recent police reforms were also examined. Such reforms were guided by the recommendations of Professor Stephen Mastrofski, and aimed to improve the legitimacy, accountability, external and internal management capability, and technical capability of the Trinidad and Tobago Police Service.

While the public often focuses on the performance of the police service in evaluating crime rates, the other arms of the criminal justice system play equally important roles. Inefficiencies in the judiciary and the prison service will also translate into problems with crime and insecurity. The judiciary of Trinidad and Tobago faces the overwhelming task of adjudicating at a rate expected to be fast enough to keep up with the large number of offences which occur on a daily basis. Consideration should be given to alternatives which may reduce the caseload of the judiciary, at least where less serious offences are concerned. For example, a restorative justice model, where there is provision for mediation, counselling, and other facilities which allow for out-of-court solutions to disputes, is encouraged. This model, quite apart from freeing the judiciary from dealing with less serious matters, has the advantage of enabling dialogue between victims and offenders and possibly initiating a rehabilitation process for offenders. Offenders who are encouraged to empathize with victims and to make reparations for wrongdoing in a social context which is more accepting of the offender, but which at the same time signals social disapproval for the wrongdoing, may be more willing to desist from reoffending. Social pressures exert as much, or perhaps even more influence on behaviour than the threat of punishment from the criminal justice system. This determines the degree to which the vast majority of citizens abide by the laws. Where offenders are allowed opportunities to reintegrate into the community, this reduces the likelihood that such persons may be forced into lives of crime due to a lack of legitimate opportunities which are typically provided by society.

A reduction in the caseload of the judiciary should be accompanied by the streamlining of the processes which affect the efficiency of judicial functioning such that cases which must be adjudicated are addressed in a timely manner. A number of suggestions were offered in this respect. The system of legal aid should be improved by increasing the fees paid to attorneys-at-law. At present, the fees paid attract very few attorneys and there is typically a three to four-month delay in appointing legal aid counsel. In addition, the system of police prosecutors should be revisited. Many police prosecutors are not trained attorneys, which results in serious disadvantages for the prosecution. Qualified attorneys should be appointed to conduct all cases in the magistrates' courts, or alternatively, police prosecutors should be qualified attorneys. A special system of remands via a video link would reduce the need for the transport of prisoners to court. This would reduce costs and time spent. In the alternative, additional remand facilities could be constructed. Such facilities should be located in close proximity to the major courts. There is also the need for an increase in compensation to be paid to witnesses and jurors who attend court. Current fees reduce witness participation and juror dedication.

Trivial cases such as expired licences and parking tickets should be heard by lay magistrates. A system should be put in place which ensures that police officers attend court when they function as witnesses or complainants. At present, police absenteeism results in delays in the administration of justice. Notwithstanding the foregoing, it is recognized that police absenteeism occurs because of poor case management, where officers are forced to attend court several times for the same case, with the case being postponed each time for any number of reasons. These occurrences result in wastage of the officers' valuable time. A case management system should be put in place where cases are allowed to proceed only when all documentation, personnel and other requirements are ready and in place for the case to proceed.

Plea bargaining legislation, which offers the possibility of sentence discounts, should be considered. This would allow at least some cases to circumvent the process of lengthy court trials by the admission of guilt. Consideration should also be given to the increased usage of paper committals as opposed to preliminary inquiries. Victim and witness protection are also important in the Trinidad and Tobago context. Witnesses as well as victims may fail to testify because of fear of reprisals by offenders. Better protection would improve the chances of successful prosecution. Consideration should also be given to the use of witness testimony via video link. Where narcotics cases are concerned, there is a need for revision of the sentencing options. Currently drug addicts and drug traffickers are treated in a similar manner. Addicts are in need of rehabilitation and medical treatment. Prison sentences do little or nothing to treat addiction. Alternatives to imprisonment, such as mandatory treatment in drug rehabilitation centres should be considered. There should also be a thorough evaluation of the key constraints to the effective and efficient operation of the judiciary of Trinidad and Tobago. Such an evaluation should rely heavily on magistrates and judges to develop suggestions to streamline the processes involved in the administration of justice.

The prison service represents the third major component of the criminal justice system in Trinidad and Tobago. If not properly managed, prisons could become the breeding ground for persistent criminality and recidivism as opposed to being institutions where rehabilitation occurs. Currently, in Trinidad and Tobago, people who have committed non-serious offences are housed with serious offenders while on remand. This increases the likelihood of criminal socialization where less serious offenders learn the skills, values and attitudes required to become more proficient and committed to offending. This also facilitates social networking whereby alliances may be developed between non-serious and serious offenders, or where offenders may be given the contact information of other offenders who are not in the correctional system. While some segregation is afforded once convicted, a more carefully graded system of segregation would ensure that similar effects are not operative among the inmate population. This, of course, necessitates an expansion of current facilities which would also serve to reduce overcrowding and improve the working conditions of prison officers.

Imprisonment should only be used as a last resort in Trinidad and Tobago. Incapacitation strategies should be employed only for serious offences and for offenders who are likely to recidivate (as evidenced by a culture-appropriate risk assessment). Alternatives to imprisonment should be available for people who are unlikely to reoffend or who have not committed serious offences. Alternatives could include community service, mandatory rehabilitation or some form of reparation. Selective incapacitation would reduce the strain on the prison system and would maximize the cost-efficiency of imprisonment while protecting the public.

Youth violence was another important issue which was considered in this book. Past research in Trinidad and Tobago has found that serious acts of delinquency begin even when youths are in primary school. Lall (2007) collected data from 589 nine- to eleven-year olds and found that within the six months prior to the exercise, 64 per cent had been involved in fist fights, 45 per cent had consumed alcohol, 26 per cent had assaulted someone with a weapon, 17 per cent had stolen something, 7 per cent had smoked cigarettes, and 2 per cent had used illegal drugs. While delinquency may be initiated at an early age, policymakers should be aware that intervention strategies must avoid the processes of labelling and stigmatization and, whenever possible, must avoid strategies based on institutionalization.

There is the real danger in Trinidad and Tobago that public perceptions about youth violence may fuel the implementation of inappropriate measures for dealing with youthful offenders and delinquents. International research (Moffitt 1993; 2003; 2006) shows that the vast majority of youthful offenders engage in acts of delinquency as a result of imitative behaviour. These offenders experience what Terrie Moffitt (1993) calls a 'maturity gap' and, in trying to compensate for this maturity gap, they imitate the delinquent behaviour of a numerically much smaller group of persistent delinquents. The persistent delinquency of such youths, according to Moffitt (1993), is rooted in neuropsychology. The average youth who imitates delinquent behaviour will naturally desist from such behaviour once they become more mature. No special intervention is, therefore, needed for the vast majority of delinquent youths, though more serious measures are required where persistent delinquents are concerned. Intervention strategies which stigmatize youths who engage in imitative delinquency, or which provide opportunities for interaction with persistently delinquent youths may interfere with the naturally occurring desistance process, and may ensnare a 'normal' youth into a life of delinquency.

Data from Trinidad and Tobago indicate that, at present, inappropriate strategies are being employed in dealing with delinquency. Ramesh Deosaran and Derek Chadee (1997), for example, interviewed the entire population of three juvenile institutions in Trinidad and Tobago and quite alarmingly found that 58.5 per cent of youths at the St Michael's School for Boys, and 92.8 per cent of youths at the St Jude's School for Girls were institutionalized for non-illegal acts. Indeed, a strong case could be made that many of the youths who were institutionalized were actually in need of counselling, support and care, as opposed to being placed in an institutional setting. 'Offences' for which these youths were institutionalized included attempted suicide, being victims of physical and sexual abuse, having no one to take care of them, running away from home and being beyond control.

Deosaran and Chadee's findings (1997) are consistent with other data from Trinidad and Tobago. For example, Ministry of National Security data for the period 1986–95 indicate that, of all juvenile offences which were adjudicated, destitution (having no parent or other fit person to provide for the youth) accounted for 30 per cent of the cases, while being beyond control accounted for 22.7 per cent. Deosaran and Chadee (1997) found that even the youths who were institutionalized for committing illegal acts exhibited characteristics which indicated a strong potential for rehabilitation.

The institutionalization of youths who are in need of protection and counselling, or youths who are not serious offenders, is contrary to the objective of reducing crime and violence. Such youths will be channelled into lives of continued delinquency and eventual criminality for a number of reasons. Institutionalization is accompanied by stigmatization, socialization into antisocial norms and values, labelling and stereotyping. Once institutionalized, the life chances of youths are negatively affected and opportunities for advancement via pro-social means are reduced or eliminated. Furthermore, an institutional setting is one in which the effects of socialization may encourage the adoption and acceptance of counter-normative values, attitudes and lifestyles by youths who may otherwise eventually desist from delinquency.

The laws of Trinidad and Tobago allow for wide discretion in the sentences handed down to youths, and institutionalization is only one among a range of options. Where there is a lack of alternatives, the decisions of adjudicators are constrained. There is at present an urgent need for the development of alternative options for youths so that magistrates and judges are not forced to use incapacitative strategies which are not justified. Consideration should also be given to the use of mediation in youth justice, and the use of family circles and community courts where youths are concerned, since this also provides alternatives to sending youths through the formal court system. In cases where youths have committed offences and have been convicted and have served their sentences, consideration should be given to the possibility of sealing or expunging their juvenile records so that their future life chances are not hampered by acts committed when they were younger. This latter suggestion may be more applicable where less serious offences are concerned. Careful consideration is also warranted in cases where youths are drug addicts or users. While these may be in the minority, if special attention is not given to these cases, these youths have a greater than average likelihood of graduating to serious criminality when they get older.

The issue of criminal gangs is one which is becoming increasingly important in Trinidad and Tobago. Ignoring the potential threat posed by gangs, or deemphasizing the magnitude of the problem increases the possibility of inaction when action is needed. Inaction may lead to a situation where the gang problem becomes so overwhelming that it can no longer be controlled. Data from the Ministry of National Security indicate that as of 2014 there were approximately 95 gangs with a total of 1,269 gang members in Trinidad and Tobago. The majority of gangs are concentrated in the Port of Spain, Western and Northern police divisions, while the gang problem appears to be minimal to non-existent in Tobago. Available data also indicate that approximately 83 per cent of gang members are of African descent, 13 per cent are of East Indian descent, and four per cent are of other ethnic backgrounds. All gangs in Trinidad and Tobago are male dominated and most (87 per cent) are comprised of adults. A large proportion of all gangs (88 per cent) claim some area as their turf, while 75 per cent defend their turf. While the vast majority (85 per cent) does not have any identifying symbols or clothing, recent trends indicate that the prevalence of tattoos and other symbols is increasing.

Data examined in chapter 4 indicated that gang members are engaged in a disproportionate amount of illegal behaviour. Furthermore, spatial comparison of the density of gangs and the incidence of crimes in Trinidad and Tobago revealed that violent crimes occur more frequently in areas with higher proportions of gangs. The crimes which were found to be most closely related to gang presence were murder, woundings/shootings, robbery, burglary and narcotic offences. Additionally, Ministry of National Security data on firearm usage in the commission of crimes indicate that there is a disturbing upward trend, to the point where firearms have become almost exclusively the weapon of choice for murders.

Suppressive as well as preventative strategies must be employed in the fight against gangs. Suppressive strategies alone will fail if the social conditions which encourage gang membership are not addressed.

Such conditions will ensure a steady supply of youths who are willing to join gangs and who see no other alternative for survival. Under such conditions, the most effective suppressive strategies will be met with a steady supply of replacements for gang members who are incarcerated or murdered. Preventative strategies should focus on the social dynamics in communities with a gang presence, as well as on external societal factors which result in the social isolation and exclusion of such communities and their members from the wider society.

The social isolation of gang-affected communities stereotypes such communities and their members, resulting in a reduction of prosocial alternatives and opportunities. When the legitimate opportunity structure is blocked, community members may resort to illegitimate means to achieve upward social mobility. In addition, social isolation may result in a withdrawal or reduction of public services otherwise provided in Trinidad and Tobago; examples here include law enforcement and access to social services. Gangs may usurp such functions and could be perceived by community members as essential to the functioning of their communities. If this occurs, gangs may become entrenched in such communities. Once this happens, the eradication of gangs will become extremely difficult, if not impossible. Victimization survey data gathered for this study indicate that gangs have not yet become entrenched in communities in Trinidad and Tobago. Of the people who indicated that there were criminal gangs in their communities, only 3.2 per cent indicated that the gangs had made their communities safer places. Despite this, however, consultation with security experts in Trinidad and Tobago indicated that communities are becoming more closely associated with gangs and their leaders and, in some instances, are beginning to see gangs as beneficial.

Initiatives should be adopted which facilitate interaction between people from socially marginalized communities and the wider society. Such interaction can sensitize the public to the ills of stereotyping and can be used to highlight successes from within marginalized communities. This would assist with challenging negative stereotypes, especially those associated with communities with a gang presence. Educational, social and economic opportunities must also be provided to people in marginalized communities such that there are available legitimate pathways to upward social mobility. Social dynamics in at-risk communities must also be addressed. Emphasis must be placed on reorienting the value systems of community members if there is to be a commitment to prosocial behaviour and norms. Isolation from the wider society may facilitate the development of alternative value systems and subcultures in marginalized communities. Once such subcultures become established, they may become self-reinforcing since the adoption of an alternative value system and culture may seem appropriate where community members perceive that they do not belong to, or are not allowed to participate fully in, the wider society. Antisocial norms would be reinforced by gangs or may even facilitate the development of gangs. Furthermore, socialization processes would facilitate the perpetuation of these antisocial values.

Systematic research is needed in crime-prone communities in order to understand the social dynamics and to uncover the risk factors which predispose youths to join gang. In this respect, the work of Charles Katz and Andrew Fox (2010) was used to examine risk factors in the community, school, family and peer-individual domains. An understanding of which factors are relatively more important would allow policymakers to design interventions that target those variables which have the greatest likelihood of achieving the intended effect. Katz and Fox (2010) found that factors in the peer-individual domain were more important than factors in the family, school and community domains. Despite this, there were a number of variables in the latter three domains which were important. Future research should widen the range of variables in each domain and should include an additional domain to capture larger structural processes.

Suppressive strategies should not be neglected where the elimination of gangs is the objective. The Anti Gang Bill (2010) is a step in the right direction and indicates the resolve of state agencies in the fight against gangs. The explanatory note to the Bill states that:

> The Bill seeks to make it a serious offence, *inter alia*, to be a member of a gang, to be in possession of a bullet-proof vest, to participate in or contribute to the activities of a gang, to support or invite support for a gang, or to harbour or recruit children in a gang. The Bill also seeks to confer on a Court the power to order the forfeiture of personal property in certain circumstances (4).

While some of the provisions of the Bill are uncontroversial, others merit careful consideration. It may be extremely difficult, for example, to establish, uncontrovertibly, that a person is a member of a gang or that, even where illegal activity has taken place, such activity is gang-related. Even more troubling is the possibility that it may be difficult to establish the most basic fact of whether or not a gang exists. The Bill states that:

> For the purpose of this Act, it shall not be necessary to show that a particular gang possesses, acknowledges or is known by any common name, insignia, flag, means of recognition, secret signal or code, creed, belief, structure, leadership or command structure, method of operation, criminal enterprise, concentration or specialty, membership,

age or other qualification, initiation rites, geographical or territorial situs, boundary or location, or other unifying mark, manner, protocol or method of expressing or indicating its membership when the gang's existence can be demonstrated by a preponderance of other admissible evidence, but any evidence reasonably tending to show or demonstrate the existence of or membership in a gang shall be admissible in any action or proceedings brought under this Act (Section 2, 10).

This lack of clarity with respect to establishing that a gang exists leaves space for the possibility of the inappropriate use of evidence in attempting to demonstrate the existence of a gang. It also signals that where such 'evidence' is seen to be inadequate, then the existence of a gang, may be difficult to establish. Given the very lengthy sentences imposed for gang membership and gang activity, jurors may be unwilling to convict if they are not absolutely certain that the existence of the gang could be established and, where established, that gang membership could be established.

Perhaps even more controversial is Clause 9 (1) (a) which makes it an offence to harbour or conceal the child of a gang member. This appears to indicate that the children of gang members should not be afforded the same rights and protections which are expected for children in general. Indeed, it may be argued that the children of gang members are especially vulnerable and may be in need of protection and care by other persons. Despite these limitations, the Anti Gang Bill (2010) signals that the threat which gangs pose is receiving careful consideration and that suppressive strategies will not be overlooked in Trinidad and Tobago.

Crime policies in Trinidad and Tobago must be based on empirical evidence. While popular opinion may exert some effect on policy decisions, this opinion often is not sufficiently informed and may be based on emotion, desperation at the escalating crime situation, or a desire for revenge. Despite this, as indicated in chapter 6, the population of Trinidad and Tobago recognizes that punitive policies alone will not solve the crime problem. Indeed, the analysis of primary data in this study indicates that the population is strongly in support of a range of educational, social and other non-punitive types of approaches to dealing with the crime situation. That notwithstanding, however, a large proportion of the population is also in support of increasingly punitive approaches to dealing with crime. There is always the risk that the emotion which underlies such tendencies could lead to less than optimal solutions to the crime situation.

It is reasonable to argue that the obvious solution to the issue of crime and security in Trinidad and Tobago can be found in support of both punishment-based as well as preventative approaches. However, the best way to determine how to proceed in developing crime policies is to rely on rigorous empirical research which assesses a range of risk factors, including those related to typical criminal justice system type approaches, and those related to alternative, more 'social' type approaches. In its assessment of risk factors, chapter 5 conceptualized such factors both within a 'levels of analysis' framework and within a temporal framework. With respect to levels of analysis, these sensitize researchers and policymakers to the fact that important predictors of crime and insecurity may be situated at a range of levels, including the societal/structural, community, family, school and individual levels of analysis. It may even be arguable that larger international/global processes impact on social and economic circumstances in Trinidad and Tobago and thus influence crime rates. Admittedly, however, such factors may be difficult or impossible to manipulate since they may be outside the sphere of control of any one nation state. Superimposed upon the levels of analysis is a temporal framework. This temporal framework sensitizes the researcher to the fact that interventions to reduce crime could occur before the crime has occurred (preventative), where there is a risk that crime could occur (preventative actions targeting at-risk persons or communities) or after the crime has occurred (reactive). These three temporal phases have been labelled primary, secondary and tertiary prevention (Brantingham and Faust 1976). The superimposition of the temporal and levels of analysis frameworks is shown in table 7.1 and sensitizes researchers and policymakers to the various possibilities for risk factors.

Chapter 5 also examined victimization survey data, as well as previous research to determine which risk factors may be important in Trinidad and Tobago. Two important factors which emerged in the analysis of the victimization survey data were community cohesion and societal cohesion. The former refers to a sense of belonging and trust at the community level, while the latter refers to the same construct, but at the societal level.

Table 7.1: Conceptual Framework for Risk Factors

	Societal/ Structural	Community	School	Family	Individual	Other
Primary prevention		Risk factors within each cell				
Secondary prevention						
Tertiary prevention						

Both factors were found to act as buffers against crime. High levels of cohesion ensure that informal social processes are operative and that citizens are willing to come to the aid of others who may be in need of assistance. High levels of cohesion also indicate a collective commitment to values which are considered normative, including standards of behaviour which avoid illegality. This ensures that children are socialized into a law-abiding lifestyle and that informal means of behaviour regulation are operative and act on children as well as adults at both the community and societal levels. Societal cohesion is critical, not only because it provides a buffer against crime but also because low levels of social cohesion could result in the social isolation of some communities, facilitating feelings of exclusion and ostracism directed against these communities and their members (much as is the case with communities such as Laventille, Beetham, Sealots and environs). When this occurs, values which are counter to those of the wider society may develop and may lead to counter-normative behaviours. Indeed, primary data used in this study indicated that, where societal cohesion was low but community cohesion was high, there was an increase in self-reported offending. The social exclusion and isolation of some communities may lead to a strengthening of relationships within such communities since the members of these communities may feel that they have only themselves to rely on. Social isolation may encourage, or even mandate, the development of norms which are contrary to those of the wider society. These norms become self-reinforcing and continued social exclusion of these communities will increase resistance to adopting wider prosocial values.

Prior research has also uncovered a range of additional factors which are important in understanding and controlling crime in Trinidad and Tobago. Randy Seepersad (2009), for example, discovered that personal and group economic deprivation (egoistic and fraternal relative deprivation), as well as criminal values and attitudes, having criminal peers, the availability of illegal opportunities, and low self-control were all consistent predictors of crime and counter normative behaviours. Katz and Fox (2010) further found that important predictors of gang membership include having antisocial peers, early initiation into antisocial behaviour and having peers who use alcohol and illegal drugs. Within the community domain, Katz and Fox (2010) found that the availability of handguns and residential mobility were important predictors of gang membership, while within the family domain it was found that parental attitudes favourable to antisocial behaviour predicted gang membership. Within the school domain, low commitment to school was found to be an important predictor.

Systematic research needs to be conducted on risk factors using the framework in table 7.1. Past research must also be reviewed to determine what is currently known about risk factors. In addition, evaluation research is required to assess the utility of existing intervention programmes; this includes an evaluation of the cost effectiveness of such programmes. Such an evaluation, in conjunction with research on risk factors and a review of past studies, will indicate which risk factors and approaches are useful in the local context and will offer suggestions for future interventions.

Current Programmes in Trinidad and Tobago

The previous chapters examined the issue of crime and security in Trinidad and Tobago and have offered a number of suggestions aimed at reducing crime and improving security. The remainder of this chapter highlights two programmes which represent promising initiatives in Trinidad and Tobago. These programmes are the Citizen Security Programme and the Community Safety and Enhancement Programme. Both programmes have a preventative orientation and utilize some of the ideas suggested in this report.

The Citizen Security Programme

The Citizen Security Programme in Trinidad and Tobago represents an example of an emerging best practice related to the control of crime and insecurity. The Citizen Security Programme Project Profile Report (2007) notes increases of serious crimes in Trinidad and Tobago since 2000. The homicide rate more than tripled, from 9.2 per 100,000 inhabitants in 2000 to 28.2 per 100,000 in 2006. Homicides were concentrated in a few neighbourhoods (the North West tip of the island through Port of Spain, Chaguanas and San Fernando), occurred mainly at night and involved the use of firearms. Robberies showed an increased from 210 per 100,000 in 1998 to 375 per 100,000 inhabitants in 2002. The Trinidad and Tobago Police Service reported that 13 per cent of homicides committed between 2000 and 2002 were domestic violence related. Reported sexual offences against children increased from 166 in 2000 to 258 in 2002. The data support the assertion that Trinidad and Tobago was experiencing an upsurge in violent crime.

The increasing crime rate brought to the fore citizens' fears for their personal safety and its impact on their quality of life. According to the Report (2007), this fear was reflected in the results of a victimization survey conducted by the Citizen Security Programme within the same period. The findings underscored that fear for personal safety was relatively widespread. Twenty-eight per cent of those surveyed reported witnessing someone wounded by a sharp weapon or firearm. Four in ten persons felt very unsafe in their neighbourhoods at night, which impacted the quality of their community life. One in five respondents limited where they shopped and curtailed recreational activities they formerly enjoyed as a result of their fear for their personal safety.

The increasing crime rate also contributed to the society's lack of satisfaction with the performance of the Police Service and facilitated feelings of insecurity among the citizenry. According to the Report (2007) the situation was further exacerbated by the fact that the society held a negative view of the community-police relationship. In fact, according to the victimization survey, the highest incidence of victimization reported (45 per cent) related to mistreatment of a family member by the police. Almost half of those surveyed believe that the police were not doing a good job. Among assault victims who reported incidents to the Trinidad and Tobago Police Service, 70 per cent were unsatisfied with the way the police dealt with their report. These victims felt that the police did not do enough (34 per cent); seemed uninterested (24 per cent), or did not treat the victims correctly or politely (14 per cent).

The Report (2007) postulates that the lack of a coordinated and collaborative approach to the many dimensions of the crime situation in Trinidad and Tobago and the failure to place sufficient emphasis on prevention, constrained the ability of the Ministry of National Security to respond to crime effectively. In an attempt to address the crime situation and to implement its Vision 20/20 Crime and Violence Reduction Strategies, the government of Trinidad and Tobago requested the assistance of the Inter-American Development Bank (IDB) in preparing a Citizen Security Programme. The goal was to significantly reduce crime by using a holistic sustained approach that addresses the root causes of crime, to reduce the involvement of young people in crime, to instil a culture of law, order and respect for human life among all citizens and to restore public trust and confidence in the protective services.

The Objectives and Components of the Citizen Security Programme

As an initiative of the Ministry of National Security, the Citizen Security Programme (CSP) seeks to contribute to the reduction in crime and violence by addressing the most proximal risk factors – firearms, unsafe neighbourhoods, and violent personal behaviours in 32 'high needs' communities; 29 in Trinidad and 3 in Tobago. These communities are recognized as high-crime or crime hot spot areas. Alberto Gonzales, Regina

Schofield and Sarah Hart (2005) define a 'crime hot spot' as an area that has a greater than average number of criminal or disorder events, or an area where people have a higher than average risk of victimization. In the local context, the Trinidad and Tobago Police Service defines a 'crime hot spot' as a specific geographic location where an unusual amount of criminal activities are committed by one or more offenders.

To further its goals, the CSP also attempts to strengthen the diagnostic, policy, monitoring and evaluation capacity of the Ministry of National Security. There are four main objectives of the programme. These include:

- the reduction in the number of homicides, robberies and woundings in partner communities;
- an increase in the perception of safety in partner communities;
- a reduction of injuries related to firearms, child maltreatment, domestic violence and youth violence, and
- an increase in collective efficacy to prevent violence in the partner communities.

The CSP has three components which seek to improve the capacities of the three stakeholders involved in the citizen security process. The three stakeholders are the Ministry of National Security, the Trinidad and Tobago Police Service and the members of the targeted communities. The components are:

  i. institutional strengthening of the Ministry of National Security by improving its ability to plan, coordinate, manage and execute violence- and crime-prevention projects, and monitor crime and violence trends;

  ii. institutional strengthening of the Trinidad and Tobago Police Service to increase public confidence by improving performance, training, management and supervision, thus enhancing the quality of police interaction with the public and victims of crime and complementing the ongoing transformation efforts of the service, and

  iii. co-ordination and implementation of community-based preventive strategies through eight separate but interrelated programmes:
    - Community Action Councils (CAC)
    - Rapid Impact Projects (RIP)
    - Community Peace Promoters (CPP)

- Community-Based Social Intervention (CBSI)
- School-based violence reduction programmes
- Youth-friendly spaces (YFS)
- Public education messages
- Inspiring Confidence in Our Neighbourhood (ICON)

Community Safety and Enhancement Programme (CSEP)

The Community Safety and Enhancement Programme (CSEP) was established by Cabinet Minute No. 3168 dated December 18, 2003. This programme was established in the then Ministry of Community Development, Culture and Gender Affairs to promote community safety and security through the development of crime prevention strategies and the implementation of projects with resource support from internal and external sources. The Programme was formally launched on July 5, 2004 in the presence of an audience of approximately 500 people comprising government ministers, officials of government ministries, officers of the police service, representatives of the business community, members of non-governmental organizations and community-based organizations, the media and emerging safety and enhancement groups.

The programme's focus was to support strategies and structures employed by people in their communities to make their communities and neighbourhoods safer. The activities aimed at promoting the programme ranged from training workshops on character development and themes related to safety awareness and crime prevention and involving unemployed youths in community enhancement activities as alternatives to crime and deviance. Complementing the training were information dissemination exhibitions at Point Fortin, San Fernando, Siparia, Couva, San Juan, Sangre Grande, Rio Claro, Trincity and Gulf City. Community safety and enhancement groups have been engaged in more than 80 projects to date. Some of the major projects are as follows:

1. Peace concert in Red Hill, Morvant, followed by peace march from Port of Spain to Laventille by gang members.

2. Workshop with the theme *Developing Manhood* where approximately 85 young men (gang members) benefited from the Defining Masculine Excellence Programme. They went on to be trained in the use of heavy equipment.

3. An employment-generating training programme in food processing and management conducted by the Caribbean Agro-

Business Association at the University of the West Indies, St Augustine for 23 young women from Morvant, Beetham Estate and Laventille.

4. An ongoing agriculture programme in Carlson Field initiated by members of the St Barb's Safety and Enhancement Group, involving 25 young men and women from the Laventille district.

5. Lectures in 25 communities on community safety and crime prevention.

6. Regional crime workshops at Sangre Grande, Mayaro, Princes Town, Penal and Arouca.

7. Street theatre on crime prevention in the communities of Laventille and Morvant.

8. Crime prevention through the sport of boxing in Smith Hill, Carenage.

9. Home work, remedial assistance and risk identification projects; Youths from Covigne, Patna, Bagatelle and environs participated.

10. Gang Resistance Education Programme (Pilot) with Restorers Safety and Enhancement Group, Diego Martin. Young men benefited by being trained to resist joining gangs and engaging in violent behaviour.

The officers of CSEP have also established and sustained close working relationships with other public and private sector organizations and agencies involved in crime reduction initiatives. An assistant coordinator of the programme has been serving on the steering committee of the Citizen Security Programme since its inception. Officials of CSEP also serve on police regional councils and partner with the National Drug Council on a number of projects, including mobilization work related to the commemoration of International Day against Drug Abuse and Drug Trafficking. The nationwide coverage of the programme and the nature of the work to be undertaken, however, require additional officers. As of 2014, the existing staff includes two assistant coordinators and four liaison officers. An increase will provide the programme with the capacity required to advance efforts in the East Port of Spain area, including Laventille, Morvant and other vulnerable districts which are inadequately serviced. In light of the fact that the Community Safety and Enhancement Programme's mandate is to promote community safety and security through the development of crime prevention strategies, all efforts should be taken to ensure that the Programme's mandate is implemented.

Conclusion

Crime and insecurity impact negatively on human development and represent one of the biggest concerns of the population and government of Trinidad and Tobago. Any worthwhile solution requires careful consideration of the many issues which potentially affect the functioning of the criminal justice system, but also requires the integration of ideas from criminology and criminological research within other institutions. The foregoing chapters offer an assessment of some of the issues and challenges facing Trinidad and Tobago in the fight against crime and insecurity. Recommendations were offered within each of the substantive areas. Areas examined included the criminal justice system, crime and victimization trends, youth violence, gangs in Trinidad and Tobago, risk factors for crime and insecurity and state policies. It is anticipated that these topics will stimulate thinking about the many challenges which presently exist, and will offer some insight into possible solutions.

Appendices

	Murder	Wounding shooting	Incest, Sexual offences[1]	Rapes	Serious Indecency[2]	Kidnapping	Burglaries & Break-ins	Robbery	Fraud[3]	Larceny & Larceny Motor Vehicles	Larceny Dwelling House5	Narcotics Offences
1990	84	391	-	-	67	13	7546	3115	245	2331	299	1211
1991	97	453	-	-	77	16	7313	3099	396	2434	318	1078
1992	109	420	-	-	98	16	7938	3786	415	2545	390	963
1993	111	608	92	192	87	41	8419	4722	332	2743	355	1080
1994	140	533	79	175	70	46	7635	4490	447	2834	367	1098
1995	122	501	132	177	99	56	6542	3858	399	2781	326	1118
1996	107	505	125	170	116	81	6835	4075	537	3196	352	1259
1997	101	370	288	226	206	80	6682	3393	572	2686	432	1209
1998	97	319	322	250	156	100	6112	2780	417	2686	379	1300
1999	93	340	236	240	180	136	5475	3629	411	2882	388	1334
2000	120	387	284	261	167	156	5623	4094	522	3042	400	1225
2001	151	499	271	274	134	135	5016	4269	308	2961	323	485
2002	171	655	339	302	149	235	4930	4675	425	3164	403	509
2003	229	784	326	317	88	235	4863	4590	459	3210	365	505
2004	261	643	276	305	52	177	5214	3885	329	3364	429	589
2005	386	801	404	334	59	280	4548	4883	300	4081	408	495
2006	371	657	644	259	81	214	4973	5633	322	4560	452	542
2007	391	680	508	317	76	178	4958	4965	236	5365	453	604
2008	547	771	488	236	55	155	4855	5043	234	6157	446	536
2009	506	689	513	247	44	155	5744	6040	548	5415	606	549

Appendix 1:   Serious Crimes in Trinidad and Tobago, 1990–2014 (contd)

	Murder	Wounding shooting	Incest, Sexual offences[1]	Rapes	Serious Indecency[2]	Kidnapping	Burglaries & Break-ins	Robbery	Fraud[3]	Larceny & Larceny Motor Vehicles	Larceny Dwelling House5	Narcotics Offences
2010	473	623	481	215	61	119	5207	5075	211	5438	623	519
2011	352	535	450	200	59	122	4220	3718	225	4018	481	486
2012	379	579	647	286	95	185	4321	4436	219	4652	536	437
2013	407	542	338	212	70	116	2967	2958	307	3650	370	474
2014	403	558	485	344	80	97	2592	2672	223	3106	289	439
Average: all years	248.3	553.7	351.3	251.8	97.0	125.8	5621.1	4155.3	361.6	3572.0	407.6	801.8
Average: last 5 years	402.8	567.4	480.2	251.4	73.0	127.8	3861.4	3771.8	237.0	4172.8	459.8	471.0
Average increase	13.3	7.0	18.7	7.2	0.5	3.5	-206.4	-18.5	-0.9	32.3	-0.4	-32.2

Source: Crime and Problem Analysis Branch of the Trinidad and Tobago Police Service.

1. Prior to 1993, data for rapes, incest and other sexual offences (except serious indecency) were not disaggregated. The total number of rapes, incest and other sexual offences for this period was 367 in 1990, 384 in 1991 and 485 in 1992.
2. Serious indecency, which is a major crime, is 'an act, other than sexual intercourse (whether natural or unnatural), by a person involving the use of the genital organ for the purpose of arousing or gratifying sexual desire.' This is distinguished from indecent assault, which is a minor crime and which means 'an assault accompanied by words or circumstances indicating an indecent intention' (Sexual Offences Act of Trinidad and Tobago [Act 27 of 1986, amended in 1994 and 2000]: Chapter 11:28, Sections 15 and 16).
3. Fraud over $TT2,000 is a serious crime while fraud of $TT2, 000 and under is a minor crime.
4. Prior to 2004, data for general larceny and larceny motor vehicles were not disaggregated. For consistency, the data presented here for all years is the sum of both categories.
5. The category of 'larceny dwelling house over $TT2,000' is a serious crime while 'larceny dwelling house $2,000 and under' is a minor crime.

Appendix 2: Minor Crimes in Trinidad and Tobago, 1990–2014

	Indecent Assault[1]	Assault on Police and Peace Officer	Possession of Housebreaking Implement	Embezzlement, False Pretence, Fraud[2]	Larceny	Larceny Dwelling House[3]	Praedial Larceny	Unlawful Possession[4]	Malicious wounding	Possession of Firearm and Ammunition	Possession of Narcotics	Possession of Apparatus
1990	153	269	15	178	13041	2659	981	532	1454	464	1710	-
1991	150	316	15	268	13382	2992	899	348	1670	465	1628	-
1992	148	270	10	226	13610	2527	968	269	1596	617	1349	-
1993	131	259	8	186	12775	3195	979	210	1588	705	1428	-
1994	130	252	6	194	12077	2832	1157	207	1482	639	1830	-
1995	129	250	5	224	11625	2572	1118	174	1316	554	1850	-
1996	99	249	8	249	10844	2914	976	164	1337	429	1968	-
1997	151	257	22	206	10780	2630	862	155	1331	518	2512	-
1998	197	274	4	201	10615	2714	661	152	1356	418	2989	
1999	190	270	6	188	9624	2278	654	95	1173	398	2969	-
2000	154	243	1	241	7667	2080	443	83	1083	487	2857	-
2001	139	205	5	236	7188	1719	417	79	856	617	4002	-
2002	146	189	7	354	6810	1666	441	81	872	707	4044	-
2003	151	280	3	237	6525	1535	333	82	1139	773	4718	-
2004	189	264	4	288	6137	1441	374	94	1086	858	6142	-
2005	200	227	3	122	5972	1143	261	49	1126	767	4671	478
2006	185	241	4	151	5977	1167	205	74	933	711	4986	430
2007	199	305	7	107	5114	874	154	59	922	600	4920	398
2008	237	303	3	103	4389	623	171	69	886	573	5105	408
2009	208	354	3	82	4317	699	179	61	872	500	3526	283

Appendix 2:   Minor Crimes in Trinidad and Tobago, 1990–2014 (contd)

	Indecent Assault[1]	Assault on Police and Peace Officer	Possession of Housebreaking Implement	Embezzlement, False Pretence, Fraud[2]	Larceny	Larceny Dwelling House[3]	Praedial Larceny	Unlawful Possession[4]	Malicious wounding	Possession of Firearm and Ammunition	Possession of Narcotics	Possession of Apparatus
2010	172	174	6	158	4314	578	184	40	580	536	3564	302
2011	179	229	7	106	3797	451	205	46	481	527	3806	278
2012	245	227	6	44	3809	387	203	34	475	471	3462	256
2013	198	134	4	33	2645	293	146	39	386	526	4031	274
2014	200	118	6	33	2105	235	93	16	299	740	3481	191
Average: all years	171.2	246.4	6.7	176.6	7806	1688	522.6	128.5	1052	584.0	3342	329.8
Average: last 5 yrs	198.8	176.4	5.8	74.8	3334	389	166.2	35.0	444.2	560.0	3669	260.2
Average increase	1.9	-6.3	-0.4	-6.0	-456	-101	-37	-21.5	-48.1	11.5	73.8	-31.9

Source: Crime and Problem Analysis Branch of the Trinidad and Tobago Police Service.

1. Serious indecency, a major crime, is 'an act, other than sexual intercourse (whether natural or unnatural), by a person involving the use of the genital organ for the purpose of arousing or gratifying sexual desire'. Indecent assault is a minor crime defined as 'an assault accompanied by words or circumstances indicating an indecent intention' (Sexual Offences Act of Trinidad and Tobago [Act 27 of 1986, amended in 1994 and 2000]: Chapter 11:28, Sections 15 and 16).

2. Fraud over $TT2,000 is a serious crime while fraud of $TT2,000 and under is a minor crime.

3. The category of 'larceny dwelling house over $TT2,000' is a serious crime while 'larceny dwelling house of $2,000 and under' is a minor crime.

4. Unlawful possession refers to the possession of any item that a person has but does not belong to them.

References

$5,000 Grant for Ex-Prisoners. 2011. *Daily Express*, February 1.

Agnew, Robert. 1985. A Revised Strain Theory of Delinquency. *Social Forces* 64, no. 1:151–67.

———. 1992. Foundation for a General Strain Theory of Crime and Delinquency. *Criminology* 30, no. 1:47–88.

———. 1999. A General Strain Theory of Community Differences in Crime Rates. *Journal of Research in Crime and Delinquency* 36, no. 2:123–55.

Alvi, Shahid, and Kevin Selbee. 1997. Dating Status Variations and Woman Abuse: A Test of the Dependency, Availability, and Deterrence (DAD) Model. *Violence against Women* 3, no. 6:610–28.

Andrews, Bernice, and George W. Brown. 1988. Marital Violence in the Community: A Biographical Approach. *British Journal of Psychiatry* 153:305–12.

Anyanwu, Eugene. 2011. Exploring Domestic Violence Against Women in Trinidad and Tobago: Analysis of the Barriers That May Hinder Abused Women from Seeking Help. MSc thesis, University of the West Indies.

Bagoo, Andre. 2008. To Community Police or Not Community Police? *Trinidad and Tobago Newsday*, January 27.

Bailey, William C. 1984. Poverty, Inequality, and City Homicide Rates: Some Not So Unexpected Findings. *Criminology* 22, no. 4:531–50.

Bailey, William C., and Ruth D. Peterson. 1999. Capital Punishment, Homicide, and Deterrence: An Assessment of the Evidence. In *Studying and Preventing Homicide: Issues and Challenges*, ed. M. Dwayne Smith and Margaret A. Zahn, 223–45. Thousand Oaks, CA: Sage Publications, Inc.

Baptiste, Cipriani, and Trinidad and Tobago. 2002. Cabinet Appointed Task Force On Prison Reform and Transformation. *Final Report of the Cabinet Appointed Task Force On Prison Reform and Transformation*. Port of Spain: Ministry of National Security.

Barlow, Hugh D. 1995. *Crime and Public Policy: Putting Theory to Work*. Boulder, CO: Westview Press.

Barnes, Annmarie, and Randy Seepersad. 2008. *Beyond Boundaries: A Comparative Study on Criminal Deportation in Antigua and Barbuda, Guyana, Jamaica and Trinidad and Tobago*. Port of Spain: CARICOM Implementation Agency for Crime and Security.

Bissessar, Ann Marie. 2000. Policy Transfer and Implementation Failure: A Review of the Policy of Domestic Violence in Trinidad and Tobago. *Caribbean Journal of Criminology and Social Psychology* 5, nos. 1 and 2:57–80.

Black, Michele C., Kathleen C. Basile, Matthew J. Breiding, Sharon G. Smith, Mikel L. Walters, Melissa T. Merrick, Jieru Chen, and Mark R. Stevens. 2011. *The National Intimate Partner and Sexual Violence Survey: 2010 Summary Report*. Atlanta, GA: Centers for Disease Control and Prevention, National Center for Injury Prevention and Control, Division of Violence Prevention.

Blau, Peter M., and Reid M. Golden. 1986. Metropolitan Structure and Criminal Violence. *The Sociological Quarterly* 27, no. 1:15–26.

Braithwaite, John. 1989. *Crime, Shame and Reintegration*. New York: Cambridge University Press.

Brantingham, Paul J. 1976. A Conceptual Model of Crime Prevention. *Crime and Delinquency* 22, no. 3:284–96.

Brantingham, P. and F. Faust. 1976. A conceptual model of crime prevention. *Crime and Delinquency*, 22(3):284–96.

Brearley, H.C. 1932. *Homicide in the United States*. Chapel Hill, NC: University of North Carolina Press.

Bridges, George S., and James A. Stone. 1986. Effects of Criminal Punishment on Perceived Threat of Punishment: Toward Understanding of Specific Deterrence. *Journal of Research in Crime and Delinquency* 23, no. 3:207–39.

Browne, Angela, and David Finkelhor. 1986. Impact of Child Sexual Abuse: A Review of the Research. *Psychological Bulletin* 99, no. 1:66–77.

Bryant, Kevin M., and J. Mitchell Miller. 1997. Routine Activity Theory and Labor Market Segmentation: An Empirical Test of a Revised Approach. *American Journal of Criminal Justice* 22, no. 1:71–100.

Busch, Noël Bridget, and Deborah Valentine. 2000. Empowerment Practice: A Focus on Battered Women. *Affilia* 15, no. 1:82–95.

Buzawa, Eve S., and Carl G. Buzawa. 1993. The Impact of Arrest on Domestic Violence. *American Behavioral Scientist* 36, no. 5:558–74.

Carroll, Leo, and Pamela Irving Jackson. 1983. Inequality, Opportunity, and Crime Rates in Central Cities. *Criminology* 21, no. 2:178–94.

Chamlin, Mitchell B., and John K. Cochran. 1995. Assessing Messner and Rosenfeld's Institutional Anomie Theory: A Partial Test. *Criminology* 33, no. 3:411–29.

Cid, José. 2009. Is Imprisonment Criminogenic? A Comparative Study of Recidivism Rates between Prison and Suspended Prison Sanctions. *European Journal of Criminology* 6, no. 6:459–80.

Cloward, Richard A., and Lloyd E. Ohlin. 1960. *Delinquency and Opportunity: A Theory of Delinquent Gangs*. New York: The Free Press.

Cohen, Lawrence E., and Marcus Felson. 1979. Social Change and Crime Rate Trends: A Routine Activity Approach. *American Sociological Review* 44, no. 4:588–608.

Cooley, Charles Horton. 1902. *Human Nature and the Social Order.* New York: Scribner.

———. 1998. *On Self and Social Organization,* edited by Hans-Joachim Schubert. Chicago, IL: University of Chicago Press.

Cullen, Francis T. 1994. Social Support as an Organizing Concept for Criminology: Presidential Address to the Academy of Criminal Justice Sciences. *Justice Quarterly* 11 (December): 527–59.

Davies, James C. 1962. Toward a Theory of Revolution. *American Sociological Review* 27, no. 1:5–19.

———. 1969. The J-Curve of Rising and Declining Satisfactions as a Cause of Some Great Revolutions and a Contained Rebellion. In *Violence in America: Historical and Comparative Perspectives,* ed. Hugh Davis Graham and Ted Robert Gurr, 547–76. New York: F.A. Praeger.

De Fronzo, James. 1983. Economic Assistance to Impoverished Americans: Relationship to Incidence of Crime. *Criminology* 21, no. 1:119–36.

Dearwater, Stephen R., Jeffrey H. Coben, Jacquelyn C. Campbell, Gregory Nah, Nancy Glass, Elizabeth McLoughlin, and Betty Bekerneier. 1998. Prevalence of Intimate Partner Abuse in Women Treated at Community Hospital Emergency Departments. *JAMA* 280, no. 5:433–38.

Decker, Scott H., and Barrik Van Winkle. 1996. *Life in the Gang: Family, Friends, and Violence.* Cambridge: Cambridge University Press.

Deosaran, R., and D. Chadee. 1997. Juvenile Delinquency in Trinidad and Tobago: Challenges for Social Policy and Caribbean Criminology. *Caribbean Journal of Criminology and Social Psychology* 2, no. 92:36–83.

Deosaran, Ramesh. 2002. Community Policing in the Caribbean: Context, Community, and Police Capability. *Policing: An International Journal of Police Strategies and Management* 25, no. 1:125–46.

Dobash, R. Emerson, and Russell Dobash. 1979. *Violence against Wives: A Case against the Patriarchy.* New York: Free Press.

———. 1992. *Women, Violence and Social Change.* London: Routledge.

Dollard, John, Leonard W. Doob, Neal E. Miller, Orval Hobart Mowrer, and Robert R. Sears. 1939. *Frustration and Aggression.* New Haven, CT: Yale University Press.

Doob, Anthony N., and Cheryl Marie Webster. 2003. Sentence Severity and Crime: Accepting the Null Hypothesis. *Crime and Justice: A Review of Research* 30:143–95.

Dutton, Donald G. 1986. The Outcome of Court-Mandated Treatment for Wife Assault: A Quasi-Experimental Evaluation. *Violence and Victims* 1, no. 3:163–75.

————. 1995. Intimate Abusiveness. *Clinical Psychology: Science and Practice* 2, no. 3:207–24.

Erlanger, Howard S. 1976. Is There a Subculture of Violence in the South? *Journal of Criminal Law and Criminology* 66, no. 4:483–90.

Farrington, David P. 1987. Early Precursors of Frequent Offending. In *Families, Schools, and Delinquency Prevention*, ed. James Q. Wilson and Glenn C. Loury, 27–50. From Children to Citizens, III. New York, NY: Springer-Verlag.

Ferraro, K. J., and L. Pope. 1993. Irreconcilable Differences: Battered Women, Police, and the Law. In *Legal Responses to Wife Assault: Current Trends and Evaluation*, ed. N. Zoe Hilton, 96–123. Newbury Park, CA: Sage Publications.

Ferraro, Kathleen J. 1989. The Legal Response to Woman Battering in the United States. In *Women, Policing and Male Violence: International Perspectives*, ed. Jalna Hanmer, Jill Radford and Elizabeth A. Stanko, 155–84. London: Routledge.

Festinger, Leon. 1957. *A Theory of Cognitive Dissonance*. Stanford, CA: Stanford University Press.

Fischer, Claude S. 1975. Toward a Subcultural Theory of Urbanism. *American Journal of Sociology* 80, no. 6:1319–41.

Flango, Victor Eugene, and Edgar L. Sherbenou. 1976. Poverty, Urbanization, and Crime. *Criminology* 14, no. 3:331–46.

Fowles, Richard, and Mary Merva. 1996. Wage Inequality and Criminal Activity: An Extreme Bounds Analysis for the United States, 1975–1990. *Criminology* 34, no. 2:163–82.

Gang Violence in School: Students Hold Silent Protest. 2010. *Trinidad and Tobago Express*, December 9.

Gartner, Rosemary. 1990. The Victims of Homicide: A Temporal and Cross-National Comparison. *American Sociological Review* 55, no. 1:92–106.

Gastil, Raymond D. 1971. Homicide and a Regional Culture of Violence. *American Sociological Review* 36, no. 3:412–27.

Gelles, Richard J. 1976. Abused Wives: Why Do They Stay? *Journal of Marriage and the Family* 34, no. 4:659–68.

Gonzales, Alberto R., Regina B. Schofield and Sarah V. Hart. 2005. Mapping Crime: Understanding Hot Spots. US Department of Justice, Office of Justice Program 810 Seventh Street N.W. Washington, DC.

Gopaul, Roanna, and Maureen Cain. 1996. Violence between Spouses in Trinidad and Tobago: A Research Note. *Caribbean Quarterly* 43, nos. 2–3:28–40.

Gopaul, Roanna, Paula Morgan, and Rhoda Reddock. 1994. *Women, Family and Family Violence in the Caribbean: The Historical and Contemporary Experience with Special Reference to Trinidad and Tobago*. St Augustine: University of the West Indies, Women and Development Studies Group/Centre for Gender and Development Studies.

Greenwood, Peter W., and Allan F. Abrahamse. 1982. *Selective Incapacitation*. Santa Monica, CA: Rand Corp.

Gurr, Ted R. 1970. *Why Men Rebel*. Princeton, NJ: Princeton University Press.

Handwerker, W. Penn. 1997. Universal Human Rights and the Problem of Unbounded Cultural Meanings. *American Anthropologist* 99, no. 4:799–809.

Hardwick, Linda T. 1995. The Relationship of Youth Gang Membership to Academic Achievement: A Comparative Analysis. PhD, University of Akron, College of Education.

Hilberman, Elaine, and Kit Munson. 1977–1978. Sixty Battered Women. *Victimology: An International Journal* 2, nos. 3–4:460–70.

Hirschi, Travis. 2002. *Causes of Delinquency*. New Brunswick, NJ: Transaction Publishers.

Horney, Julie, and Ineke Haen Marshall. 1992. Risk Perceptions among Serious Offenders: The Role of Crime and Punishment. *Criminology* 30, no. 4:575–94.

Huff-Corzine, Lin, Jay Corzine, and David C. Moore. 1986. Southern Exposure: Deciphering the South's Influence on Homicide Rates. *Social Forces* 64, no. 4:906–24.

Humphreys, Catherine, Audrey Mullender, Pam Lowe, Gill Hague, Hilary Abrahams, and Marianne Hester. 2001. Domestic Violence and Child Abuse: Developing Sensitive Policies and Guidance. *Child Abuse Review* 10, no. 3:183–97.

International Centre for Prison Studies. 2010. World Prison Brief, 2010. London.

Jankowski, Martín Sánchez. 1991. *Islands in the Street: Gangs and American Urban Society*. Berkeley, CA: University of California Press.

Johnson, Devon, William R. King, Charles M. Katz, Andrew M. Fox, and Natalie Goulette. 2008. Youth Perception of the Police in Trinidad and Tobago. *Caribbean Journal of Criminology and Public Safety* 13, nos. 1–2:217–53.

Johnson, Julie. 2007. *Bullies and Gangs: Thoughts and Feelings*. Mankato, MN: Stargazer Books.

Jouriles, Ernest N., Renee McDonald, Amy M. Slep, Richard E. Heyman, and Edward F. Garrido. 2008. Child Abuse in the Context of Domestic Violence: Prevalence, Explanations, and Practice Implications. *Violence and Victims* 23, no. 2:221–35.

Katz, Charles M. 2009. Diagnosing Gang Problems in the Caribbean. PowerPoint presented at CARICOM Conference on Violence Prevention: Confronting the Challenge of Youth Violence in Society, St Kitts and Nevis, June 2009.

Katz, Charles M., and David Choate. 2010. Diagnosing Trinidad and Tobago's Gang Problem. PowerPoint presented at Annual Meeting of the American Society of Criminology, Los Angeles, California. https://cvpcs.asu.edu/sites/default/files/content/products/Katz%20Choate%20ASC_TT%20Presentation_short%20version_10_30_06.pdf.

Katz, Charles M., David Choate, and Andrew Fox. 2010. *Understanding and Preventing Gang Membership in Trinidad and Tobago [unpublished report]*. Phoenix, AZ: Arizona State University.

Katz, Charles M., and Andrew M. Fox. 2010. Risk and Protective Factors Associated with Gang-Involved Youth in Trinidad and Tobago. *Revista Panamericana De Salud Pública* 27, no. 3:187–202.

Kawachi, Ichiro, Bruce P. Kennedy, Kimberly Lochner, and Deborah Prothrow-Stith. 1997. Social Capital, Income Inequality, and Mortality. *American Journal of Public Health* 87, no. 9: 1491–98.

Kawachi, Ichiro, Bruce P. Kennedy, and Richard G. Wilkinson. 1999. Crime: Social Disorganization and Relative Deprivation. *Social Science and Medicine* 48, no. 6:719–31.

Kennedy, Leslie W., and Robert A. Silverman. 1990. The Elderly Victim of Homicide: An Application of the Routine Activities Approach. *The Sociological Quarterly* 31, no. 2:307–19.

Kennedy, Leslie W., Robert A. Silverman and David R. Forde. 1991. Homicide in Urban Canada: Testing the Impact of Economic Inequality and Social Disorganization. *Canadian Journal of Sociology* 16, no. 4:397–410.

King, Keron, and Terence Bartholomew. 2007. Identifying and Predicting the Correctional Orientation of Trinidad and Tobago's Correctional Officers: Implications for Prison Reform. Paper presented at Crises, Chaos, and Change: Caribbean Development Challenges in the 21st Century, SALISES 8th Annual Conference, St Augustine, March 26–28, 2007.

King, William R. 2012. Estimating and Investigating Gang Homicide in the Caribbean: Lessons from Trinidad and Tobago. PowerPoint presentation to the Symposium on Gangs and Gang Violence in the Caribbean, 2012. Available from https://www.american.edu/spa/djls/upload/King-presentations.pdf.

Kirton, Raymond Mark, Marlon Anatol, and Niki Braithwaite. 2010. *The Political Culture of Democracy in Trinidad and Tobago: 2010: Democracy in Action*. St Augustine: Institute of International Relations, University of the West Indies.

Klein, Malcolm W., and Cheryl L. Maxson. 2006. *Street Gang Patterns and Policies*. New York, NY: Oxford University Press, Inc.

Koss, Mary P. 1990. The Women's Mental Health Research Agenda: Violence against Women. *American Psychologist* 45, no. 3:374–80.

Kowlessar, Geisha. 2011a. New Prisons' Inspector: Don't Expect Magic. *Trinidad and Tobago Guardian*, January 23.

————. 2011b. Volney: Justice Will Be Served. *Trinidad and Tobago Guardian*, January 7.

Krahn, Harvey, and Trevor Harrison. 1992. 'Self-Referenced' Relative Deprivation and Economic Beliefs: The Effects of the Recession in Alberta. *Canadian Review of Sociology* 29, no. 2:191–209.

Kukis, Mark. 2009. Is Baghdad Now Safer Than New Orleans? May 1.

Lall, Vidya. 2007. Bullying, victimization, and delinquency in primary schools in Trinidad and Tobago: Some preliminary results. *Caribbean Journal of Criminology and Social Psychology*, 12:155–76.

Land, Kenneth C., Patricia L. McCall and Lawrence E. Cohen. 1990. Structural Covariates of Homicide Rates: Are There Any Invariances across Time and Social Space? *American Journal of Sociology* 95, no. 4:922–63.

Loeber, R., and T. Dishion. 1983. Early Predictors of Male Delinquency: A Review. *Psychological Bulletin* 94, no. 1:68–99.

Loeber, Rolf, and David P. Farrington. 1997. Strategies and Yields of Longitudinal Studies on Antisocial Behavior. In *Handbook of Antisocial Behavior*, ed. David M. Stoff, James Breiling and Jack D. Maser, 125–39. Hoboken, NJ: John Wiley & Sons, Inc.

Lyon, Eleanor. 2002. *Welfare and Domestic Violence against Women: Lessons from Research.* Harrisburg, PA: National Resource Center on Violence against Women.

Maguire, Edward R. 2013. Exploring Family Risk and Protective Factors for Adolescent Problem Behaviors in the Caribbean. *Maternal and Child Health Journal* 17, no. 8:1488–98.

Maiese, Michelle. 2003. Restorative Justice. Last modified June 2013 by Heidi Burgess and Sarah Cast. [Online] *Beyond Intractability*, edited by Guy Burgess, and Heidi Burgess. http://www.beyondintractability.org/essay/restorative-justice.

Mastrofski, Stephen D., and Cynthia Lum. 2008. Meeting the Challenges of Police Governance in Trinidad and Tobago. *Policing: A Journal of Policy and Practice* 2, no. 4:481–96.

Mastrofski, Stephen D., Roger B. Parks and Craig D. Uchida. 2008. *Model Stations Initiative in the Trinidad and Tobago Police Service: Interim Report. Report to the Ministry of National Security, Trinidad and Tobago.* Manassas, VA: Center for Justice Leadership and Management, George Mason University.

McCree, Roy. 1998. Violence: A Preliminary Look at Gangs in Trinidad and Tobago. *Caribbean Journal of Criminology* 3, nos. 1–2:155–73.

McDonald, I.S. 1989. *Something's Wrong at My House: Children in Domestic Violence Workbook.* Brisbane: Brisbane Department of Family Services & Aboriginal & Islander Affairs.

McDougall, L., S. Patel, N. Leepow, S. Sankar, D. Mohess, S. Khan, et al. 1999. Prevalence and Factors Associated with Physical and Emotional Abuse against Pregnant Women in Central Trinidad. *West Indian Medical Journal* 48:1–68.

Merton, Robert King. 1968. *Social Theory and Social Structure*. New York: The Free Press.

Messner, Steven F., and Richard Rosenfeld. 1997. *Crime and the American Dream*. Belmont, CA: Wadsworth Pub. Co.

Messner, Steven F., and Kenneth Tardiff. 1985. The Social Ecology of Urban Homicide: An Application of the Routine Activities Approach. *Criminology* 23, no. 2:241–67.

Moffitt, Terrie E. 1993. Adolescence-Limited and Life-Course-Persistent Antisocial Behavior: A Developmental Taxonomy. *Psychological Review* 100, no. 4:674–701.

———. 2003. Life-Course Persistent and Adolescent-Limited Antisocial Behaviour: A Ten-Year Research Review and a Research Agenda. In *Causes of Conduct Disorder and Juvenile Delinquency*, ed. Benjamin B. Lahey, Terrie E. Moffitt and Avshalom Caspi, 49–75. New York: The Guildford Press.

———. 2006. Life-Course Persistent versus Adolescence-Limited Antisocial Behavior. In *Developmental Psychopathology Volume 3: Risk, Disorder, and Adaptation*. 2nd ed., ed. Dante Cicchetti, and Donald J. Cohen, 570–598. Hoboken, NJ: John Wiley & Sons.

Montoute, Annita. 2010. Violence and Insecurity in Trinidad and Tobago: The Impact of Gang Violence. Presentation Given at the Institute of International Relations, UWI, St Augustine, Trinidad on December 13, 2010.

Morrison, Denton E. 1971. Some Notes toward Theory on Relative Deprivation, Social Movements, and Social Change. *American Behavioral Scientist* 14, no. 5:675–90.

Morrison, Denton E. 1973. Some notes toward theory on relative deprivation, social movements, and social change. In Zaltman, G. (Ed.). *Processes and phenomena of social change*. New York: J. Wiley

Ohene, Sally-Ann, Marjorie Ireland and Robert Wm Blum. 2005. The Clustering of Risk Behaviors among Caribbean Youth. *Maternal and Child Health Journal* 9, no. 1:91–100.

Patel, S., N. Lee Pow, R. Kawal, and S. Khan et al. 1999. *Prevalence and factors associated with physical and emotional abuse against pregnant women in central Trinidad*. Presentation by medical students, Caribbean Health Research Council Conference, Barbados, April 1999.

Peled, Einat, Zvi Eisikovits, Guy Enosh, and Zeev Winstok. 2000. Choice and Empowerment for Battered Women Who Stay: Toward A Constructivist Model. *Social Work* 45, no. 1:9–25.

Peterson, Dana, Terrance J. Taylor and Finn-Aage Esbensen. 2004. Gang Membership and Violent Victimization. *Justice Quarterly* 21, no. 4:793–815.

Piaget, Jean. 1953. *Logic and Psychology.* Manchester: Manchester University Press.

Pino, Nathan W. 2009. Developing Democratic Policing in the Caribbean: The Case of Trinidad and Tobago. *Caribbean Journal of Criminology and Public Safety* 14, nos. 1–2:214–58.

Piquero, Alex, and Nicole L. Piquero. 1998. On Testing Institutional Anomie Theory with Varying Specifications. *Studies on Crime and Crime Prevention* 7, no. 1:61–84.

Pleck, Elizabeth. 1987. *Domestic Tyranny: The Making of American Social Policy against Family Violence from Colonial Times to the Present.* New York: Oxford University Press.

Plichta, Stacey. 1992. The Effects of Woman Abuse on Health Care Utilization and Health Status: A Literature Review. *Women's Health Issues* 2, no. 3:154–63.

Procope-Beckles, Marilyn. 2007. *Global School-Based Student Health Survey (GSHS) 2007: Trinidad and Tobago Report.* World Health Organization.

Rawlins, Joan. 1998. Domestic Violence: Reviewing the Situation with Special Reference to Spousal Abuse. From The Situation of Domestic Violence in Trinidad. Presented at a Health Forum, Hoilo City, The Philippines, November 06, 1998.

Rawlins, Joan. 2000. Domestic Violence in Trinidad: A Family and Public Health Problem. *Caribbean Journal of Criminology and Social Psychology* 5, nos. 1–2:165–80.

Robinson, Matthew B., and Christine E. Robinson. 1997. Environmental Characteristics Associated With Residential Burglaries of Student Apartment Complexes. *Environment and Behavior* 29, no. 5:657–75.

Rosenfeld, Richard. 1986. Urban Crime Rates: Effects of Inequality, Welfare Dependency, Region, and Race. In *The Social Ecology of Crime*, ed. James M. Byrne and Robert J. Sampson, 116–30. New York: Springer-Verlag.

Savitz, Leonard D. 1967. *Dilemmas in Criminology.* New York: McGraw-Hill.

Schechter, Susan. 1982. *Women and Male Violence: The Visions and Struggles of the Battered Women's Movement.* Boston: South End Press.

Schiefelbein, Ernesto. 1981. Analysis of the Role of Preschool Education in Reducing Scholastic Failure. *Revista Paraguaya de Sociología* 18, no. 52:7–32.

Seaby, Graham. 1993. *Final Report for the Government of Trinidad and Tobago on Investigations Carried Out by Officers from New Scotland Yard in Respect of Allegations Made by Rodwell Murray and Others About Corruption in the Trinidad and Tobago Police Service.* London: Metropolitan Police Office.

Seepersad, Randy. 2007. *A Study of Youth Involvement in Crime and Violence in Jamaica*. Commissioned by the Ministry of National Security, Jamaica.

—————. 2009. *Mediators and Moderators in the Relative Deprivation – Crime/Counter-normative Actions Relationship*. PhD Criminology thesis, University of Toronto. Available at ProQuest Dissertations.

—————. 2013. *Drug Use and Criminal Behaviour among the Prison Population in Trinidad and Tobago*. Washington, DC: Organization of American States.

—————. 2014. *Bullying and Victimization in Selected Primary Schools in North Trinidad*. Citizen Security Programme, Ministry of National Security and Ministry of Education.

Shannon, Lyle W. 1991. *Changing Patterns of Delinquency and Crime: A Longitudinal Study in Racine*. Boulder, CO: Westview Press.

Shaw, Clifford R., and Henry D. McKay. 1942. *Juvenile Delinquency and Urban Areas: A Study of Rates of Delinquency in Relation to Differential Characteristics of Local Communities in American Cities*. Chicago: University of Chicago Press.

Sheldon, Hackney. 1969. Southern Violence. *The American Historical Review* 74, no. 3:906–25.

Sigelman, Lee, and Miles Simpson. 1977. A Cross-National Test of the Linkage between Economic Inequality and Political Violence. *Journal of Conflict Resolution* 21, no. 1: 105–28.

Similar Challenges. 2010. *The Barbados Advocate*, December 12.

Singh, H., and N. Mustapha. 1994. Some Factors Associated with Substance Abuse among Secondary School Students in Trinidad and Tobago. *Journal of Drug Education* 24, no. 1:83–93.

Sookraj, Radhica. 2011. Form One Student Beats His Teacher. *Trinidad and Tobago Guardian*, February 19.

Spivack, George, and Norma Cianci. 1987. High-Risk Early Behaviour Pattern and Later Delinquency. In *Prevention of Delinquent Behavior*, ed. John D. Burchard and Sara N. Burchard, 44–74. Newbury Park, CA: Sage Publications.

Stiles, Beverly L., Xiaoru Liu and Howard B. Kaplan. 2000. Relative Deprivation and Deviant Adaptations: The Mediating Effects of Negative Self-Feelings. *Journal of Research in Crime and Delinquency* 37, no. 1:64–90.

Strube, Michael J., and Linda S. Barbour. 1983. The Decision to Leave an Abusive Relationship: Economic Dependence and Psychological Commitment. *Journal of Marriage and the Family* 45, no. 4:785–93.

Sykes, Gresham M., and David Matza. 1957. Techniques of Neutralization: A Theory of Delinquency. *American Sociological Review* 22, no. 6:664–70.

Thompson-Ahye, Hazel. 1999. Youth and Crime in the Caribbean. *Caribbean Journal of Criminology* 4, nos. 1–2:169–91.

Trinidad and Tobago Committee on the Restructuring of the Police Service. 1984. Report of the Committee on the Restructuring of the Police Service. Port of Spain.

Trinidad and Tobago Prison Service. 2002. *Golden Grove Prison Annual Administrative Report, 2002.*

———. 2006. *Women's Prison Administrative Report, 2006.*

———. 2010. *Youth Training Centre, Quarterly Report, January–March, 2010.*

Tunnell, Kenneth D. 1990. Choosing Crime: Close Your Eyes and Take Your Chances. *Justice Quarterly* 7, no. 4:673–90.

Two Choices: Educate or Incarcerate Them. 2011. *Trinidad and Tobago Guardian*, April 24.

United Nations Development Programme. 1990. *Human Development Report 1990*. Oxford: Oxford University Press.

———. 2009. *Opening Spaces to Citizen Security and Development: Human Development Report for Central America; HDRCA, 2009–2010*, ed. Marcela Giraldo. UNDP.

———. 2012. *Caribbean Human Development Report 2012: Human Development and the Shift to Better Citizen Security*, ed. Robert Zimmermann, Carol Lawes and Nanette Svenson. New York: UNDP.

United Nations Development Programme. Regional Bureau for Arab States (RBAS). 2009. *Arab Human Development Report 2009: Challenges to Human Security in the Arab Countries*. New York: United Nations Publications.

United Nations Economic Commission for Latin American and the Caribbean. 2008. *Economic Survey of Latin America and the Caribbean 2007–2008: Macroeconomic Policy and Volatility*. New York: United Nations.

United Nations Office on Drugs and Crime, and World Bank. Latin America and the Caribbean Regional Office. 2007. *Crime, Violence, and Development: Trends, Costs and Policy Options in the Caribbean*. New York, NY; Washington, DC: United Nations; World Bank.

Wells, William, Charles M. Katz and Jeorglim Kim. 2008. *Illegal Gun Markets in Trinidad and Tobago*. Huntsville, Texas: Sam Houston State University.

Wolfgang, Marvin E., Robert M. Figlio, and Thorsten Sellin. 1972. *Delinquency in a Birth Cohort*. Chicago: University of Chicago Press.

Women and Development Studies Group. 1994. Women, Family and Family Violence in the Caribbean: The Historical and Contemporary Experience with Special Reference to Trinidad and Tobago. Prepared for The CARICOM Secretariat for The International Year of the Family.

University of the West Indies, Women and Development Studies Group/Centre for Development Studies.

World Health Organization. 1997. *Violence against Women Health Consequences*. World Health Organization.

World Health Organization. 2007. Global Student-Based Health Survey 2007. World Health Organization in collaboration with the US Center for Disease Control and Prevention.

World Health Organization. 2011. *Global Student-Based Health Survey 2011*. World Health Organization in collaboration with the US Center for Disease Control and Prevention.

Wright, Richard A. 1994. *In Defense of Prisons*. London: Greenwood Press.

Zellerer, Evelyn. 2000. Domestic Violence in Trinidad and Tobago: Some Comments. *Caribbean Journal of Criminology and Social Psychology* 5, nos. 1 and 2:209–27.

About the Authors

Randy Seepersad, PhD

Randy Seepersad is a criminologist in the Department of Behavioural Sciences at the University of the West Indies, St Augustine, Trinidad and Tobago. Dr Seepersad holds a PhD from the University of Toronto and an MPhil degree from the University of Cambridge. He specializes in research methodology and statistics and has a research interest in economic deprivation and crime, gang violence, youth crime and justice, and penology. Dr Seepersad co-authored the Jamaican National Crime Victimization Surveys (2006 and 2013), and *Beyond Boundaries: A Comparative Study on Criminal Deportation in Antigua and Barbuda, Guyana, Jamaica and Trinidad and Tobago* (2008). Dr Seepersad was also co-author of a 13-country CARICOM IMPACS assessment of forensic science capacity in CARICOM member states (2011) and was lead consultant for Trinidad and Tobago in the 2012 United Nations Development Programme's Caribbean Human Development Report on Citizen Security. More recently in 2013, along with Professor Ann Bissessar, Dr Seepersad published a 290-page book entitled *Gangs in the Caribbean*.

Dianne Williams, PhD

Dianne Williams is the coordinator of the Unit for Social Problems Analysis and Policy Development (USPAP), a research unit under the umbrella of the Department of Behavioural Sciences at The University of the West Indies, St Augustine. She is a certified criminal justice specialist, certified by the American College of Certified Forensic Counselors since 2004 in the Division of Counseling. She is currently a consultant criminologist for the Ministry of National Security of Belize and one of the Caribbean criminology experts of record for the Organization of American States. Current and recently completed projects include authoring the Analysis of Firearms Legislation for the Caribbean, and providing the expert opinion on the risks faced by homosexuals in Trinidad and Tobago for the Refugee and Migrant Justice Service of the United Kingdom.

Index

www.ingramcontent.com/pod-product-compliance
Lightning Source LLC
Chambersburg PA
CBHW070911270326
41927CB00011B/2529